Strivings Within – The OCD Christian

Strivings Within—
The OCD Christian

Overcoming Doubt in the Storm of Anxiety

Mitzi VanCleve

Copyright: January 2015 Mitzi VanCleve
All rights reserved.
Cover art by Lindsey VanCleve

ISBN: 1517678447
ISBN 13: 9781517678449

Scripture quotations marked NIV are taken from: "The Holy Bible, New International Version, Copyright 1973, 1978, 1984 by International Bible Society, Zondervan Publishing, Grand Rapids, Michigan. Used by permission.

Scripture quotations marked KJV are taken from: "The New Scofield Reference Bible, Holy Bible, Authorized King James Version", Copyright 1967 By Oxford University Press, Inc.

Disclaimer: This book is not intended to be used as a substitute for, or replacement of the professional services of a physician who is trained in the management of anxiety disorders. If you or a loved one are suffering from or debilitated by severe anxiety, please seek help from a professional who specializes in the treatment of anxiety disorders.

Table Of Contents

	Foreword	ix
	Part One	1
Chapter 1	Sudden Onset	3
Chapter 2	Shame and Blame	9
Chapter 3	Horrible Thoughts and Hideous Images	12
Chapter 4	"And Now unto Him who is Able"	17
Chapter 5	Dysfunctional	22
Chapter 6	You Can't Call a Time Out in the Middle of War	27
Chapter 7	The Unexpected	31
Chapter 8	Thankful for Thanksgiving	35
Chapter 9	Be Still	38
Chapter 10	Fighting Back	41
Chapter 11	Pride and Presumption	45
Chapter 12	Still Loony After all These Years	51
Chapter 13	Scary Pills	56
Chapter 14	A Humbling Step	59
Chapter 15	Intolerable Testing	64
Chapter 16	The Towering Terror	68
Chapter 17	A Successful Medication Plunge	72
Chapter 18	Just When You Think You Know it All	75
	Part Two	79
Chapter 1	When Anxiety Chooses You	81
Chapter 2	Misguided Counsel and Stinging Blame	92
Chapter 3	Causes of Anxiety Disorders	103

Chapter 4	Strivings Within – OCD	117
Chapter 5	Risky Business	134
Chapter 6	Common OCD Questions	161
Chapter 7	Practical Matters	169
Chapter 8	Purposeful Affliction	197
	Appendix	239
	About The Author	257
	Helpful Resources	259

Foreword

WRITING THIS BOOK has been one of the most challenging undertakings of my life. I've dragged my feet throughout the whole process, dreading each revisiting of some of the most painful days of my disorder. More disturbing than that was the knowledge that by exposing my innermost thoughts and struggles, I would be opening myself up to the possibility of harsh criticism and judgment. I knew there would likely be some folk whose only mission in reading this book would be to find fault with it. I knew there would be others within the Christian community who might read it hoping to find more reasons to dismiss the validity of mental disorders by chalking them up to things like a lack of faith, sin, or spiritual weakness.

If that happens to be your sole purpose in reading this book, then you might as well put it down right now. It wasn't written for you. If you are determined to disbelieve it or find fault with it at the outset, then I'm quite certain you shall have no trouble in your quest. If, on the other hand, you could set aside some of your preconceived notions and approach this book with prayerful discernment and a teachable heart then by all means, press on. Perhaps your only education about anxiety disorders has come from the pulpit of a pastor or a person for whom you have the utmost respect and yet that individual has absolutely no medical training in diagnosing and treating mental disorders. Maybe *that* "education" has led you to attempt to help a person who suffers from a mental disorder by pointing out their lack of faith or their need to confess or abandon their sinful practice of worry. Although your motives may be pure, your efforts have been misguided and more than likely counterproductive to this person's recovery process. If you're interested in learning what I mean by that statement, then this book was written for you.

Or you might be reading this from the perspective of someone who is desperate to find help and encouragement for your own tortured and isolated experience of living with an anxiety disorder. If that describes you, then this was *especially* written for you. You may be a pastor who has experienced lengthy and confusing counseling sessions with a small number of people in your flock who seem to be stuck in an endless cycle of anxiety and despair which seems resistant to the application of scriptural truth. If you are open to gaining new insight as to how you might be able to help those individuals, then this was written for you.

This book deals with the confusing dilemma of understanding how a disorder that causes intense anxiety and fear can coexist in a person of faith. I have put forth my best effort to explain the difference between chosen worry and the non-chosen instinctive fear response of the person who is afflicted with an anxiety disorder.

I am not insisting that the suffering of folk with anxiety disorders is worse than that of other disorders. I only intend to show that these disorders are *true* afflictions which create tremendous suffering and distress and, therefore, should be viewed through the lens of compassion.

It is my sincere hope that the reader will come away with the clear understanding that the road of this affliction is not unlike many other diverse roads of suffering that God permits or orders in the lives of His children. Indeed, it is often the case that these circumstances are allowed to bring us to a fuller knowledge of who He is and who we are in relation to Him.

I write for the thousands of other Christians who share my affliction hoping that within these pages, they will find a soul mate. My great desire is to offer up hope, encouragement and education to those who are thus afflicted so that they may be better able to live with and manage these distressing disorders.

It is also my goal that the reader will come away with a new perspective on mental disorders. That rather than dismissing, denying or ignoring them they will bravely acknowledge them as valid afflictions. I pray that the knowledge gained from reading this book will open up hearts of empathy and compassion in the Christian community rather than judgment and disdain. Yet, it is my uppermost goal to convince the individual sufferer that the activity of God in their lives is in no way limited by the presence of an anxiety disorder. It is, in fact, the exact opposite. The most radical change in my own perspective concerning my anxiety disorder has been in my being able to say that God has done a work in my life not, *in spite* of it, but rather, *because* of it. This change has come about as I've gained a deeper understanding of the following scripture; "But He said to me, 'my grace is sufficient for you for my power is made perfect in weakness.'" 1.

The first section of this book highlights some, though not all, of my own personal journey of living with an anxiety disorder. I'm not sharing these private struggles to drum up sympathy. In fact, it would have been far easier and way more comfortable for me to never have done so. However, one of the greatest encouragements I've had concerning my own suffering has come from the open and transparent testimonies of others who share my affliction. Reading their comments or hearing from their own lips about their thoughts and struggles has been like hearing my own voice. It removes the sense of isolation that the disorder creates. Suddenly I'm blessed with the knowledge that I'm not alone. I'm not the singularly freakish anomaly that I thought I was. Someone else really understands; really knows just how intense and agonizing the mental pain of my disorder is. That understanding creates unbelievable empathy and compassion as well as provoking a great desire to reach out in loving support and fervent prayer for one another. This indeed, is a thing that God desires for His children to do for one another. The book of Corinthians prompts us in this way; "Praise be to the God and Father of our Lord Jesus Christ. The Father of all compassion and the God of all comfort who comforts us in all our troubles, so that we can comfort those in any trouble with the comfort we ourselves have received from God." 2.

The second portion of this book offers some practical suggestions for the sufferer. I will be delving into things like symptoms, causes and types of anxiety disorders as well as treatment recommendations and practical measures that can greatly benefit people who are afflicted. In this section of the book, I will be sharing some techniques and practices that have greatly assisted me in managing my own disorder. **This portion of the book in not intended to be used as a substitute for or replacement of the counsel or recommendations of professional physicians who diagnose and treat these disorders. I strongly recommend that all people who experience debilitating anxiety seek professional help for their disorders.** I will even go a step further in suggesting that the things you read in this book be discussed with your own doctor to ascertain whether he or she concurs with it.

I feel the need to comment on something that will be obvious to the reader, which is the redundancy in this book. There will be times as you are reading that you might think: "She already made that point." The redundancy in this book is on purpose. Anxiety disorders and in particular OCD are so stubbornly repetitive and redundant in nature that one must attack them with the same measure of stubborn and redundant persistence that they dole out. The lessons must be repeated over and over until the sufferer becomes persuaded to accept them and the behavior modifications must be practiced again and again until they become second nature. Therefore, the redundancy in this book serves to remind and persuade the sufferer to keep at it until they get it right.

Further on in the last chapter of the book I will be sharing how I've come to view my affliction as *purposeful*. I am now able to see it as a tool which God has used to deepen my relationship with Him rather than a hindrance to growth or a thing that I need to be cured of so that I'm able to live a life that bears fruit for His kingdom. I will also be devoting a rather large chapter solely to the most distressing and confounding thing that a Christian afflicted with anxiety might experience which is called "Religious OCD." My own Religious OCD really threw me for a loop. It is extremely difficult for a person with this form of OCD to distinguish and separate the manifestations of the OCD theme from a spiritual problem. Yet amazingly, even in the intense agony of this type of OCD God has taught me even more about the sufficiency of His grace. One big lesson that I've learned, (okay – I'll admit, I am *still* learning), is that to be able to experience the fullness of His grace, I really need to keep on admonishing myself in this way: "Get over yourself, Mitzi!" What do I mean by that? Well, I suppose the only way for you to find out is to read this book.

I will be praying for each and every one of you who ventures on in this book hoping to find help for your own mental pain, that God might see fit to use it as a tool of His grace whereby He might reach out in love and encouragement to you.

Notes:

1. 2 Corinthians 12:9, NIV
2. 2 Corinthians 1: 3-4, NIV

Part One

CHAPTER 1

Sudden Onset

A DAY FILLED with cleaning, cooking, laundry, chasing after a toddler and caring for an infant can cause the bedtime hour to be the most favored of the day. Such was the case for me one winter evening back in 1980. Sleep wasn't playing any hide and seek games with me, as I drifted off the moment my head hit the pillow. Little did I know that this would be the last night for well over a year that sleep would cooperate with me in such a willing manner. Within fifteen minutes of falling asleep I was jolted to consciousness by the physical sensations of a racing heart, trembling, sweating, difficulty breathing, ringing in my ears and a strange sensation that I struggle to describe to this day of floating outside of my own body. Accompanying these physical sensations was an overwhelming feeling of sheer terror. This nocturnal episode, as I would learn much later on, was my very first panic attack. I'd never felt such an overpowering sensation of fear. Even the fear that I'd experienced when I'd climbed the face of a vertical cliff in the mountains of Colorado as a teen paled in comparison to this. I was frightened beyond belief of – something. Yet I couldn't identify the target to which the fear was aimed. *Am I dying?* I wondered. After a few minutes nearly all of the symptoms subsided but as they passed the tracks they left behind were those of impending doom and dread.

As I lay back down for a second attempt at sleep, my mind continued to ponder the event to try and come up with an explanation as to what had just happened to me. Unable to answer that question, I decided that I would let it go until morning and tried to encourage myself with the thought that *even the smallest of worries loom larger in the middle of the night. The morning will surely bring clarity to my mind and I'll be able to figure it out then.*

Shortly after that I managed to fall back to sleep, but before I got into a very deep sleep, I was assaulted by yet another episode exactly like the first. I sat up in bed trying to breathe and calm my racing heart. I hated that it was the middle of the night because I wanted to get up, turn on a light and pace around the room. I thought of waking my husband but couldn't imagine how I could begin to describe what was happening to me without him thinking I'd gone totally nuts. Then it hit me. *Maybe I am having some sort of nervous breakdown. Maybe this is just the beginning of it and before long I'll wind up in a mental hospital.* Sickening nausea gripped me at this horrible possibility. I sat there mentally challenging that notion. I had been feeling just fine, functioning normally and I loved my role of homemaker, wife, and mother. So I couldn't come up with any reason that I should suddenly go insane. Fully awake with my mind racing in circles I lay staring at the ceiling until just before dawn when I finally managed to drift off for another hour or so.

The morning was a welcome sight and I got up determined to put the night's events behind me. Yet there would be no escape or avoidance of the manifestations of that night as they began to haunt my days also. When they materialized, they would completely overwhelm my mind and body. With each passing day, they increased in number and severity.

In retrospect, most of these attacks included every single one of the known symptoms of Panic Disorder. At that time, however, I'd never heard the term Panic Disorder so I was wholly in the dark as to what was happening to me. I was unaware and uneducated about all types of anxiety disorders and, in this instance; my ignorance certainly did not lead to bliss.

It wasn't that I didn't have a way of speaking to myself about the attacks. I referred to each one of them as **IT** - ugly nightmarish **IT'S** used in my daily thought life with frantic statements such as: *Oh no, here* **IT** *comes again, I wish **IT** would stop, why can't I make **IT** stop and always – Dear God, please make **IT** go away!*

I began to spend all of my waking hours with fear as my constant companion and nights with terror as an ever-present monster. Only the monster wasn't hiding in the closet or behind the curtains like the fears of my childhood. Instead, it was haunting the realm of my mind. I felt as if I was living with a lunatic in my head.

Years later I would awake from a dream with these words on my lips; "I am my own stalker." It struck me funny when I heard myself muttering them, but as I pondered them, I had to admit that those words were very descriptive of what it's like to live with an anxiety disorder that has set up camp in your brain.

As time wore on I began to not only fear the attacks but to live in dread of when and where they might happen. I was scared to death to tell anyone about them for fear that to do so might lead to my being committed to a mental institution. Therefore, being out in public or around family and friends became an exhausting exercise of faking normalcy. My life was soon consumed with a constant striving within.

There may be someone reading this account who is might be thinking: *why didn't she just go to the Lord in prayer, lay this burden at His feet, turn around and just leave it there?* I wish to make it clear that from the moment of my first attack I sought the Lord's help continually. I went to Him in prayer every hour of every day and I spent countless hours poring over His Word. Many times - for most of the night, while everyone else in the entire city lay peacefully asleep. That was how I felt – utterly alone in my suffering. *"I am weary with my groaning all the night I make my bed to swim."* 1. *"When I lie down, I think; 'how long before I get up?'"* 2.

Another unpleasant effect of my condition was that it caused me to feel isolated from everyone else whom I deemed to be "normal folk." It caused me to withdraw into a tight little bundle of self, but there was no comfort to be found there. Night after night as I kneeled on the cold floor of our living room, my Bible open, with a blanket thrown over my shoulders, I would dwell within the pages of the Psalms desperately seeking the comforting presence of my God. *"Whom, have I in heaven but thee? And there is none upon earth that I desire beside thee."* 3. There, I found words that spoke directly to my feelings; words that caused me to know that although I felt utterly alone in my suffering there had been others who experienced similar pain. *"Why are you downcast, O my soul? Why so disturbed within me? Put your hope in God, for I will yet again praise Him, my Savior, and my God."* 4.

Why indeed was I so troubled? I asked myself this question innumerable times as well as others such as; "Why is your faith so small and weak? Why can't you just let go of this and stop allowing this fear to attack and control you?" There was this strange dichotomy within me of knowing rationally that I could trust God just as I had in the past yet not being able to get my emotions to line up with that knowledge. This confused me and made me desperate to try and figure out why I couldn't find a sense of peace. But the more I struggled to muster up those emotions of faith, peace and calmness, the more aware I became of just how lacking I was in them. On one of many sleepless nights I was reading a passage in the book of Timothy when a familiar verse seemed to leap off the page. *"God has not given you the spirit of fear, but of power and love and a sound mind."* 5. This verse struck and stabbed at me as never before and seemed to drive me further into the dark pit of self-accusation. Much later on, this verse, when placed within its proper context would prove to be of tremendous encouragement to me. Yet, at *that* time I could only view it as more evidence of my failure to trust in God.

My situation, I concluded, was my own fault. It was obviously not of God and if not of God then clearly I was somehow to blame for it. I began to believe that I was reaping the harvest of my past tendencies toward fear and worry. I pleaded with God in earnest to forgive me for my lack of faith and to help me to trust in Him for peace and comfort. I begged Him to take away the horrid attacks of fear so that I could live with a sound mind instead of the insanity that I felt certain would eventually envelope me. After praying, I would begin to feel somewhat hopeful and encouraged. But these feelings were always short lived as each new day brought on more and more of the attacks and with them deep wounds of anguish and despair. I could only cling to the hope that eventually God would show me the way out of this dark pit. *"My comfort in my suffering is this; your promise preserves my life."* 6.

As time wore on, I found that the only way I could cope was to be in constant motion. Although I was able to carry out my duties as wife and mother I did so in a sort of robotic way, going through the motions while my mind was wholly preoccupied with the war that raged within. And, in *that* war I was most often cowering and hiding. This was eventually evidenced by an outward posture of stooped shoulders and downcast eyes. Although I hid, I couldn't break free of or take my focus off the ghoul within my head.

Nights were always far worse as I was usually only able to get a maximum of three hours of fitful sleeping. Eating became a big challenge for me. Food tasted like sand and my stomach was constantly churning with nausea. "My heart is blighted and withered like grass; *I forget to eat my food. Because of my loud groaning I am reduced to skin and bones."* 7.

There were rumors circulating that I might be anorexic as my weight dropped dramatically to 115 pounds. At nearly five feet eight inches tall, I actually *did* take on the appearance of an anorexic. People often make flippant remarks and careless statements about this type of weight loss saying things like: "I wish *I* had that disorder so *I* could lose some weight." One should be careful what they wish for. The mental pain of a severe anxiety disorder is excruciating and most that experience it would gladly trade off a few extra pounds in exchange for rightly balanced brain chemistry.

Alongside of reading my Bible I began to search within some Christian books for a solution to my inability to find peace. One of the books that I picked up was titled, "The Power of Positive Thinking" by Norman Vincent Peale. Hoping to tap into that power I diligently studied each and every page and did my level best to apply the techniques therein. Yet nothing that I did served to minimize the problem in any way. Feeling more disheartened than ever I eventually turned away from this book and went straight back to the Word of God praying that He would, in time, show me the door that would lead me out of this unending nightmare.

Notes:

1. Psalm 6:6a KJV
2. Job 7:4 NIV
3. Psalm 73:25 KJV
4. Psalm 45:5 NIV
5. 2 Timothy 1:7 KJV
6. Psalm 119:50 NIV
7. Psalm 102:4-5 NIV

CHAPTER 2

SHAME AND BLAME

OVER THE NEXT few months, I began to spiral further down into the quicksand of despair. The more I struggled to break free from the grips of anxiety and those horrible thoughts of insanity the more mired I became. Feelings of abandonment began to overtake me. *"My God! My God! Why have you forsaken me? Why are you so far from saving me, so far from the words of my groaning? O, my God. I cry out by day, but you do not answer, by night, and am not silent."* 1. This feeling of being cut off from the comforting presence of God eventually led me to believe that He was angry with me. *There must be something*, I pondered, *which I have done to bring this oppressive condition on myself.* Perhaps God was punishing me. To my mind, this was not because God was mean or cruel but rather because He is a just and righteous judge. Therefore, I came to suspect that I must have been receiving my just deserts for some hidden sin. *"Be not deceived, God is not mocked, for whatever a man soweth, that shall he also reap."* 2.

This led to many hours of self-examination and poring over past sins. I revisited the sins of my past; all those things that had been motivated by rebellion, willfulness, selfish choices, pride, and stubbornness; for all of that, I would plead with God to forgive me and restore the joy of my relationship with Him. *"For I am about to fall, and my pain is ever with me. I confess my iniquity; I am troubled by my sin."* 3. I understood the need for consequences and feared that the state of despair I was in might somehow be linked to some past sin that lay yet unrevealed to me. So I prayed for God to reveal all my sin and I diligently sought His forgiveness for every past failure that I could think of. Yet with each new confession and each new effort to somehow stir up feelings of faith and peace I only felt all the more condemned and confounded. *Would this situation go on forever?* The thought horrified me. Yet God's word struck down that notion. *"He will not always accuse, nor will He harbor His anger forever. He does not treat us as our sins deserve or repay us according to our iniquities. For as high as the heavens are above the earth, so great is His love for those who fear Him."* 4. These reassuring words should have brought reassuring feelings, but instead the struggle continued.

There were times when I would experience a few hours of blessed relief. During those times, the fear of insanity and God's anger at me seemed absurd. But then the anxiety would come flooding back with a rush of terror as if a dam had been holding it back. And the sudden swell of anxiety often seemed much fiercer than it had been before. Would stability ever return or would I live out the rest of my life as a cowering trembling wreck? *"Though we fall, we shall not be utterly cast down."*5. "Utterly cast down" – was exactly how I felt; cast down, cast aside, even shunned by my God. And although I knew deep down that God's Word was to be trusted, I could not get my feelings to validate that. If asked to honestly describe myself, my response would have been something like this: "The useless one, the weak one", and even scarier, "the crazy one." I had this horrid image in my head of how painful it might be for any member of my family to claim me as their wife, daughter or mother. I began to view myself as a blot on their good reputations – an embarrassment, and a black sheep. This was not only regarding my blood relatives but also to my extended Christian family. I would be that person that people wished to avoid because of the awkwardness of trying to converse with a nut case. There would be hushed whispers of, "isn't it so awful – so sad about Mitzi?" I began to envy every normal person that I encountered. There were times when I was even jealous of those who weren't Christians. I envied them for the confidence and calmness they seemed to possess. From my perspective, all the Christians that I knew seemed to stand far above me as giants of the faith. Oh, how I envied them! If it was a sin to do so, I didn't care. I wanted to be like them. At the very least, I wanted to live a normal and productive life. But I was unable to see how any kind of useable fruit could come out of this situation or from me. I had become a terrified pitiful heap of flesh. I was, I concluded, *"a wave of the sea driven about with the wind and tossed."* 6.

Yet even as the darkness threatened to close in and destroy me I clung desperately to the message of God's love for me. It was all I could do. I would hang on and wait for the dawn. I had heard His voice of love and peace so clearly in my past and had been greatly comforted by it. My only hope was that I would hear it again with ears of faith and a heart that chimed in.

Notes:

1. Psalm 22:1-3 NIV
2. Galatians 6:7 KJV
3. Psalm 38:17-18 NIV
4. Psalm 103:9-11 NIV
5. Psalm 37:24a KJV
6. James 1:6b KJV

CHAPTER 3

HORRIBLE THOUGHTS AND HIDEOUS IMAGES

IT WAS NO small feat of strength to do so, but somehow I managed to hide my condition from most people. Even some of those who were very close to me. I have a stubborn streak in me which when coupled with a fairly high threshold for pain allowed me to put up a façade of normalcy. But the thing which assisted me most in this effort was my pride. The fear of public humiliation over the possibility that I might be mentally ill or have to be institutionalized bolstered me in my efforts to hide my pain. Many people came in and out of our home without the slightest clue as to how disturbed I was. I also went to their houses, our church, the grocery store, restaurants and other places, yet in time every one of these outings became increasingly difficult. To go out and about only seemed to intensify and trigger my episodes of panic. I began to dread having to go anywhere.

One particular outing stands out in my memory as one of the few times that the anxiety won out over my ability to fake it. I was at a small dinner party over at my folk's house with my brother and his fiancé. My Mom is an outstanding cook but on this occasion everything on the table was revolting to my stomach. I remember the panic rising up. The ringing ears, dizziness, racing heart, trembling, cold sweat and nausea began to overwhelm me. I tried several times to shake it off by excusing myself to use the bathroom but when I would come back to the table, I would feel as if at any moment I would lose total control and turn into some sort of screaming wild lunatic. I could picture my poor family looking on in horror as they held me down to keep me from hurting myself or one of them. That was it for me. I just couldn't sit there and endure it one moment longer. In shame and humiliation,

I quietly excused myself from the table, muttering something about not feeling well and hid out in one of the bedrooms for the rest of the evening. I was angry at myself for not being able to tough it out, but the mental torture of what I had experienced at that dinner table was more powerful than the feelings of embarrassment at having to leave. The urge to get out, run and hide was so loud and insistent that resistance seemed impossible.

Over the years, I've learned that to ask yourself, "can things get any worse?" is a bad idea. This is because most often the answer always seems to end up being, "yes". Although it seemed to me that my descent into this chasm of fear and despair couldn't get any deeper, I was soon to learn that there were worst terrors yet to come. Just round the bend there lay yet another monster far uglier and fiercer than the one I'd been battling against for so long. The element of surprise is an effective tactic for scaring the wits out of someone and that was exactly how my new monster approached me.

One morning, in an effort to distract myself from the war in my head, I was thumbing through a book that I had previously read on the topic of disciplining children from a Christian perspective. As I browsed my way through this book, my eyes happened to settle on a page where the author was contrasting loving discipline with purely abusive behaviors. In order to demonstrate just how devastating certain forms of child abuse could be, they had offered up an example of a particular case of abuse in graphic detail that was so disturbing, that when I read it I experienced extreme horror and revolting nausea. This act of abuse had been committed by a young mother against her helpless infant daughter. It was at that very moment that my condition took an ugly and unexpected turn for the worse. It suddenly occurred to me that *I* might be capable of doing something like that to one of my precious children.

It's very hard for me to describe the mental torture that this doubt filled accusation caused in me. I wished that I could somehow unread the book, or unthink that thought. Instead, this thought began to haunt my every waking hour. It would torment and pummel me from the moment I woke up in the morning and it would be accompanied by horrific mental images of my going totally insane and mutilating one of my children.

In retrospect, it's revealing to note that when I'd read this same book in the past with the absence of my anxiety disorder, that I'd been able to read that description of abuse, move on and not dwell on it at all. But the experience was wholly different when my brain was flooded with intense feelings of anxiety. Due to this, my mental warfare against the thoughts and images that this account of child abuse provoked was both fierce and constant. My war tactics went like this; I would spend every hour of every day looking inside of myself for reassuring evidence that such a thing just wasn't possible of me. I would think, *The Lord would never allow you to do such a thing* and *you would definitely kill yourself before you would ever harm one of your children.*

Yet, even as I would assert these things, I couldn't get my feelings to provide any confirmation whereby I could obtain absolute reassurance that I wouldn't or couldn't do such a thing. I was unable to rid myself of that nagging doubt no matter how hard I tried. I began to wonder if the fact that the thoughts and images wouldn't leave me alone was some sort of dire warning that I would act upon them. But then I'd think; *you'd have to be totally insane to do something like that,* which would then make me think; *but isn't it true that insane people don't really know or worry that they're insane? Isn't it rather that they don't think they are?* And this thought, would lead to yet another doubt filled possibility: *Maybe it won't be like that with you. Maybe you'll just do it because you can't control the urge anymore than you can stop the thoughts from being in your head. You might even be fully aware and fully horrified right while you're doing it!*

In the midst of all this endless striving, the gut-wrenching anxiety seemed unbearable. With each new twist in the accusation, I would step up my effort at mental warfare. I felt certain that I needed to do this because if I didn't keep up the fight I feared that the horrible obsessions might just win out and take over my will. The harder I fought against the thoughts and disturbing images the more they plagued me and the more they plagued me, the more fearful I became that they just might be true. There were periods of time where, if I was intensely focused on a task, that I was able to shove them to the outer realms of my consciousness. They never really left, though. Instead it was as if they were just resting up between attacks so that, after gaining new strength, they could charge in with a vengeance that seemed even more lethal than the previous attacks.

All of this was a manifestation of an anxiety disorder that is often co-morbid with Panic Disorder called OCD, and in my case, a particular variety of OCD referred to as "purely obsessional" or "Pure O." 1. But - just as I was ignorant of the existence of Panic Disorder, so too I had not one smidgen of information available to me about the disorder of OCD so I fought it both ignorantly and blindly.

There came a day where I entertained the notion that maybe my children would be safer if I killed myself. Not that I really desired to do such a thing, but if doing so would keep them safe then perhaps, that would, in the end, be my only choice. The very fact that I could think such a thing demonstrates just how large and threatening those revolting thoughts had become. I was well aware that to take my own life would only bring tremendous pain and sorrow to every member of my family. But in the end, the knowledge that to take my own life would be very displeasing to God was the thing which forced me to turn away from contemplating it any further. My life still belonged to God as well as the number of days I would live it. Still, there loomed the sickening possibility of my slipping over the edge into the abyss of total insanity where my ability to reason would be annihilated, and *then* – I thought, that my suicide might occur outside the realm of my will.

One day shortly after these new consuming doubts had made their first appearance there came a knock on my front door which seemed to give them even more weight and validity. Upon opening the door, I came face to face with a person that I came to see as a symbol of the ghost of my future existence. There she stood, a young woman staring blankly into my face. I can't remember much of what she said to me but

I clearly discerned her total disconnect from the world of reality. She wanted to come inside, but my not knowing what she was capable of and prompted by my own present state of inner turmoil I chose to block her entrance and quickly shut the door in her face and locked it. I watched her as she headed across the street and went into the house where she lived with her mother. With her departure I slumped onto the couch; my heart pounding in horror. *That's me!* I thought. *I might end up just like her in the very near future.* Her appearance seemed to me as a prophet of doom. "Why Lord?" I cried out in anguish. "Is my terror too small that you must send me even more? When Lord? And, more importantly, h*ow will this nightmare end?*" *"How long, O Lord? Will you forget me forever?"* 2.

Notes:

1. Dr. Stephen Phillipson @ http://www.ocdonline.com, From the article: "Thinking the Unthinkable."
2. Psalm 13:1a NIV

CHAPTER 4

"And Now unto Him who is Able" 1.

Bleak and dreary winters followed up by that experience of the very first day of sunshine and warmth which heralds the approach of spring, feels, to most of us, like receiving an infusion of sudden joy. We refuse to stay indoors. We run out into the warmth of the sun, shedding constricting layers of coats and sweaters and inhaling those balmy breezes into our lungs as if breathing was something totally new and fresh to us. Usually, a day like this is followed up very quickly by another onslaught of winter weather as the "old man" doesn't die out easily. But just that one day of warm weather gives reason to hope because we know that spring is on its way. This analogy aptly describes my feelings during an event that happened to me just at the point where my disorder had nearly robbed me of any hope that I'd ever again know a moment's peace or the slightest hint of joy. I call it my "glimpse of springtime."

The unrelenting attacks had led to an ever increasing avoidance of leaving our house. The challenge of enduring and attempting to hide my symptoms in public places became too exhausting. I was able to manage short outings or brief visits to other people's homes knowing that relief would come if I could just stick it out for a little while.

Meanwhile, I had completely lost my ability to drive because doing so always triggered debilitating panic attacks and I feared that I'd lose control of the car while fighting one off. Eventually, even riding as a passenger in a car was excruciating. I felt trapped and the motion of the car made me feel as if my head might explode. I would spend the whole time pleading internally with God: *Please help me to stay calm.* Upon reaching any destination, I would generally feel completely exhausted and drained.

Each time my husband, Dennis, suggested a movie or dinner out I'd make up some excuse as to why I couldn't go. I never shared even the tiniest detail with him as to what I was experiencing. No; not to him or anybody else except God.

One morning my mom phoned me with an invitation to go on a shopping trip to Detroit's Renaissance Center with her and my two sisters in law. I knew she was aware that something was wrong with me and probably thought that the trip would do me some good. Perhaps she thought that it would cheer me up or get my mind off my troubles for a while. But the daughter who would have normally been thrilled to go on such an outing was gone and the person that I had become felt overwhelmingly terrified at the idea. The plan included doing lunch at a restaurant atop one of the two Renaissance Center towers which featured a bird's eye view of the city, complete with glass walls that went from floor to ceiling. To turn down the invitation meant that I would probably be hurting the feelings of family members that I truly loved. I knew that the guilt that would ensue from that choice would only serve to increase my embarrassment and disgust over my behavior. Not knowing how to avoid these consequences left me with no other choice but to accept the invite.

As I hung up the phone, my thoughts whirled with a storm consisting of all sorts of fear-filled questions and dreaded possibilities. *How would I get through that car ride?* I couldn't imagine that I would even be able to carry on a conversation let alone sit still for that long. *The shopping will be easier*, I thought. *Because I can keep moving and that would serve to help dampen down some of the fear. Yes*, I encouraged myself, *it will be easier for you to fake it then.*

Yet, to picture myself doing lunch perched on top of that building was something I could barely think about, let alone actually do. I hoped those glass windows were unbreakable because I figured that I might just finally lose it altogether, jump up from the table with a maniacal look on my face, run headlong right through the glass and plummet to my death. Wouldn't that serve future generations as an instructive family moment? "You darn kids better stay away from that edge! Remember your great Gramma took a nose dive off that tower in Detroit and they say that she bounced off at least four cars before she finally hit the ground. You wouldn't want to end up like her would you?"

In retrospect, it might be easy to find OCD thoughts humorous or absurd, but when you are besieged with a storm of anxiety, there is absolutely nothing amusing about them. The television character Monk might seem quirky and comical, but in the real world people afflicted with a bad flare of OCD are in tremendous mental anguish and making light of their illness as if it's nothing more than comical or quirky behavior isn't helpful. There comes a time after learning how to manage the disorder where those of us with OCD can choose to purposely treat our obsessions as outlandish or absurd as demonstrated by me in the imagined scenario above. But for others to poke fun at our illness when we're in severe pain can be very hurtful.

It wasn't that I had any desire to actually end my life by jumping off a building but rather that I feared the uncontrollable and unexplainable feelings of fear that I was continually having might just send me over the edge – quite literally.

I had developed a revulsion for any sort of wide open space. To look up into the expanse of the sky created a dizzying feeling of falling up. Any environment that was high, wide or expansive would generally bring on a severe panic attack. The auditorium of our church posed a particular difficulty for me.

When I was a little girl and before I had the attention span that enabled me to glean much from my Pastor's sermons I would handle my boredom by counting all the recessed light fixtures in the ceiling. Now, much to my dismay, I couldn't even glance up one time without experiencing the symptoms of a panic attack.

In light of all this I couldn't conceive how it would be possible for me to get through that shopping trip without acting in a bizarre manner. I didn't want to spoil the trip for the others, but I also wished desperately that I wouldn't have to go because to do so might be the tip-off to my family that I was mentally ill. I began to pray fervently that God would send me relief from this nightmare before the day of the trip. I told Him that I wasn't just asking this for my sake but also for the sake of my family. I wanted so very badly to be able to just go with them and experience a relaxed and enjoyable day. I saw no way out of it. I would just have to go and hope for the best. After praying, I had an inexplicable sense that God had not only heard me but that somehow, some way He would help me through that day.

I hadn't experienced one day of relief from the attacks of fear up until the day of our trip. That morning I awoke with a wonderfully refreshed and calm spirit. But even more surprising than that, I experienced a very tangible sense of happiness and actual anticipation regarding the trip. I can't begin to describe how wonderful it was to feel this way after so many months of dread and terror. The previous analogy of that first warm day that herald's the coming of spring is the closest I can come to it.

When my family arrived to pick me up, the joyful anticipation that I felt made me think that I might just run outside and start jumping up and down as if I were a little school girl reacting to the gift of a pony.

The trip ended up being a day which survives in my memory as a source of pure joy. Best of all I was a participant in the creation of that joyful memory rather than the dark blot I had imagined I would have been. We rode these glass elevators up the outside of one tower to the restaurant. This brief ascension even caused the others to experience an element of nervousness, but for me, it was just plain fun. It was rather like a ride at an amusement park. Even today, I'm not amused by amusement park rides. I'm generally freaked out about them, so to enjoy that particular ride was indeed a miracle. I can recall a weak attempt at humor by me as we sat at our lunch table next to one of the glass windows.

I began to point my finger at the parking lot below us and said something to the effect of; "look at that! Do you guys see that?"

I had them all straining for a little while to try and see what it was that I was referring to and asking; "what – I don't see anything. What are you looking at?"

To which I finally replied; "I don't know why you guys can't see it. It's sitting right on the back of that mouse, right there on the ground by the left rear tire of that blue car." Yes – a poor joke indeed, but the jovial atmosphere of our time together provided the fuel it needed to make it seem totally hilarious to all of us at the time.

The entire day was nothing short of blissful to me. The thoughts, the ugly images, the panic attacks and the blackness that accompanied them had been completely and wholly removed from me. It was as if a window shade that had been blocking all sunlight had suddenly sprung open and I had been embraced by the warming rays of calmness, comfort, and joy. If I had tried to force myself to be upset about something on that day, I would have found it impossible. For me, this was a demonstration of God's power to heal in an instant, yet all according to His will and in His time.

The very next day that thick, dark window shade dropped down again. The thoughts, the disturbing images, the panic attacks and the dark gloom that accompanied them all came flooding back. My brief R&R from the war in my head was over. Yet the oasis of this day provided a spark of hope that God indeed was able to heal me. My trial, however, was not over by any means. I had much left that God wanted me to learn, not the least of which was this; *"My grace is sufficient for you."* 2.

Notes:

1. Ephesians 3:20 (KJV)
2. 2 Corinthians 12:9a (NIV)

CHAPTER 5

Dysfunctional

It is often affirmed by physicians that while stress can certainly exacerbate an illness, it can also be the very vehicle by which an illness will first manifest itself in an individual who is predisposed to it. I must acknowledge that stress has certainly played a role in both the onset and severity of my Anxiety Disorder. Most Anxiety Disorders are opportunistic illnesses which usually make their entrance through doors of prolonged periods of stress.

I married at a young age, after a rather tumultuous dating period. Dennis and I were head over heels in love, but more than anything else we were in love with the *feeling* of being in love. It took me a long time to learn that while romance has her place, she also makes promises that she can't keep. Now after thirty-five years of marriage the true meaning of love has finally been realized for the both of us.

Yet when you are young, it's easy to place your confidence in those intense emotions of attraction, romance and passion to the point that you feel certain that love will conquer all and that those feelings will never fade. Dennis and I concentrated on those feelings more than anything else. We shoved aside all practical concerns that should have been dealt with before we decided to marry. The consequence of this was that when the sparks died down, we had to face the fact that we really didn't know each other very well and that we had many differing opinions and ideas about the practical aspects of married life. We weren't good at communicating these things to one another in ways that didn't feel like an insult or attack. This led to arguments and conflict which for me were so scary and unpleasant that I would usually choose avoidance over confrontation. For me, disagreeing with one another fired off an alarm signal that our marriage might be doomed to fail. Rather than face that dreaded possibility, I would often withdraw and fall silent whenever a conflict arose. The birth of our first two children, financial difficulties and the total lack of productive communication with one another created a level of inner stress and pressure within me that was truly unhealthy.

Dennis and I were total opposites. He would never hesitate to speak his mind on a matter, but if I disagreed with him, I would rarely tell him because if we fought at all I would panic inside. This characteristic of avoiding conflict wasn't a new thing for me. All through my years growing up I never once argued with my childhood friends. I was afraid to do so because they might get mad at me and not want to be my friend anymore. I was, however quite good at arguing with my brothers and my parents as I felt confident that I couldn't lose them. They were pretty much stuck with me. But in my marriage I would hold my thoughts inside and stew over them, often feeling very angry within but unable to express it outwardly.

Then, after the birth of our second child the post-partum hormone shift, combined with my longstanding inner turmoil created the spark that ignited the flash fire of my disorder. And when the disorder overtook me, my habit of not communicating effectively with Dennis made it all the harder for me to open up to him about the mental pain I was in. It was as if I lived in a padded isolation cell in my own head where I was frantically dashing here and there to try and escape the fear and torture but finding no way out. This sense of isolation and desperation eventually drove me to seek professional help from a psychologist.

I made up my mind, ahead of time, that the doctor had to be a Christian because I felt quite strongly that my problems were mostly spiritual in nature. Taking that step was scary for me because I knew that I would have a lot of difficulties being really open and transparent about the thoughts that I had been experiencing which fixated on me going insane or harming one of my children. To admit such a thing would mean I would be vulnerable to being labeled a "nutcase" and that my friends, family and the larger community of the church would somehow find out about it. I could well imagine there would be some folk who would blame me for my condition. Why shouldn't they when I certainly blamed myself? They might gossip about me, judge me or avoid me. Yet my desperation to feel better outweighed my fear of shame, so I decided to take that desperate plunge.

Before my visit to the psychologist, I laid out a game plan of how I would divulge my problem. First I would share about the difficulties in my marriage and use that as a stepping stone to get to the most difficult subject of my current mental state. I would express concern to him that these difficulties might be playing a role as instigators of the attacks of terror, dreadful thoughts, and horrific obsessions. But once I got there and after opening up about the marriage problems, my effort to describe my mental warfare was so vague that I can't imagine that the doctor even picked up on just how bad the anxiety had become. I only explained that I'd been feeling very nervous and was having great difficulty sleeping. It's not that I wasn't concerned about the lack of good communication between my husband and myself, it was that I couldn't even manage to address *that* issue until I got help to find my way out of the debilitating mental anguish that I was in. I'm quite sure that if I'd been wholly transparent with the doctor he would have been in a better position to diagnose my disorder. Instead, he zeroed in directly and only upon the marriage difficulties and what role I could play to make Dennis feel more loved and appreciated. He asked me all about Dennis, his past and current situations, his job, his stress level, etc. Then he proceeded to give me some suggestions as to practical ways in which I could be a better wife; one that loved more selflessly and compassionately. From that point on, he totally lost my attention as my level of anxiety rose to a heightened pitch while I sat there thinking; *how can I do any of these things when all I have the energy to do right now is to cling desperately to my last shred of sanity? Can't this guy see that I'm too whacked out to be of any use to anyone? Isn't it obvious to him that my current condition makes me pretty much useless as a wife or a mother and that it's me who's dysfunctional and needs healing, not my husband? I need help!*

That was my one and only appointment with that doctor. I left his office feeling all the more defeated and piled on top of that was a deep sense of shame at my inability to be the wife that God intended me to be. I felt like a pile of dirt. *"For He knows how we are formed; He remembers that we are dust."* 1. The dust that represented my life was severely disturbed. Just the slightest puff of wind unsettled me and the disturbance had grown into a frenzied tornado that whipped my emotions into a swirling and persistent nightmare of unending terror. *"Once I was prosperous and used to say, that nothing could ever shake me – when you showed me favor, Adonai, I was firm as a mighty mountain. But when you hid your face, I was struck with terror. I called to you, Adonai; pleaded for mercy; 'What gain is there in my destruction, in my going down into the pit?' Will the dust praise you? Will it proclaim your faithfulness?"* 2.

My next effort to obtain some relief was to make an appointment to see my family physician. He'd known me from birth and therefore when I walked into his office, he recognized instantly that I was experiencing some sort of mental disorder. He also encouraged me by telling me that he felt quite certain that I'd be able to work through the difficulties in my marriage because he was going to help me with my "nervousness." He then proceeded to give me a very sweet and compassionate pep talk about what a good person I was and how he just knew that with all I had going for me that I'd get through this period and have a stable and solid family just as my folks did. It felt good to hear those hope-filled statements. Then he prescribed several medications for me to try over the next few weeks. I went away from that appointment with a flicker of hope that I hadn't felt for quite some time. I took the medications faithfully in the weeks that followed, but I might as well have been eating skittles for all the good they did me. They had absolutely no positive effect at all. I still couldn't sleep. I had at least hoped they'd accomplish that much for me. Eating was still a big challenge for me. Worst of all they provided no release from the mental war. I still spent every day battling it out. *"I am bowed down and brought very low; all day long I go about mourning."* 3.

So now instead of functioning as a normal wife and mother I viewed myself as some sort of hideous zombie which replaced the old Mitzi with this shell of a body. I went through the daily motions of my duties while the inner woman – the real me had been snatched away and was being held hostage in the prison of her mind. My outer appearance even changed. My shoulders slumped, my frame grew even more skeletal and my daily activity became mechanical.

This reminds me of an amusing moment when our oldest son was first beginning to sing Sunday school songs. He was about four at the time and after church one day he was singing this familiar children's song; "Jesus wants me for a Sunbeam." Although he had the tune down perfectly, the words were just a bit off. He was singing, "Jesus wants me for a Zombie." We had quite a laugh about it at the time.

But in thinking about just how zombie-like my daily activity had become I'm pretty certain that Jesus doesn't want any of us to serve Him as zombies. Yet it was in this zombie-like state that I still kept up the normal routine; the chores, caring for the children, cooking – yes, all the things that homemakers do. But there was a huge disconnect from my outward activity and that which was going on inside of me. Inwardly, I was intently focused and engaged in the unseen war that raged on and on without reprieve. There were no backup troops to call in so I could retreat or rest. I had to fight no matter how exhausted I was. At times, my battle tactics were cowardly. Instead of rushing the enemy I would cower or scream in silent terror. But most of the time I wrestled with the tortured thoughts. I couldn't let them win. I must win or die trying! I wanted the Lord to come rushing in and rescue me, but He seemed unwilling to do so. I knew that He was able, but I couldn't comprehend why He wouldn't. *"Why are you so far from saving me, so far from the words of my groaning?"* 4.

Notes:

1. Psalm 103:14 NIV
2. Psalm 30:9-10a NIV
3. Psalm 38:6 NIV
4. Psalm 22:1b

CHAPTER 6

You Can't Call a Time Out in the Middle of War

THE REASON WE humans love to go on vacation is that it provides a time of relief and release from the toil and labor of everyday life. It's a time of refreshment. We walk away from our regular work, schedules and phone calls to take a much needed time out.

Our family has a tradition of going to one special locale for vacation. I've been going there on a regular basis since I was a little girl. Over the years, it's become a home away from home for me. Being there stirs up wonderful memories of laughter, love, joy and the sweet companionship of family. In that place, the pace of our lives slows down. There are no schedules to keep and no pressure of daily obligations. There we engage in our favorite pastime. We fish! Every year we compile new family fishing history which will be passed down from generation to generation complete with photographs and detailed accounts of each extraordinary catch. Everyone looks forward to their moment of fame; "This year maybe I'll be the one who catches the big one."

When I'm in that place, I even dream about fishing in my sleep and often I've spent so much time on the water that I can still feel the gentle rocking of the small choppy waves that pass beneath the boat long after I've returned to the cottage. This place is still quite pristine. The air is fresh and invigorating. The wildlife is abundant and diverse. We call it "God's country." We indulge ourselves with the best food ever known to mankind; freshly caught, deep fried Northern Pike, which we top off with our favorite dessert – strawberry shortcake made with the locally grown berries that we pick while we're there. In the evenings, we will often gather together in one cottage to play cards or board games. We go to bed when we feel like it and get up when we feel like it. The sleep I've experienced while there is like the deep relaxed sleep of a baby. There's no middle of the night restlessness which I think may be attributed to the purity of the air. Yet the summer of my mental warfare placed an ugly mark on what should have been yet another blessed memory. In the weeks before our trip, I began to dread the car journey.

As I mentioned before, riding in a car had become a huge challenge for me and now I realized that compared to the short trips around town which I had learned to endure, the drive to our vacation spot would likely feel like a marathon of torture. There was no way that I would back out of it, though. I would not punish my family because of my condition. I would go and do my best to fake it while I was there. That five-hundred-mile journey was the longest and most arduous I've ever endured but much my surprise I arrived with my sanity still intact. I began to hope that the change of scenery might be just what I needed to break free from the endless cycle of fearful attacks, horrid thoughts and the intense striving that I experienced every day. But apparently you can't call a timeout when you're in the midst of war.

Dennis' folks came up to stay with us for a portion of the time that we were there. I managed, although I don't know how, to hide my mental condition from them. To them I probably just seemed a bit quieter than usual. I dreaded the nights because in the close quarters of the cottage with just curtain doors separating us from one another I was unable to get up, turn on a light, pace the floor or read for hours on end as was my practice while at home. So instead, I would just lie there staring into the darkness - listening to the deep rhythmic breathing of everyone else as they slept peacefully in their beds. I wished that I could go back in time and be that little girl who had slept in that same cottage with my family. Back then I had fought the closing of my eyelids not wanting to miss one moment of the sweetness of our time together. But sleep always won out and I'd drift off with a smile still plastered on my face as I reviewed the events of the day.

Oh… if only there were such a thing as "Never, Neverland" where a person doesn't have to grow up. But reality insists that we grow up and now as a grown up woman, the fear I was experiencing was far greater than any I had known as a child. I *would* hide it though and hope for that day when it would finally leave me. So I gritted it out as each and every night I forced myself to lie there, stiff as a board, determined not to disturb anyone else – not because I was unselfish but rather to protect my reputation. No one could know the truth; that I had become a total basket case. In this self-imposed loneliness, I mentally accused myself; *"I'm a freak. There's no one like me who can hear or understand my cries of anguish, no one to run to for comfort, I am utterly alone."* As a rebuttal to this the words of scripture would fly at me. *"I will never leave thee, nor forsake thee."* 1. To which I would reply; *"But Lord I can't find you in this darkness, I need so badly to feel your presence and the comfort of your healing touch!"*

Once again those haunting questions from the scriptures rang out in my head. *"My God, my God, why hast thou forsaken me? Why are thou so far from helping me, and from the words of my roaring? O my, God, I cry in the daytime, but thou hearest not; and in the night season, and am not silent."* 2.

When it came time to head out fishing I had hopefully anticipated that getting out on the lake would provide some measure of relief. I had this idea that if I could get away for just a bit from the exhausting task of faking it while around Dennis' folks and let the fresh air, the sunshine and gentle motion of the boat embrace me that I might be able to experience a few hours of respite. But I was sorely mistaken.

The whole setting; the wide open expanse of water and sky when coupled with the confinement of being trapped on a boat with nowhere to hide took my level of anxiety up to a frenzied pitch. It became so intense that I felt certain I wouldn't be able to bear it. I felt dizzy, nauseated and certain that I would pass out at any moment. I considered offering to swim ashore and walk back to the cottage but changed my mind because to do so would divulge the secret of my disturbed mental state. So I sat there, rigid and trembling gripping my fishing pole and staring at the bottom of the boat. And it was at that very moment that I began to give in to thoughts of despair. *Is this how I will spend the rest of my life?* The question horrified me. *Will this nightmare ever end?* Then; *if I don't get relief soon I will run out of strength to bear this any longer.* In this dread state of hopelessness, I approached God with a proposal. "Lord, I cannot go on like this anymore. If I must be afflicted, then please give me a different affliction – one that doesn't rob me of my mental stability. Please, Lord, I want to make a trade. You can even take my life if need be. Give me terminal cancer, take me home, but please release me from this endless nightmare. At least then I'll know that the end of pain is near."

In my mind, the release that death would bring seemed the better choice than continuing on for the rest of my days in that state. Yet I still knew that God must decide these matters. I could only make the petition. I couldn't choose the answer. So I waited; clinging desperately to that meager shred of faith in His promises that yet remained in me. *"And the God of all grace, who called you to His eternal glory in Christ, after you have suffered a little while, will Himself restore you and make you strong, firm and steadfast."* 3. I only hoped that His plan to restore me might take place while I was still on the earth rather than after my death.

Notes:

1. Hebrews 13:5b KJV
2. Psalm 22:1-2 KJV
3. 1 Peter 5:10 NIV

CHAPTER 7

The Unexpected

I've come to understand something about God that had escaped me for many years and I must confess that it's still something that I need to remind myself of more often than not. It is this; God works in and through the unexpected. *"For as the heavens are higher than the earth, so are my ways higher than your ways and my thoughts than your thoughts."* 1. This lesson has taught me that I need to rely on *who* God is more than on what is going on in and around my life circumstances. It means that the answer to my prayers to Him will often be very different from what I expect them to be. It means that there will be periods in my life when I won't be able to comprehend what He is doing, but even without that information, I can rely on who He is, on His character, on His unswerving promises, and on His perfect love.

The answer that He gave to my desperate cry for relief that day in the boat was not what I expected. God did not send relief to me in the form of a different affliction or death. He sent relief to me in the form of life. Not *my* life but rather the new life of another.

Later in that same summer I became pregnant with our third child. Now, at first glance this may not have seemed to be a good thing considering the mental and physical shape I was in. Yet God had allowed it and some of the things that happened as a result of the pregnancy served as a turning point in the long road toward recovery. The first was that I finally developed an appetite and started eating regularly. The challenge of eating which for me had been like gagging down a mouthful of sand was suddenly over. Just being able to actually enjoy the simple act of eating was a huge relief to me. More importantly it made me feel normal and feeling normal in even the smallest of ways gave me hope that I might feel *wholly* normal again. Normal was what I wanted. I wasn't asking for anything more than that. I just wanted to be part of the common folk who lived common, balanced and regular lives. (I was asking for mediocrity which is really nonsensical as there is nothing mediocre about the work of an Almighty God in the life of His child.)

Later on, I would learn that my inability to eat which caused many episodes of low blood sugar had exacerbated the intensity and frequency of my panic attacks. Once I began to eat regularly, the second good thing occurred. The number of panic attacks dropped off to the point where I could actually sleep through the night on many evenings. Every one of those nights was experienced as a time of refreshment and healing. The blessing of sleep which I had taken for granted in my past was now viewed as a gift from the hand of a loving shepherd. Often I would visualize myself curled up in His hand and imagine Him whispering to me, "sleep child, just sleep and I shall keep watch over you."

The third thing that happened was that I was able to focus on something else other than the continual terror in my head. Since the health of the baby depended on my health, I realized that I would need to take good care of myself. I began to pray for him daily. I petitioned God by asking specifically that He would give me a little boy and prayed that God would lay hold of his life and use him to glorify Christ in extraordinary ways. I was even so bold as to ask God to please make him take after my dad because I adored his fun nature and sweet disposition. *"Before I formed you in the womb I knew you, before you were born I set you apart."* 2.

Anxiety disorders push the attention ever inward. They create an overwhelming state of self-absorption. But the self that you are absorbed in is terrifying. It's like having a monster in your head that is roaring so loud that it takes a tremendous amount of effort to turn your attention toward anything else.

Having this other person living within my body who depended on me for life support provided me with another focus – a real mission. I would do everything and anything I could to make sure that I kept him safe. He was living in me, but he was not mine. He belonged to God and God had entrusted me to carry him. The pregnancy gave me yet another reason to hope. It seemed that God wasn't finished with me yet and I clung to that knowledge with every fiber of my being.

On my first visit to the obstetrician's office, I was told that I would likely have a difficult pregnancy. The doctor told me that I had a 50/50 chance of developing a condition called Preeclampsia and that this might mean that I would end up spending a great deal of time in bed and possibly even in the hospital during the final trimester of my pregnancy. The prediction of this illness didn't frighten me for myself, but it did cause me to have even greater concern for the welfare of the child I was carrying. Now I would have to be even more vigilant in caring for myself. This shift in my focus was a much-needed event. It provided just one of many ways that I could learn how to better manage my Anxiety Disorder. God was teaching me. But the lessons were coming in unexpected ways. I asked to be healed, but I would eventually understand that He was in the process of teaching me that He had a plan, not just for my child, but also for me. He was opening my eyes to His sufficiency which included working in and through affliction. My eyes were slow to open, but thankfully He is also a very patient Father, who is willing to wait for the lessons to sink in, no matter how hard headed the child. Years later I penned the following poem which was inspired by all this hard-won knowledge. It serves me well as a reminder of those times when I must trust in who He is in all circumstances and rely on His character to define truth rather than the faulty signals of an affliction that wreaks havoc on my emotions.

THE UNEXPECTED
I expect the unexpected,
When God is working in my life,
Oft times His plans are best effected,
By the things that I have viewed as strife.
He's not some small ingredient,

Poured from a spoon within my hand,
For flavors that He never meant,
As I my life, try to command,
For He is the creating source,
Of all those things I try to test,
And so it is I see, of course,
That He knows how to use them best.
For in the mix of trials He sees,
The blending to be good,
Though bitter it might seem to me,
As He adds in things, I never would.
Just as in youth when I lay ill,
The medicine I'd shove away.
Not knowing that the bitter pill,
Would free me to resume my play,
Now, I've learned to let Him cook,
With any recipe He would,
And to His promises I'll look,
For all the tastes are for my good.

"And we know that all things work together for good to them that love God, to them who are the called according to His purpose." 3.

Notes:

1. Isaiah 55:9 KJV
2. Jeremiah 1:5 NIV
3. Romans 8:28 KJV

CHAPTER 8

Thankful for Thanksgiving

I WAS FOUR months into my pregnancy when we received an invitation to spend the Thanksgiving holiday at my aunt and uncle's cottage along with extended family members. As a child, I had spent quite a few family vacations at this location and not unlike our favorite fishing spot it also held many dear memories for me. Although there had been some marked improvements in my condition, I was still nowhere near to feeling normal. The attacks of fear and disturbing thoughts were still fairly regular visitors and it remained quite difficult for me to be out in social settings for very long periods. The uncertainty that I still might be on the path to insanity was still an ever present possibility. One thing, however, that encouraged me about this trip was that the drive would be much shorter and having survived the other trip I felt pretty certain that I could handle this one.

Our sleeping quarters in the partially finished basement of the cottage were being shared with my brother and his wife. Once again, I was in a situation where the only thing separating us from them were curtains. Just as I had been unable to rest on the other trip, I spent the vast majority of this two night stay wide awake, staring at the ceiling, yet refusing to get up for the fear that someone might ask questions and catch on to my disturbed condition.

During the day, we would spend time in conversation or playing board games. This was quite the challenge for someone who just wanted to crawl away and hide. The second day of our visit the men decided that it would be entertaining to watch a popular horror movie titled, "Alien." I tried very hard to sit calmly and watch, but the last thing I needed was any kind of trigger to rev up the engine of my fight or flight response. I already had enough adrenaline coursing through my body to catapult me through the roof if need be.

Deciding that it would be better for me to focus on something else, I picked up a Readers Digest magazine from the coffee table and began thumbing through it. As I scanned the pages searching for something interesting to read my eyes lit upon the title of an article that peaked my curiosity. The words "Panic Disorder" jumped off the page at me and quickly flipping to the beginning of that article, I began to read with intense interest. It related the experiences of a woman who lived with the disorder. It spoke of what she had to endure before finally obtaining a diagnosis. Alongside the article, there was a checklist of the symptoms and manifestations of Panic Disorder. As I sat there absorbed in this woman's account, it was as if the author was penning an account of my own suffering. Going over the checklist of symptoms I found that I had not just a few of them, but every single one! The article went on to state that if you experienced more than three of these symptoms several times a month you were likely suffering from Panic Disorder. *Several times a month*, I found that statement startling. *How about so many times in a day that you lose count*, I thought to myself. There are no words to describe the flood of relief that came over me as I read this article. I wasn't alone after all. I was especially encouraged to read that although people with Panic Disorder feel as if they might be going crazy, they aren't and never do. It gave an overview of the underlying causes and triggers for the disorder, the genetic predisposition and the role that stress played in not only bringing on the condition but exacerbating it. But the thing that gave me the greatest hope was the portion of the article that spoke of successful treatment for the disorder.

If someone had offered me a million dollars at that moment, that gift would have paled in comparison to the gift that this magazine article was to me. I don't know if the woman who shared her story will ever read this book, but if she does, I wish for her to know that I owe her an enormous debt of gratitude for having the courage to share so openly and publicly about her disorder.

God had finally given me an answer – an explanation for all that I'd been going through and along with that a reason to hope which was something that had been absent in my life for a very long time.

Thanksgiving was the perfect setting to receive this gift of knowledge and as I sat there reading the article over and over trying to absorb and retain as much information as I could, I was also shedding tears of relief. Deep down inside of me there had always been a tiny spark of knowledge that God had not wholly abandoned me, even though the intensity of my fear had often driven me to question His presence. All along I had lived with the dread that I was some sort of lone freak, an anomaly that stood isolated and trapped within suffocating walls of inner terror. The thing had seemed beyond the scope of any explanation to me and well out of the reach of any sort of help or recovery. Now I knew those conclusions had been errant and *now* I had an explanation as well as a new path to follow which would teach me how to take up and employ the tools that I would need to battle this consuming monster.

"I waited patiently for the Lord, and He inclined unto me, and heard my cry. He brought me up also out of a horrible pit." [1].

Notes:

1. Psalm 40:1-2 KJV

CHAPTER 9

BE STILL

ANYONE EXPERIENCING A panic attack will tell you that one of the most difficult things to do while in the midst of it is to be still. This is why I avoided situations where I had no choice but to sit for very long periods without being able to get up. One hour of sitting in a church service felt like eternity to me. But sometimes God asks us to be still; *"Be still and know that I am God"*[1]. Other times He even puts us in a place where we have no choice but to be still. That's what happened to me in the last trimester of my pregnancy.

My doctor's predictions of pre-eclampsia had come true and I was forced into the unwanted experience of being still. My two little children had to be sent off to stay with their grandparents while Dennis was out of the house working because the doctor said I couldn't take care of them till the pregnancy was over. This was terribly hard for me. I felt robbed of my role of motherhood and missed them desperately while they were away. I was instructed by the doctor to go to bed, lie on my left side and to only get up to use the bathroom. During the last six weeks of the pregnancy, I was put on a medication called Phenobarbital which was to help prevent the seizures that can occur with eclampsia. This drug assisted me a little bit in my efforts to lie still, but I still struggled tremendously with episodes of panic from time to time. I also had to endure a few stays in the hospital. Being away from home for any reason at all was stressful and these visits to the hospital were no exception. During one of the hospital stays, I found myself once again in the miserable position of not being able to fall asleep at all. When I was discharged, I remember going home, climbing into my bed and falling asleep for nearly two whole days with very few moments of wakefulness. For me, that kind of long interrupted sleep was actually quite blissful.

It was during this period of forced stillness that God was showing me that although it was difficult for me to be still, that He could provide the strength I needed to protect the life of my baby. *"God is our refuge and strength a very present help in trouble."* 2.

I was also gradually learning to believe one of the things that I'd read in the article on Panic Disorder, which stated that even though you feel as if you are going crazy, you won't. After many, many days of forced stillness my rational mind still remained intact.

During this time, I began to plan for the day when I could begin to employ many of the tools that I'd read about which would help me manage the disorder. I was already practicing some of the breathing techniques which would help me to ride out a panic attack. I learned that my panic attacks caused me to breathe very shallow and would even cause me to hold by breath, though I had been unaware that I was doing that. This lack of oxygen to the brain only served to increase the symptoms of an attack. The breathing exercises taught me to be mindful of what was happening to my breathing during an attack and to make a conscious effort to not only slow my breathing down but to breathe deeply into my abdomen. With practice, I was actually learning how to ride out a panic attack, but more importantly I was often able to avert many attacks from becoming full blown by employing the breathing techniques at the first sign of their appearance.

Yet the thing that I was really looking forward to the most was being able to use aerobic exercise to raise the level of circulating serotonin in my brain, which, according to the article was lacking in the brains of most people with Anxiety Disorders. This lack of circulating serotonin was said to be one of the major contributors to the development of the disorder.

When my due date finally arrived, my doctor induced my labor. The labor lasted for the majority of the day which was surprising to me since this was the birth of my third child. When it came time for me to deliver, the fetal monitor began to indicate that the baby was in distress. His heart rate dropped with every push and didn't recover as expected in between contractions. This disturbing development when coupled with my doctor's sudden suspicion that the baby may have grown too large for me to deliver him, led him to decide that I would have to undergo an emergency C-section. My long period of being still was finally over and was joyously rewarded with the birth of a robust nine-pound fourteen-ounce baby boy. This precious child is now a grown man and has started a family of his own. He and his brother and sister have been a constant source of blessing and joy. Yet God would prove His tenderness and attentiveness to my prayers even more so by answering them so specifically. As this little baby boy grew into a man, He eventually chose to go into the ministry by reaching out to teens with the gospel of Jesus Christ through the gift of teaching and the gift of music. *And* he does take after his Grandpa in so many ways. Oh, how very good God is! *"Now unto Him who is able to do exceedingly abundantly above all that we ask or think, according to the power that worketh in us, Unto Him be glory."* 3.

Notes:

1. Psalm 46:10a KJV
2. Psalm 46:1 KJV
3. Ephesians 3:20-21a KJV

CHAPTER 10

FIGHTING BACK

My discharge from the hospital came on one of the most beautiful spring days in my memory. It was on that very day that I began my efforts to return to the world of the living. Our other two children were still at their grandparent's and Dennis had plans to head out to the grocery store to stock up on baby items, so I decided to wrap up out new little boy and go along with him. Before we went, he informed me that after we had finished shopping, he planned to head over to a local park which had a large hill which was used for sledding in the winter. There, he intended to do some heavy duty leg work to enhance his running ability. I told Dennis that there was no way I was going to miss out on a chance to be outdoors after being cooped up inside for so many months. So off we went.

I think of all the times that I've been outdoors nothing has yet measured up to the beauty of that day. The fresh spring air, the warmth of the sun and the soft new carpet of grass all spoke of new beginnings to me. I hadn't felt such a stab of joy over the wonder of creation in a very long time. Calmness came over my spirit and then a new resolve to do everything in my power to fight back against the disorder and reclaim the joy of everyday living. Hope was reignited within me and I was giving thanks to my God for surrounding me with such visions of victory and renewal. I saw it all in one breathtaking moment; the baby, my seat atop that lovely hill, the blueness of the sky that had been wiped totally clean of even the slightest trace of a cloud. I felt the refreshing, gentle breezes that had replaced the biting winter winds and the rebirth of all that had been waiting just beneath the surface to burst forth in a blossom of praise to the hand which created it. *"He set my feet on a rock and gave me a firm place to stand. He put a new song in my mouth, a hymn of praise to our God."* 1.

Some years later I would pen this poem as a reminder to myself that the clouds of my trials are not permanent or too thick for God to see me. What is always there even when I can't see it is the faithfulness of my God.

CLOUDS
I've never known a cloud to *stay*,
And cast its shadows every day,
Upon a certain place or town,
To ever all the sun's light drown.
But I've known dark banks that long have hovered,
And weeks or months the sun's light covered,
Till people mourned the hidden light;
That warm and glowing cheerful sight.
Yet without clouds above our heads,
All that's green would soon be dead.
Just as to us with failing hearts,
Our God must oft His clouds impart,
For clouds must come to bring the rain,
And though to us the drops cause pain,
It's just *then* we'll turn our eyes,
To seek the Light, that calms our cries.
For there's no gloom God's love can't lift,
No shadow that His grace won't rift.
For His light shall cause our hearts to say,
That in our nights we still see day.

"For our light affliction which is but for a moment, is working for us a far more exceeding and eternal weight of glory, while we look not at the things which are seen, but at the things which are not seen, for the things which are seen are temporary. But the things which are not seen are eternal." 2.

I can't recall exactly how long I waited post-delivery to begin jogging except that I know that my desire to start fighting back likely caused me to begin much earlier than my doctor had recommended. I figured it would be okay since I'd have no choice but to take it very slowly at first. Six weeks of continual bed rest had left me feeling pretty weak physically. It was many months before I was able to get to the point where I could run non-stop for four to five miles. I never got to that place which other runners speak of where running became "fun." No, for me the best part was when I could say, "Thank the Lord that's over!" I kept at it though because the benefits far outweighed my temporary discomfort.

Within a few months of consistent running, I began to notice that my panic attacks were decreasing in frequency as well as in intensity. This was more proof to me that the disorder wasn't a chosen attitude but rather something that was biological in nature. The running had begun to affect a biochemical change within my brain which finally convinced me that I could stop blaming myself for my past inability to keep the attacks from coming through sheer willpower. I continued on with that form of exercise for probably close to a year. During that time, I enjoyed many weeks and even months totally free from anxiety or panic attacks. In time, I found other forms of aerobic exercise that were more enjoyable to me. I engaged in speed walking, aerobic dance and even kickboxing, all of which had the same effect as the jogging but had the added benefit of enjoyment.

The account that I've shared thus far is of one long and particularly difficult flare of my Anxiety Disorder. I have experienced other episodic flares, some of them difficult and some of them just "mini-flares". For most people, these disorders are chronic conditions which wax and wane over time and are often exacerbated by stress. In light of this knowledge, it should have been no surprise to me that I would have to go through yet another really big flare – but it was - and shockingly so.

Notes:

1. Psalm 40:2b
2. 2 Corinthians 4:17-18 KJV

CHAPTER 11

Pride and Presumption

Twenty-five years under my belt of living with and learning to manage my Anxiety Disorder left me feeling rather confident that I'd never be as debilitated by it as I had in the past. It's not that I stopped having panic attacks entirely, or that I was completely rid of the occasional unwanted, disturbing or fearful thought, it was just that I felt that I'd learned to tolerate their presence to the degree that I lived a fairly normal, mostly happy and productive life. I became comfortable with the level of my anxiety especially in comparison to what it had been in the past.

It was at this point that Dennis and I began to go through a barrage of unexpected trials and big life changes. Our youngest son became ill simultaneously with Grave's Disease and a lung disorder that required back to back lung surgeries. Our daughter and eldest son both married within a year of each other. Then Dennis, the picture of perfect health – a marathon runner/triathlete suddenly fell ill with a chronic condition that forced him into disability. It took nearly a year and a half to get him on Social Security Disability as well as State Retirement Disability. During this period, we were forced to sell our home in Lansing in order keep up our health insurance cobra payments and to downsize our financial obligations since we were living within a very limited budget. Our Lansing home held so many joyful family memories and I'd planned that we would probably stay there until we died. It was my comfort zone, situated close to my folks and my daughter's family and the church which I had attended my entire life. Over the years, my ability to drive had returned and I could get all over Lansing with little or no difficulty although highway driving was still a big challenge for me.

We had an enormous garage sale where we were forced to part with far more of our belongings than we wanted to. Then we packed up and moved, along with our youngest son, Lindsey, into our rustic little cottage, which was located way up in the northwest finger of Michigan's Upper Peninsula on Lake Superior's Keweenaw Bay. The move was difficult for me, but I tried to keep my chin up about it knowing that I couldn't change what was happening to us.

Lindsey's health wasn't at all stable for the first year we lived up there. He was still having some problems with his lungs and the treatment for his Grave's disease had been ineffective in alleviating his symptoms. Shortly after having his thyroid irradiated he was placed on several different drugs to replace the thyroid hormones that his body didn't make anymore. But those drugs weren't working for him. He experienced debilitating fatigue, low body temperature, frequent colds, sinus infections, facial swelling and the agonizing symptoms of clinical depression which were all caused by severe hypothyroidism. His lab tests would always appear normal, but he had every clinical sign of a person who was severely lacking in thyroid hormones. He struggled to get through each day. His weight continued to drop and I was desperate to find some way to help him.

The physicians that were treating Lindsey's Grave's Disease would only rely on his blood tests as a measure of how he was doing and simply refused to acknowledge his deteriorating condition. So I took it upon myself to be an advocate for him and began to do research on my own to find out just why he was still so sick. I eventually learned that although his labs indicated that his thyroid levels were normal he was still severely hypothyroid at the cellular level. This was because he was on a drug that made only one kind of thyroid hormone called T4. For some people, this is enough as their body will convert the T4 drug into the other essential thyroid hormone T3. But in some cases, like Lindsey's, a person's body won't do this and they need to go on a drug that contains both of these hormones. After discovering this, I began my search to find a physician who would treat Lindsey's Grave's disease by addressing his clinical symptoms. That physician, Dr. Walter Woodhouse, ended up being located way down at the southernmost corner of the lower peninsula of Michigan some six hundred miles away. I called his office and related Lindsey's symptoms to the nurse and after she had consulted with Dr. Woodhouse, he saw the urgency of his condition and agreed to see him right away.

Lindsey and I hurriedly packed our bags and made the long drive down with the prayerful hope that Dr. Woodhouse would be able to help him.

Twenty-four hours after Lindsey's first appointment and after Dr. Woodhouse started him on a new thyroid medication that contained both T4 and T3 hormones Lindsey's debilitating symptoms of severe fatigue and clinical depression began to lift. I still give thanks to God for directing us to Dr. Woodhouse - a physician who was willing to listen to and actually believe what his patient was telling him.

Within a year of Lindsey's recovery, he *also* married and moved away. And therefore, within a two-year period we endured the frenzied, albeit exciting, planning for all three of our children's weddings.

It was a sudden and difficult adjustment for me to have all the kids leave home in such a short period of time. This was especially true since I had been a stay at home mom and considered the raising and training my children my full-time occupation. I experienced the deep sadness of empty nest syndrome. It was rather like retiring from a full-time job that had been one of the most fulfilling experiences of my life.

Meanwhile, Dennis and I were adjusting, much earlier than expected, to him being retired and home with me full time. His illness, Mixed Connective Tissue Disease, robbed him of his ability to run and caused severe and chronic fatigue. He went from being a guy who got up at four a.m. and never stopped moving until he hit the sack at about ten p.m. to a guy who struggled to stay awake for a whole day and lacked the energy to keep up with yard work and the numerous projects that the cottage required. What used to be a vacation get away had now become our primary place of residence. It didn't have a washer or dryer, a garage, a good heating system and many other comforts that we'd had at our Lansing home. There was so much to do and very little cash on hand to do it.

Then there was the driving. I found out very quickly that I was right back to square one with my driving challenges. Every trip into town took at least a half hour or more and took our vehicle up and down steep and winding roads at higher speeds than my brain seemed to want to accept. I even experienced some panic attacks with Dennis driving, especially in winter, but when *I* took the wheel the panic attacks were overwhelming and oppressive. I could only stand this intense level of anxiety for very short drives which meant that I lost my independence and once again had to rely on Dennis to take me everywhere. I was angry as well as humiliated by this.

Then - winter set in. If you've never experienced winter in the U.P. of Michigan and you think that you might like it, I'm not the person you'll want to hear an opinion from. I absolutely loathe living up there in winter. It snows nearly every day; it's bitterly cold and extremely windy. The days are short and the nights are long. White out conditions are weekly occurrences. Getting out is always a chore and consequentially you might end up holed up in your house wrapped in blankets for most of the winter. This was especially true for us due to the primitive heating system we had for the first year we lived there. One winter up there was enough for me and I pleaded with Dennis to see if we could find a place in Lansing that we could afford to live in during the winter months.

After looking into several possibilities, we managed to find a single wide manufactured home for five thousand dollars in a senior community in a suburb just outside of Lansing. We had refinanced the cottage to build a garage and used the money left over from that to purchase this home. The rent didn't seem too high and we thought we might just be able to fit it into our budget.

Although I was happy to be back in Lansing for the winter the financial strain of keeping both places began to take its toll on me. I was in charge of paying the bills and as we began to fall behind in our monthly expenses, I found myself lying awake at night trying to figure out how to make ends meet. I would wonder, "Should I get a job?" This presented a problem because our presence in Lansing was seasonal and no one would hire me for only six months at a time.

Meanwhile, I had allowed myself to become complacent about my need for regular exercise making excuses that I just didn't have the time for it anymore. In spite of this I started to lose weight and was experiencing periods of insomnia in the middle of the night. I chose to ignore this too figuring that I could get by fine on four to five hours of sleep per night.

My panic attacks became more frequent visitors, but I just shrugged them off, telling myself that I could tough them out. I ignored the fact that I was having episodes of digestive upset nearly every morning. When I'd do my morning Bible study, I began to notice that my hands trembled slightly and that I was experiencing cold sweats. In addition to this I had cut my hormone replacement dosage in half thinking that it might help to lower my rapidly rising high cholesterol.

Hormone shifts can be triggers for women with Anxiety Disorders and although I was educated about that I didn't give it much thought. All of these things were dire warning signals – tremors that were signaling the fast approach of another eruption of my disorder that would shake me to my very core. But instead of heeding their warnings I chose to willfully ignore them.

I was actually proud of my ability to endure these things and just keep on going. I would tell myself that in comparison to what I'd been through before these things were nothing more than minor nuisances. I felt that they certainly weren't worthy of taking any real or aggressive counter-action against to nip them in the bud. I really considered myself an "expert" at dealing with the symptoms of my Anxiety Disorder. I thought I'd learned all I needed to know as a result of living with it for so long. After all God had just recently provided me with several opportunities to share the testimony of His grace toward me in the process of my recovery from my past experience with this disorder. Hearts had been encouraged by this and people had opened up to me about their own struggles with Anxiety disorders. Surely I was doing well.

But all those minor nuisances were just about to morph into a monster whose roars would send me reeling into another deep pit of despair. I had been foolish, presumptuous and proud in ignoring these signals and would soon be shocked to find out that God hadn't finished teaching me the deeper meaning of "My Grace is sufficient for you." The tool He would use to further my education came clothed in the return of the very affliction that I'd thought I'd licked.

"Pride goes before destruction, a haughty spirit before a fall." 1.

Notes:

1. Proverbs 16:18, NIV

CHAPTER 12
Still Loony After all These Years

With the approach of Christmas 2006 all of those aforementioned "minor nuisances" suddenly became so intense and distressing that I could no longer ignore them. My digestive upset was so severe that I was nauseous most of the time. I would actually gag just trying to eat a few spoonful of yogurt in the morning. The mild trembling turned into horrible periods of uncontrollable full body shaking. I can remember going into my bedroom, sitting in a chair and doing deep breathing to try and get my body to calm down. When that didn't work, I'd lie down and try to do some progressive muscle relaxation exercises but more often than not the intensity of the anxiety would drive me to get right back up again.

My logical mind told me that I was experiencing some sort of flare of my Anxiety Disorder and that all of these physical manifestations were caused by an overabundance of fight or flight chemicals, but even with that knowledge I began to question whether or not there might be something else more ominous and dire wrong with me. Suddenly, the fact that my gut was in a knot all the time and that I was waking up each night with episodes of abdominal pain made me wonder if I might have an ulcer or something worse.

I remembered that my Aunt Lucille had nearly died from a bleeding ulcer when I was a child. For all I knew that could happen to me too. Then I remembered that, last summer, a routine blood test, that my physician ordered, had shown some mildly elevated liver enzymes. *What if this means I have liver cancer?* I began to turn this thought over and over in my mind.

One day after my bath I was studying my abdomen to see if there was any swelling on the side where my liver was and I noticed that there was a definite difference from one side to the other. What's funny is that the side where my liver is actually stuck out less than the other side but that didn't matter. What mattered was that it looked different *and* it felt different. This really freaked me out because I thought it meant that my liver was somehow misshaped, maybe due to cancer. The real cause of the very subtle difference is that one side of my rib cage is pushed back farther than the other side because of my last pregnancy and I have a lot of rib cage pain on my right side that I've lived with for years due to that.

I remember thinking that it was so strange to be obsessing over health problems as I hadn't done that sort of thing in years. I had even undergone several breast biopsies and had my gallbladder removed without losing one night's sleep over the procedures.

Yet even while being completely aware that I was likely overreacting, I still couldn't manage to stop myself from the endless mental questioning that something very serious might be wrong with me.

All these threatening "what ifs" eventually drove me to my computer where I would spend literally hours doing internet searches on stomach/intestinal diseases and liver disorders. The more I read the worse I felt. The vast majority of what I read seemed to indicate that I didn't have any of these disorders yet my mind would always seem to latch onto even the tiniest symptom that I'd experienced as a possible indicator that I might really be very sick. This would leave me with a dreaded feeling of uncertainty that I found intolerable. In response to that feeling, I would continue to search the internet for more proof that I wasn't really ill. There were those times when I'd just get really mad at myself and admit that I was behaving in a nonsensical way and I'd slam my laptop shut in disgust. Yet the doubts and questions would still haunt me endlessly.

Even when I had periods where I wasn't obsessing about my health I had this free-floating anxiety which was like living in a continual state of gloom and dread. Every minor issue became a major one. When my little grandson picked up a common stomach bug, I developed an intense fear that he might vomit or have diarrhea so bad that the resulting dehydration might kill him. A few days later when he bounced back like any normal healthy toddler, I recognized that my fears had been greatly exaggerated and kicked myself for the time I'd wasted torturing myself about it.

My loss of appetite sparked new fears that I hadn't pondered before. Once again although my logical brain told me that loss of appetite was a common symptom of Anxiety Disorders and that I should know this better than anyone else due to my past experience with that symptom, instead of finding comfort in that I began to fret endlessly over my inability to eat enough food. I started weighing myself and as the pounds continued to drop off, I started worrying about whether or not I'd ever be able to eat normally again. I actually needed to shed some weight and should've been happy to see it go but instead I began an intense effort to keep my weight from dropping any further. I thought about things like how anorexic people can actually die from starvation. Even though I dreaded stepping on the scales for fear that they might show yet another pound of weight loss, I just had to do it. I needed to check to be sure I wasn't losing too much weight. Then I had this idea that I could force myself to eat enough calories to maintain my current weight. So after doing another internet search to find out just how many calories I needed to eat to do this I began to write down everything I ate each day and tallied up the calorie count to be sure that I'd eaten enough.

Some days I was unable to gag down enough food to meet my quota so I started drinking Boost or Ensure to maintain my weight. There were moments where I would chide myself about my bizarre behavior with thoughts like, *Mitzi, this is totally irrational, you could actually stand to lose a few more pounds without being too thin, so why all the fuss?* At one point during the course of my caloric intake computations, I sat there contemplating how I could find a foolproof way to be certain that I wouldn't starve to death. It was at that moment that I suddenly had the temporarily *comforting* thought that *even if I stopped eating altogether I could always have a feeding* tube – big sigh of relief! In retrospect, when I think about how I found *that* particular thought comforting I have to laugh at just how whacked out and ludicrous obsessions can get. But at *that* time I took it all very seriously.

Eventually, I chose to listen to the rational part of my mind and had to admit that everything I was experiencing was likely a relapse of my Anxiety Disorder. It seemed different, though. It felt confusing and maybe even more intense. I think this reaction was because I had been so certain that I'd completely conquered it and the idea that I hadn't really scared me. *What if this means that I'll never get well again?* That thought sent shock waves of terror through me.

I got out some of my old books on Anxiety Disorders and read up on all its subtypes. I began to think that maybe what I had was something called "Generalized Anxiety Disorder." The free-floating sense of doom and dread seemed to fit the diagnosis. Desperate to feel better I decided to be more aggressive in my efforts to get well and made an appointment with my GP with the intention of finding out if there might be some type of medication that could help to speed up my recovery. During this appointment, I filled her in on my past history with Panic Disorder and then attempted to vaguely describe some of the current things I was experiencing. I kept it as vague as possible because I was really embarrassed about how obsessed I'd become about my health. The last thing I wanted was to be labeled a hypochondriac. I could well imagine the staff at her office reacting to my every visit with comments like; "Oh… great…here she comes again, I wonder what made up ailment she has today? What a nut job!"

Even with my vague description my doctor was able to ascertain that the likeliest cause for most of my symptoms was a relapse of my Anxiety Disorder. Still, she insisted that to be thorough I should get some testing done to rule out any sort of liver or intestinal illness as a possible source of my abdominal distress. She set up an appointment for me to see my gastroenterologist and then wrote me a prescription for an anti-anxiety medication called Paxil.

I left her office encouraged and hopeful that I'd taken my first big step toward recovery from the misery I'd been experiencing. *Soon*, I thought, *you'll be right back to normal.* There it was again, that longing to be *normal* – to feel normal, act normal and above all else to *seem* normal to other people. Instead, I would soon discover that obsessing over my health couldn't hold a candle to the new doubts and fears that would assail me before this nightmare would reach its peak.

CHAPTER 13

Scary Pills

ALTHOUGH I WENT to the pharmacy right away and filled the prescription for Paxil, I was, to say the least, a bit leery of taking it. I'd never been on that type of drug before. I knew it was a Selective Serotonin Re-Uptake Inhibitor, (SSRI) and that sounded good to me. This was because I was aware that a lack of circulating Serotonin in the brain is usually implicated as one of the causes of Anxiety Disorders. Still, I had all these questions and concerns floating around in my mind about it; *Could I become addicted to it? What if I was allergic to it? Would it make me gain weight or lose weight?*

The patient information leaflet prompted many more concerns but even more disconcerting than those was my fear that I'd take it only to find out that it wouldn't work for me. This, I figured could serve as evidence that there might not be any hope for my recovery. This notion was prompted by just one small statement in a book that I'd been reading about Anxiety Disorders which suggested that some people might live with the chemical imbalance of the disorder for so long without getting any help that their condition could become permanent. *That*, I thought, *could very well be me.* So in light of all these fearful considerations I shelved the medication thinking that if I didn't take it I wouldn't have the risk of side effects or the even greater risk of discovering that my condition was irresolvable.

There were many days when the anxiety was so intense that I'd almost give in and take the Paxil. But then I'd convince myself that I didn't need it. I'd been able to get better without medication in the past – surely I could do it again.

Eventually, these mental debates about whether to start the Paxil or not became a big obsessional theme. I would look up the medication on the internet, (bad idea), and read page after page of patient ratings. There were a plethora of positive comments about the use of Paxil in comparison to negative comments, but my mind would make a beeline straight for all the negative ones. Then my highly exaggerated anxiety response to all of this would cause me to become even more terrified of taking it.

There came a day, though when the intensity and misery of the anxiety outweighed my fear of the Paxil and I made the decision to give it a try. A couple of hours after swallowing the first pill, the level of my anxiety went right through the roof. I began to experience severe panic attacks and found it hard to even sit down. Then that evening in bed I had the most awful whole body trembling. Then when I happened to drift off to sleep for a few moments, I woke up with horrible attacks of panic that were worse than the daytime episodes. It was as if I was experiencing a nonstop panic attack while I was on Paxil.

After two days of this torture, I called my doctor's office to report what was happening to me. She decided that since the Paxil didn't agree with me that she'd switch me to a different medication called Zoloft.

Although it was very difficult for me to get up the courage to give the Zoloft a try, I was slightly encouraged by the fact that my doctor decided to start me out on a very low dose with the plan to increase it gradually to a therapeutic level. After taking a few pills at that dosage, I found that I was still having bouts of greatly increased anxiety so I lowered the dosage even more and decided that it would take baby steps for my body to adjust to the drug.

From my reading, I had learned that some people experience something called paradoxical anxiety when they first start taking these types of medications. It seemed, to me, that I was one of those unlucky few. Determined to try and give the medication a full six to eight-week trial to see if it would help me, I dug my heels in and forced myself to tough it out. I was hanging on desperately to the hope of recovery, but the fear that I might have to live with the anxiety for the rest of my life was always in the back of my mind.

CHAPTER 14

A Humbling Step

MAKING THE DECISION to seek professional help for my Anxiety Disorder was a difficult step for me. I knew that doing so meant that I would have to be far more transparent and honest with this therapist than I'd been with the other psychologist all those years ago. Doing so would also create a sense of weakness and vulnerability because it would force me into the position of admitting that I couldn't manage my disorder by myself.

I had this wrongheaded idea that toughing it out on my own meant that I was a strong individual. All of my life I'd honed the skills of toughing it out, grinning and bearing it and not showing weakness. I was actually proud of my ability to do these things and considered myself to be someone who had a very high level of pain tolerance, both mental and physical.

But now the pain had the upper hand over my pride. This put me in the position of finally admitting that I needed help. So although I made an appointment with a psychologist my attitude at having to do so was a mixed bag of embarrassment over my weakness and anger at myself for being debilitated by the same old problem that I'd thought I'd conquered all those years ago. I'd made a promise to myself that I'd been unable to keep. After coming out of the nightmare of my past I'd proclaimed; "I will never, ever let anxiety get the upper hand with me again." But the ambush had been successfully executed and now it was as if that menacing monster whom I'd declared dead had resurrected itself, grabbed me by the throat and hurled me right back into the same dungeon where it had been able to torture me so effectively in the past. I could picture it grinning down at me gleefully, mocking my weakness and doing a celebratory victory dance at its ability to defeat me yet again. Even more disturbing was the knowledge that Satan was most likely in cahoots with it. *"How long must I wrestle with my thoughts and every day have sorrow in my heart? How long will my enemy triumph over me? Look on me and answer, O Lord my God. Give light to my eyes, or I will sleep in death; my enemy will say, "I have overcome 'her'."* 1.

My first visit with my new psychologist, Dr. Jeanne Brickman, was like opening up a pressure valve little by little as I gradually revealed to her bit by bit what I'd been going through. She offered up some very helpful insight about the effect of cumulative stress on people with Anxiety Disorders. She also questioned me as to whether I held in my emotions and feelings especially when I felt hurt or wounded by someone else. I had to admit that fear played a big role in my habit of bottling emotions. I had always been afraid of conflict. Therefore, it was far easier for me to back down or shut down in any situation where there was a disagreement. We discussed the panic attacks and then moved on to the scarier topic of my disturbing obsessions. I told her that I was accustomed to having panic attacks so it is was easier for me to accept their presence than the presence of the unwanted thoughts.

These obsessional themes had been so constant and crushing in intensity that I just couldn't seem to escape them no matter how hard I tried. It's strange to me that I recognized the panic attacks as a part of my past experience but didn't connect the dots between the pattern of my former obsessions about possibly harming my children with the current ones I was having.

In the following weeks, I opened up to Dr. Brickman about a new obsession that had pushed a lot of the others aside and was, at that moment, the most unsettling to me. I had read that depression was often comorbid with Anxiety Disorders and was even aware that it was quite likely that I'd been severely depressed back in the eighties, but now the idea of – or even the actual word, depression, would instantly put my stomach in a knot. I didn't want to be depressed because I was very fearful that I'd never be able to pull out of it.

Dr. Brickman would ask me what proof or evidence I had that I might stay depressed and although I had no proof, I could still manage to come up with reasons that I might. Reasons like; "The medicine might not work", to which Dr. Brickman would reply; "Then you'll try another till you find one that does." What she didn't know was that I'd seen a television documentary on depression years ago and although it didn't disturb me even the tiniest bit at *that* time, now I would play scenes from it over and over in my brain. It featured a young woman, whose depression was unresponsive to any type of treatment, including electroshock therapy. The program didn't end on a hopeful note. It ended with this scene of her wrapped up in a blanket on the couch still enduring the unending pain of depression. *What if I end up just like her?* The thought horrified me.

Even now, as I write these words, I can still feel the familiar stab of anxiety that accompanied these thoughts.

There was also another woman I'd known who had eventually taken her own life after struggling for years and years with depression. These images would plague me constantly and sometimes I would even have to ask Dennis if he thought I was *acting* depressed. He would say that I acted anxious and distracted and was a little quieter than usual, but he didn't think I was depressed because I didn't' cry at all. I began to try and take notice of whether or not I had laughed at some point during each day. One time I tried to watch a Christian comedian on TV in order to see if I would laugh or not. About half way through the show I became so anxious about the fact that I hadn't yet laughed that I had to shut it off.

Dr. Brickman would ask me to try and use logical counter statements to fight this obsession. I was supposed to try and find evidence or proof that this fear would come true and then write down all the reasons or logical counter statements as to why it wasn't very likely that it was true. After that, I was to write down all the steps or measures that I could take to prevent it from happening. I began to make a list of my fearful obsessions and then each day I'd make a determined effort to try and write down a whole bunch of logical counterstatements next to them in an attempt to convince myself that I was exaggerating the fear. Yet instead of this making me feel better it actually fixated my thoughts even more so on the obsessions. They became even more embedded and stuck in my conscious mind and their presence seemed all the more foreboding. It became harder and harder to dismiss them.

One day that stands out in my memory as one of those "you've really hit bottom now" moments, was the day that Dennis needed to go out to his folks for the afternoon. My fear about depression had expanded and morphed into this new fear that due to the depression I might possibly commit suicide. It wasn't that I actually *desired* to kill myself, but rather that I feared that I might not be able to control myself or fight the urge to do so. Just as Dennis was walking out the door, I had the sudden thought; *What if you just get up, go to the bathroom and swallow a whole bottle of pills?* The very fact that such a thought crossed my mind terrified me because it seemed impossible to separate the fact that I had the thought from the possibility of my acting upon it.

For a very long time after that I tried to make sure that I was never left alone because I thought, *it might not be safe*. It didn't' seem to matter that when Dennis returned from his folks I was still alive and kicking because I thought, *maybe next time will be the time that the thought might turn into reality – how could I be certain whether it would or not?*

There was one other thing that Dr. Brickman had suggested that *did* have a very positive effect. This suggestion had its basis in just three little words that I could use from time to time in response to all my fear filled obsessions. The words were "act as if". She said, "if you're feeling anxious *act as if* you're not. If you feel, you lack confidence act as if you *are* confident." When I could actually apply this technique, it would serve to minimize or take the edge off the anxiety because it would cause me to focus on *acting* in a positive manner while choosing to ignore the disturbing thoughts that were buzzing about my brain. It gave me a choice. I could cower in the corner or I could stand up to the fear and not let it bully me around. I still use those three little words as part of my arsenal against my disorder. Therefore, I'm very glad that I put my pride in my pocket and decided to seek professional help for my disorder. It was a humbling realization for me to discover that I still had so much to learn about living with my disorder. *"He that refuseth instruction depiseth his own soul."* 2.

Notes:

1. Psalm 13:2-4 NIV
2. Proverbs 16:32a KJV

CHAPTER 15

Intolerable Testing

I PUT OFF making my appointment to see my gastroenterologist for a while because even though I wanted to know if I had a liver disorder or some other serious stomach or intestinal disorder, I was also afraid to find out. And in this case, I figured, ignorance might be bliss. I had this odd mixture of avoidance and the need for reassurance. Finally, the need for reassurance won out, so I made the appointment.

My "gut" doctor as I like to refer to him, was fairly certain that all of my symptoms were due to irritable bowel syndrome which he thought was likely being exacerbated by my Anxiety Disorder. Yet not wanting to jump to any false conclusions he still recommended that I have several tests done to rule out any other causes for all my abdominal distress. I would have to undergo a Barium enema, a small bowel x-ray, and a liver biopsy because my liver enzymes were mildly elevated. Honestly, I didn't feel mentally or physically strong enough to go through any of those tests, but in the end I decided that having them might finally put some of my health obsessions to rest. This would be a way that I could feel reassured that I wasn't dying of liver cancer, or an ulcer or something even worse.

Although none of the tests were physically painful to me the mental torture that they caused felt nearly unbearable. My efforts to act normal and hide my anxiousness from the medical staff totally wore me out. The liver biopsy was the most difficult because I was asked to lie still in the recovery room for three hours after the procedure. The ever-present panic response in my brain made me want to leap out of the hospital bed and pace the floor. Every time I have any sort of medical procedure where someone instructs me to, "lie very still and don't move," my brain instantly insists that I'm going to move, that I won't be able to control myself and that if I move something horrible will happen during the test.

The actual liver biopsy went very well and the nurse who was attending me commented that the doctor was impressed with how quickly the tiny incision had stopped bleeding. This was a good sign as a few people develop bleeding complications from liver biopsies, but it looked as if I wasn't going to be one of them. This news should have put my fears to rest about *that* complication, but instead I spent the next three days at home checking the site over and over just to be sure that it wasn't bleeding. I would try so hard to just ignore it, but the urge to check it was so powerful that I usually gave in to it. Sometimes I'd be able to put if off or limit the checking to two or three times an hour but I still couldn't get my mind off it even then. Thankfully this need to check the incision site died off after about three days.

After all of these procedures were completed I couldn't help but contrast just how different my reaction to them was compared to how I would have acted in the past. My reaction to such things in the past was quite the opposite. I had an almost reckless or careless attitude about medical procedures. They were nothing more than a nuisance to me, an intrusive interruption in my plans and daily life. When I'd had my C-section all those years ago, I began to engage in really intense physical exercise well before my doctor gave his approval. When I had my breast biopsies, I didn't lose one wink of sleep pondering whether I might have cancer or not. When my gall bladder had been removed, I was more annoyed by it than anything else. I didn't like to be forced to slow down for any reason. But now *everything* in my life seemed to carry the weight of a big, fat, ugly, hairy deal. Even the smallest things spelled imminent disaster. *"The grasshopper shall be a burden."* [1].

During this period of my life, I felt like I was enduring a plague of burdensome grasshoppers.

When my tests results came back, I went in to discuss them with the doctor. He told me that they were all completely negative which should have created a sense of calm and relief in me but at that moment I had found something else to freak out about. Earlier that same day I had developed an ominous, although faint, rash on my forearms. I showed this to the doctor and he recommended that I stop in to see my GP just in case the rash was an allergic reaction to the Zoloft that I'd been taking.

My GP was out of town. And, therefore, I had to make an appointment the next day to see a colleague of hers. When he looked at the rash, he recommended that I go ahead and quit the Zoloft because I might be having an allergic response to it. I couldn't believe it! My fear about being allergic to the medication that could help me had come true! "Now," I mulled over this dreaded possibility, *there's not going to be anything else to help me get through this. I could be stuck in this state of mind forever.*

The doctor thought otherwise and proceeded to write me a new prescription for another medication called Remeron. He said it was a safe and gentle drug that he prescribed quite often to "skinny little old ladies who had trouble eating and sleeping." I know he was trying to reassure me, but his comment made me feel as though I must have appeared to be a complete basket case. It really bothered me a lot to think that he felt he had to talk to me that way.

It never helps a person who is afflicted with an Anxiety Disorder to handle them with kid gloves. This only serves to reinforce a sense of weakness, failure and incompetence. Empathy and understanding have always been welcome to me, but as soon as someone starts to act in a condescending manner toward me my hackles go up. Their pampering words convey a lack of understanding concerning people with anxiety disorders. For me it makes me feel as if they are thinking; "don't upset the crazy lady. We don't want her going off the deep end."

Immediately after my appointment I went to the pharmacy and filled the prescription, but put off taking it until I could research it online. (This, once again, was a very bad idea.) Along with my fear that I might be allergic to it I also found a whole lot more to be afraid of as my mind latched onto every single negative comment and blew them way out of proportion. If I dared to take it I would risk having one of the following negative side effects: First, that it might turn me into a walking zombie, second that it might make me gain a ton of weight, third that it might drive up my cholesterol, fourth that it wouldn't fix my anxiety at all and fifth that I'd still become dependent on it and never be able to stop taking it.

So fueled by the fear of these seemingly dire possibilities I shelved these new "scary pills", unable to muster up the courage to give them a try. Meanwhile, Dennis, being aware of the level of my suffering would try on a daily basis to convince me to give the medication a chance. There were days when I came very close to doing so but then my anxiety would shoot up so high that I'd chicken out. I finally made the decision to postpone taking the Remeron until my regular GP came back from her trip. I told myself that it was probably wise to get her opinion on the medication to see if she concurred with her colleague that it would be a good drug for me. It would be several weeks before I could get in to see her, but I was willing to wait just to be able to get some sort of reassurance that it would be okay for me to start taking those new pills.

Notes:

1. Ecclesiastes 12:5b KJV

CHAPTER 16

THE TOWERING TERROR

"Of all the temptations that ever I met with in my life, to
question the being of God, and the truth of his gospel,
is the worst, and the worst to be borne."

JOHN BUNYAN 1.

IT WAS DURING those weeks while I was waiting for my GP to come back that my disorder took the ugliest of all turns. My inability to sit still for very long made it hard for me to relax enough to focus on studying my Bible so I decided that a good alternative might be to listen to some sermons on CD. My son had given me a sermon series that had impressed him and which he wanted to share with me, so I decided to start with those. I figured that I could listen and do other things at the same time to try and distract myself.

At first I found the sermons encouraging and insightful but then about mid-way through the series I encountered a sermon that prompted a new obsession that would lay me lower than I'd ever been before.

In retrospect, I've given this sermon a new title that fits the way my disorder twisted it and used it to torture me. I call it the; "You might not really be a Christian – if," sermon. I remember *that* day so clearly. I was doing the dishes while listening when just this one phrase grabbed my attention and dealt me such a vicious blow that I thought I'd never be able to get up again. It was like having a big bully sneak up from behind you, tap you on the shoulder and just as you turn to see who it is, he sucker punches you. You stagger backward, reeling with dizziness and collapse on the floor in a heap unable to get up and fight back. The "sucker punch" that my bully used against me came wrapped up in a particular phrase that went something like this; "There are a lot of folks who *think* they are Christians but if they are still struggling with sin, then they might not be." *Whoa!* My brain felt as if it might explode in reaction to that statement and a cold fist of terror wrapped around my heart. Those words, when they'd had the chance to sink in ignited a barrage of horrifying accusations which would soon morph into an all-consuming dread of the possibility of hell and eternal separation from God. *What if I'm not a Christian after all? I struggle with sin in some way nearly every day! What if I've just been fooling myself all along? What if my belief isn't good enough? Maybe that's why I have all this fear and anxiety. Is this God's way of warning me? I need to know. How can I know for certain?* The questions and doubts poured out like water from a burst dam. And the aftermath that this torrent left behind was a deep gouge in my brain of confusion, dread, and incredible sorrow.

This new mental war was far worse than any that I'd engaged in before. I wanted to turn back the clock and erase my thoughts. I wanted to unthink these things, but I knew that short of having my memory erased that was impossible. These hissing and menacing accusations would come at me relentlessly and I felt that I had no choice but to fight back. I would work very hard to gather evidence against these condemning notions. I would use scripture after scripture to reassure myself that I still belonged to God. Yet every time I'd think I'd won the war, a new question would pop into my head. These doubts and questions were so frequent and so diverse in their method of attack that it would be impossible for me to account for them all on paper. But in an attempt to reveal to the reader just how they operated I'll give one example.

The backdrop for this particular episode was the exhaustion I'd felt from the continual inner turmoil. This kind of exhaustion would often lead to periods of utter despair where I just wanted to give up and give in. During these times, I would often wish that I could die. Yet to actually die was a fearful prospect because the feeling of uncertainty about my salvation might mean that I could end up in hell. So then I began to wish that I could be an animal instead of a human. I would watch a bird sitting in a tree outside the window and think, *oh...if I could only be like him, to just instinctively exist without all these questions and doubts and the fear they create. "I said, 'Oh that I had wings like a dove! I would fly away and be at rest'."* 2.

Then, just after that, came the next brutal twist; *Atheists don't see themselves as being any different from animals.* The thought leaped up in my mind like the unexpected charge of a lion out of the midst of the tall grass. *Does this mean that I want to be or actually already might be an atheist?* The question demanded an immediate answer. *No, it can't mean that!* I shouted back at it in my head. The possibility sickened me as I pondered how meaningless my life would become if I were to be an atheist. My argument against it continued; *If you were a true atheist, you wouldn't be at all troubled by the fact that you were.* But then I'd think, *maybe atheists really are troubled but just hide it. What if the real reason you've been reading all those apologetic books hasn't been so that you could 'give a reasoned answer for the hope the lies in you,* 3. *but rather because you really never had any hope to begin with?* To which I'd argue back; *but I have placed my hope in the Lord and the scripture states that; "whosoever shall call upon the name of the Lord shall be saved."* 4. *Yes, that may be true, but what if this only applies to those who don't doubt or disbelieve.* The inner debate wore on – *If you truly believed you wouldn't be freaking out right now. Oh, but I have believed, I really have!* My thoughts shouted back. Then I prayed in desperation; *"Lord, I believe, help thou my unbelief!"* 5.

These horrible strivings within were my desperate effort to find that one perfect reassurance which I thought could dissolve all my fear and uncertainty concerning my eternal standing with God. They were also the pinnacle – the towering terror of all the obsessive themes that my disorder had latched on to. Now, obsessing over health concerns seemed like a walk in the park in comparison.

Accompanying this nightmare was that old accusation that I had somehow sinned by publicly sharing about my Anxiety Disorder. I began to entertain the notion that my situation might be the consequence of my unbelief and that I had sinned by getting up and *acting* as if I had faith in God when now it appeared that I might not have any faith at all. *Was I a phony – a fake?* I found the notion appalling.

Words fall short of my being able to convey just how excruciating the mental pain became from these obsessional themes. Horror gripped me – mind, heart, and soul. When Sunday rolled around, I would sit in my pew feeling like a blight that had no place among the children of God. I felt like a contaminate in their midst.

This battle to gain a feeling of certainty about my salvation raged on for quite some time. There were many tangled and twisted turns along the way, but every path led back to one basic fear; eternal separation from God. Every effort or attempt to gain reassurance only led to one more doubt filled "what if?" The harder I struggled against those doubts the greater and more powerful grip they would have on me. How could I ignore these things when to do so might mean the eternal damnation of my soul? How could I find peace when my very own heart condemned me? Later on my eyes would open up to the realization that God's grace and salvation are not dependent upon the fickleness of my emotional states. *"Whenever our hearts condemn us,"* we must remember, *"God is greater than our fears, and he knows everything."* 6.

But first I needed to be educated about *why* I had become so stuck in these obsessive cycles. I needed to come to grips with the fact that I had OCD.

Notes:

1. "Grace Abounding to the Chief of Sinners," John Bunyan, Penguin Books, Page 83, #1
2. Psalm 55:6 NIV
3. 1 Peter 3:15 KJV
4. Acts 2:21b KJV
5. Mark 9:24 KJV
6. 1 John 3:21 NIV

CHAPTER 17

A Successful Medication Plunge

As soon as my GP returned to her office I made an appointment to discuss the concerns I had about the medication. She seemed confident that the Remeron could really help me to feel better to the point where I wouldn't feel so depressed all the time. Meanwhile, I had read up on another type of anxiety medication called Buspar. Of all the anxiety medications that I'd researched it seemed to be one of the few that didn't carry as many side effects as the others. It was also a drug that was easy to stop taking as I couldn't find any reports of discontinuation syndrome associated with it. When I asked my GP if this drug would be a better choice for me, she agreed, but said that I could be on both drugs at the same time. She felt that I still needed the Remeron because it would do a better job of addressing the depression as well as helping me be able to eat again.

It was extremely hard for me to muster up the courage to begin taking the medications, but I finally had to take that seemingly risky leap. Since I still had huge fears about being allergic to them, I decided to start them one at a time so that if I ended up with an allergic reaction I'd know which one was the culprit. That very evening after my doctor appointment I took my very first dose of Remeron. The anxiety when I swallowed that first pill was so intense that I was crying and trembling all over as it slid down my throat. Then I waited, expecting at any moment that some horrid unbearable side effect would kick in. Instead, I became calm and sleepy within a very short time. I went to bed and slept soundly for at least eight hours. I didn't wake up cured of my obsessions as they greeted me the very moment my eyes popped open, but I felt very encouraged to have escaped them during those eight hours of sleep. It also didn't take very long for me to be able to eat again as the side effect of an increased appetite finally kicked in.

The first evidence of this phenomenon was an experience that I had within a week of taking my first dose of Remeron. It was on a Sunday evening while sitting in church that I had an extremely intense craving for something sweet. By the time service was over I had made the decision to go home and bake a batch of peanut butter cookies. Dennis couldn't believe that I wanted to bake that late in the evening but was pretty happy at the prospect. During the baking process, I got another wonderfully decadent idea that the cookies would taste even better if I spread homemade chocolate frosting in between them to form cookie sandwiches. Again, Dennis thought this to be a terrific plan and even offered to help me by cleaning out the frosting bowl. I must admit that of all the times I've indulged in sweets that this Sunday evening of wolfing down those deliciously evil cookies ranks right up there with one of my most satisfying binges.

After surviving a whole month on Remeron, I began to feel a wee bit more confident to go ahead and add the Buspar to my treatment program. I hadn't experienced any paradoxical anxiety with the Remeron, but adjusting to the Buspar turned out to be a lot more challenging. My first full dose wreaked havoc on my nerves and kept me in a state of pretty intense anxiety for most of the day. Not wanting to give up so easily I backed myself way down on the dosage and gradually increased up to the full dosage over the next month without the paradoxical anxiety plaguing me.

Over the next six-week period, I began to notice that this combination of medications was helping me considerably. It didn't erase the obsessional thoughts, but it dampened down my anxiety response to them in such a way that I was able to take a step back from them and consider them in a calmer manner. This measure of calm allowed me to think about them but not to be as debilitated or mentally paralyzed with fear when they were present. The anxiety was far from gone, but it was certainly more bearable. Still, I didn't want to live out the rest of my life with the thought that I might not be a Christian after all so I kept up my efforts to prove to myself that this accusation wasn't true. All during this time I kept on praying that God would send me the reassurance and comfort that I still belonged to Him.

CHAPTER 18

JUST WHEN YOU THINK YOU KNOW IT ALL

THE INTERNET IS more often a foe than a friend to a person with an Anxiety Disorder. The reason being is that it's often a tool that is employed as part of the compulsive activity of a person with OCD, but I'll be addressing that further on. In this case the internet turned out to be a God send on the day that I decided to type the following words into the search engine; "doubting your salvation." Typing those words were just one more attempt on my part to find that perfect answer which I thought could finally lay all my fears to rest. A lot of Christian websites popped up which offered a plethora of scriptural reassurance on the subject of eternal security for the individual who had placed their trust in Christ. I read them all and found that they didn't provide any new insights or information than what I already knew on the subject. It was confusing and unsettling to me as to why those same scriptures which had the power to reassure and comfort me in the past couldn't seem to break through or provide relief from all those nagging feelings of doubt and uncertainty. In fact, as I read those scriptures over and over I found that instead of my being able to get past the fears I only seemed to feel even more pushed to search for more proof that I was still saved. As I frantically read and jumped from one website to another, I finally landed on a site that had an entirely different theme. The words; "doubting your salvation", were linked to a Christian forum that dealt with the disorder of OCD. "OCD," I wondered out loud – "what in the world does *that* have to do with doubting your salvation"? Curious to understand the connection I pressed on in my reading.

Within a short time of reading I was totally astonished! At that very moment, it was if I had been transported back to that day when I'd read the Readers Digest article and made the discovery that I had Panic Disorder. *This* time, though, the disorder was OCD and the thoughts and feelings that the people on this forum were expressing were so much like my own it was as if they'd been able to read my mind and then had set my thoughts and feelings down in writing.

Still, the notion that I might have OCD seemed absurd. I couldn't think of any ways in which I fit the description of a person with OCD. My perception of OCD conjured up images of quirky compulsions like repetitive hand washing, hoarding, constant checking of locks or appliances, extreme cleanliness and having to have things just so in one's environment.

Yet this was a forum specifically dedicated to the disorder of OCD. It became very clear to me in a fairly short time that although I thought I knew it all when it came to living with my Anxiety Disorder that I still had a lot to learn.

It was incredibly comforting to find out, once again, that I wasn't alone in my nightmare. These people could actually relate to my pain. In the weeks and months that followed, I would go through yet another period of learning about my disorder. I couldn't believe that I'd lived all those years with the disorder of OCD and never had the slightest inkling of it or how over the years it had beaten me down in so many ways. But, more importantly than all that, was the fact that I had been completely clueless about how to go about managing it.

For now, I'll leave off telling my story. The things I've learned about my OCD will be shared in the second portion of this book which deals with how I've learned to live with and manage my Anxiety Disorders. There will be quite a large segment in this portion of the book devoted to OCD and, most specifically to what psychologist's refer to as "Religious OCD" as this has been one of the most distressing and disturbing ways in which my disorder has afflicted me.

It's been extremely hard to revisit the pain of my Anxiety Disorder as I've set about to share some of my experiences with my readers, but if even just one person can be helped or comforted by it, then it's been well worth the discomfort. One of my greatest encouragers in my own struggle with OCD has been an individual who has been home with our Lord for over 300 earth years. His name is John Bunyan. I have thanked God over and over for this man. I look forward to the day when perhaps I will be given the great privilege of being able to tell him face to face just how much he's helped me through my journey with Religious OCD, which seems to so closely mirror his own.

If you've come this far and have found that you and I are very much alike in our experiences of living with these distressing disorders, then I would invite you to press on to the next portion of the book which I hope will be far more helpful to you than what you've read thus far. But it's good to know, isn't it, that you're not alone. I understand your pain and I'm in your corner – praying for you. I am confident that God will lift your head up again and that he will teach you that this affliction is an opportunity for you to experience His grace more fully.

"You fearful saints, fresh courage take; the clouds you so much dread are big with mercy, and shall break with blessings on your head." 1.

Notes:

1. William Cowper – "God Moves in a Mysterious Way."

Part Two

CHAPTER 1

WHEN ANXIETY CHOOSES YOU

C.S. Lewis:
"Some people feel guilty about their anxieties and regard them as a defect of faith I don't agree at all. They are afflictions; they are if we can so take them, our share in the Passion of Christ. For the beginning of the Passion – the first move, so to speak – is in Gethsemane." 1.

IN THIS CHAPTER, my efforts will be directed at contrasting Anxiety Disorders with commonplace worry or doubt. I figured that the best way to make this contrast more discernible to the reader would be to relate what the experience of having an Anxiety Disorder is like. Therefore, I've chosen to share just how mine developed as well as how it has affected me.

Anxiety Disorders differ greatly from everyday commonplace worry in that the level of anxiety that they cause is far more intense, hangs on for a very long period of time and can be so debilitating as to interfere with an individual's daily functioning. The anxiety from these disorders can crop up unexpectedly or, in the beginning, can be experienced as a general sense of free floating anxiousness without a specific theme or target as a reason to be feeling anxious. The physical and emotional symptoms of an Anxiety Disorder are the driving forces that cause a person to become stuck in specific obsessional themes which create intense doubt and fear or to withdraw from or avoid many situations. The person may then develop co-morbid conditions such as the inability to eat, insomnia, and clinical depression just to name a few. These distressing emotions are experienced as being in a continual hyped up state of fight or flight. Without these distressing emotions, a person could easily choose to just let go of their worries. However, for the person with an Anxiety Disorder the brain's insistence that something is amiss makes this task extremely difficult.

The brain of a person suffering from these disorders can be compared to a broken fire alarm that will blare out a warning signal when there is neither smoke nor fire. Imagine that you are sleeping quite peacefully all warm and snug in your bed when you are awakened with a sudden jolt to the noise of your smoke detector going off. The first thing that happens when you are jolted awake in this manner is that your heart will generally begin to pound quite fast. You will likely jump out of bed realizing that the smoke detector is warning you about a possible fire. You begin to race about the house looking for the fire, trying to find the source of the emergency only to discover that there's no fire to be found, no smoke to be detected, and yet the fire alarm is still blaring. You rip out the batteries and the very next day you replace them thinking that *this* must surely be the problem. Yet the very next night the same scenario takes place all over again. So this time you make the decision to throw out your old smoke detector and replace it with a new one. Problem solved!

When the anxiety center, or for illustrative purposes, the "fire alarm" of the brain begins to misfire at inappropriate times there are no batteries to replace and one can't throw out a malfunctioning brain and replace it with a new one. Instead, the only choice that remains is to treat the inappropriate anxiety response and also to learn to recognize and ignore the false warning signals. Trust me when I say that this is far easier said than done! The chemistry in the brain of a person with an anxiety disorder becomes imbalanced in such a way that they are constantly receiving the signals of fight or flight when there's no real need for them. It's extremely difficult to ignore these signals because our instinctive response to them is either to run from the danger or to fight to protect ourselves. Ignoring them not only feels wrong - it feels exceedingly dangerous! To tell a person with an Anxiety Disorder to "buck up – shake it off" or to "just stop worrying" can be compared to telling a person whose head is resting in a guillotine to just shrug off the fear that they're experiencing at that moment and grin and bear it. That's just how intense the fear emotions that drive these disorders can be. This fear response isn't something that a person chooses, it chooses them. The fear is an ever present feeling. It's there when their eyes pop open in the morning and it's there when they climb into bed at night. It's just there – waiting for something to latch on to – something to chew on and this is the reason that people with Anxiety Disorders will usually develop an exaggerated or disproportional fear to everyday common things, experiences or thoughts.

I've engaged in *chosen* worry and can testify to the fact that it feels entirely different than the anxiety that accompanies these disorders. Anxiety Disorders are often attributed to a person worrying too much, but this is just not so. These disorders are real afflictions and should not be labeled as the sin of worry, just as one wouldn't dare to label heart disease or diabetes as sin. It's a well-known fact that the heart and pancreas are made up of flesh and blood and, therefore, are subject to disease or malfunction. This prompts the question; why should the brain be any different?

There are many types of Anxiety Disorders and it's not uncommon for a person who is afflicted with one type to experience one or more of the other types in a kind of overlap syndrome.

The list that follows covers the range of Anxiety Disorders that have impacted my own life. Some have not been as severe as others and my list is certainly not exhaustive in that it doesn't include all the types.

Panic Disorder – Moderate to severe.
Agoraphobia – Mild to moderate.
Social Phobia – Mild to Moderate.
Obsessive Compulsive Disorder – Moderate to Severe

There are a lot of good books written by physicians who specialize in treating anxiety which cover all the subsets but for my purposes, I will only be sharing about those which I have experienced.

My **Panic Disorder** developed in my mid-twenties and has been present with me ever since. It has waxed and waned in intensity over the years. When my brain chemistry becomes severely imbalanced, my panic attacks are far more frequent. When it's more balanced, they are intermittent and less severe in their intensity. My panic attacks are experienced as a sudden shockwave of intense fear that can come on me without cause. They usually come in clusters of two or three attacks which last only a few minutes but can leave me with a generalized feeling of anxiousness that can hang on for quite a while. There are also certain situations which will often prompt or trigger my panic attacks. Some of these situations include; Driving, especially in new areas or on the highway, watching action movies on large screen theatres and looking up at tall structures or down from tall structures. I'm also triggered when thinking about or contemplating expansive or infinite topics like; outer space, the concept of eternity, the height of a mountain or the depth of the sea.

I've experienced every one of the known symptoms of a panic attack at one time or another which are as follows;

> Shortness of breath or a feeling of being smothered.
> Heart palpitations – pounding heart or accelerated heart rate.
> Dizziness, unsteadiness, or faintness.
> Feeling of choking.
> Sweating
> Nausea or abdominal distress.
> Feeling of unreality – as if you're not all there - (depersonalization).
> Numbness or tingling in hands and feet.
> Hot and cold flashes.
> Chest pain or discomfort.
> Fears of going crazy or losing control.
> Fears of dying. 2.

The symptoms of a panic attack are so distressing that a first encounter with one will often cause an individual to seek help in the emergency room of a hospital because it feels very much as if they might be dying.

Most of my experiences with **Agoraphobia** have been prompted by the presence of panic attacks, but some of it has been related to the generalized feeling of dread associated with going anywhere that is unfamiliar, new or uncommon to my experience. For instance, going on vacation is always accompanied at first by a sense of dread that something will go wrong while I'm away.

Agoraphobics are often described as reclusive people who avoid public situations or even going out of their houses. Agoraphobia, like most Anxiety Disorders, can wax and wane over time and can range from mild to severe.

My first encounter with Panic Disorder is what led to a great deal of my avoiding many public situations. I was terrified that I might have a really bad attack of anxiety and lose complete control of my sanity while out in public. The need to be able to escape in all public situations made it very difficult for me to function normally. During that time, all of the following situations were very difficult for me to endure. When I engaged in these things I felt trapped with no place to flee should my panic get the best of me: Riding in a car, sitting in church, sitting in a restaurant, going to a movie, going to concert, going to visit other people's homes and waiting in a doctor's office.

To this day, I still struggle with some lesser manifestations of agoraphobia. Driving is still a big challenge to me if it means driving somewhere I've never driven before or very far from my home, especially if I'm alone. I am still unable to drive on highways. I insist on sitting at the end of a row in theaters or in church so that I'll be able to get up and leave in case I have a panic attack that might get too intense for me to stay put. Every time I have to go into a new social situation whether it's an invite to a party or a new Bible study, I always have a strong urge to avoid it. Deep down I really want to go but I always experience a pretty strong anxiety response to new social situations. I have to push myself out the door knowing that once I get there and force myself to be friendly and social that eventually I will be glad I went.

When I was a little girl of elementary school age, **Social Anxiety Disorder** was mostly absent from my life. I look back on those days with wonder and amazement. Who was that little girl and where did she go? I was a very friendly, outgoing, and surprisingly popular little girl. I sang out loud on the school bus. I was usually one of the kids that got picked first when forming teams for softball, football or a neighborhood snowball war. I had boyfriends galore and a whole gaggle of girls that were my pals. My teachers liked me and I liked them. I helped out with the kids who struggled with their grades. I jumped rope, played tether ball, collected bugs, rode skateboards down steep hills, climbed trees, stayed the night with my cousins, kept snakes as pets and even managed, although with some difficulty, to go camping with my cousin in the summer.

My entry into Junior High brought about changes in me that transformed me from a happy, outgoing little girl into a shy introvert with just a small handful of friends. I dreaded each and every day of school. Most school day mornings my stomach was in such a knot that I found it difficult to choke down a piece of toast. My mom insisted that I eat something before I left for school. I was terrified that I'd forget my locker combination, forget my class schedule or even how to get to my classes. I could well imagine how stupid I'd feel having to go to the office and ask for help should I forget any of those things. I never raised my hand in class to answer a question or do a math problem on the chalkboard. I totally quit speaking to or flirting with boys because if I tried to I would break out in hot hives that would start on my cheeks and travel down my arms and torso. I avoided the restrooms as much as possible. Gym class was nothing short of sheer torture to me especially since I couldn't swim. I wanted to fade into the woodwork and hated for any attention to be drawn to me for fear that I might say or do something embarrassing or stupid. I managed to shove through those feelings for the most part and even forced myself to engage in things that I love such as drama or music. I could get up and sing a solo, yet not without severe abdominal distress and a racing heart, but once I was done, I couldn't talk to anyone about my performance. When I was in high school popular kids would come up to me after a concert when I'd sang a solo and compliment me on my talent. But, the most I could muster up in response was to quickly mumble, "Thanks" and then I'd rush off as I'd feel the hives starting to form.

An awakening as to just how big a role my social anxiety played during high school came at my ten-year class reunion. I was talking to one of the more popular individuals from our graduating class when they suddenly said; "Wow you're Mitzi French! I didn't know you could even talk!" I still break out in hives when speaking in public, or talking about myself to anyone. New experiences such as meeting a new group of people or having to start a new job are extremely challenging for me. I still haven't been able to pump gasoline for myself.

Yes…some of the things that my social anxiety causes are pretty weird but I just know that there is someone else reading this account who can relate. There are times when my social anxiety wins out and I avoid certain things, but I'm learning not to let it push me around and rob me of the life enriching experience of human fellowship. I've learned to "act as if" I'm outgoing and confident and in doing so I can sometimes actually begin to feel that way.

Last but most certainly not least is the mother of all my Anxiety Disorders; **Obsessive Compulsive Disorder or OCD.** This disorder has a wide range of symptoms and manifestations. Consequently, there are many, many people who suffer from this disorder who are clueless as to what is wrong with them. If, for example, you think that the character Adrian Monk from the popular television series "Monk" is an example of how OCD always manifests itself you will have a very narrow and incomplete understanding of this disorder. That was my problem. You will recall that all the knowledge that I'd gleaned about OCD was that the people with the disorder usually washed their hands a lot, or continually checked locks, or hoarded junk to the point of being nearly buried alive in it. While it's true that some of these things are symptomatic of some forms of OCD, there is a far greater list of the many ways in which this disorder can manifest itself.

Discovering that I had OCD was an unexpected and unwelcome shock to me. Once I realized that I'd been afflicted with this disorder for many years my emotions ran the gambit of relief to fear. I was relieved to finally know *why* I had suffered so tremendously from bizarre or frightening thoughts that I couldn't get out of my head.

Yet, I also had a great deal of dread about having to fight yet another battle with something I knew very little about. It also made me feel like a mental weakling, someone who was truly a "nut job."

Even though I'd gotten over my fear of being labeled as someone with Panic Disorder, I hated to think that I had a new and seemingly more embarrassing label called OCD. I think this had to do with the fact that a lot of people seem to find humor in what they perceive to be quirky behaviors of people with OCD. That TV show "Monk" is a classic example of this. But to the person in a bad flare of OCD there is nothing humorous about it. They wouldn't wish it on their worst enemy. It's an excruciating disorder and those who are afflicted with it spend enough time beating up self and, therefore, need no help from others to that end.

What follows is a list of various OCD obsessions and the compulsions that often accompany them compiled by Dr. Jeffrey M. Schwartz in his book "Brain Lock." 3. I've italicized the ones in bold which I've struggled with the most as well as the specific way in which they are manifested.

Obsessions:

Obsessions about Dirt and Contamination – unfounded fears of contracting a dreaded illness. Excessive concern about germs.
Obsessive Need for Order and Symmetry
Obsessions about Hoarding and Saving

Obsessions with Sexual Content
Repetitive Rituals
Nonsensical Doubts
Religious Obsessions (Scrupulosity) – Troublesome blasphemous thoughts. Fears and doubts of losing salvation.
Obsessions with Aggressive Content – Repeated intruding images of violence. The fear of acting out a violent thought.
Superstitious Fears – Fear of demonic influence

Compulsions:

Cleaning and washing Compulsions – This is very mild with me, but I do have to use a hand sanitizer every time I leave a store, or church or any other public setting. I don't like to touch door handles at all and will use my elbows to shove them open whenever possible.
Compulsions about Having Things "Just Right."
Hoarding or Collecting Compulsions
Checking Compulsions – My checking compulsions are mostly mental. (Explanation to follow.)

If I had stopped in my search to understand just how my doubts and fears about my relationship with Christ fell into the category of OCD, I might not have ever learned about one more type of OCD which perfectly described my experiences. This type of OCD is described by Dr. Stephen Phillipson in his online article titled; "Rethinking the Unthinkable" [4] as "Pure-O" OCD. His description of the disorder is as follows:

"In 'Pure-O' the anxiety emerges in response to an unwanted, intrusive thought or question; what I call a 'spike.' The ritual or compulsion with this form of OCD involves the non-observable, mental 'pushing away' of the thought, avoiding the recurrence of the thought, or attempting to solve the question or undo the threat that the thought presents."

Further on in the article he explains that:

"'Pure-O' has two parts: the originating unwanted thought (spike), and the mental activity in which the sufferer attempts to escape, solve, or undo the spike. This is called 'rumination.' With 'Pure-O', it is the threatening, nagging, or haunting nature of the idea, which compels the patient to engage in an extensive effort to escape from the thought. Most likely, it is not the intrusive idea, per se, that drives the response, but the associated emotional terror." 4.

This definition of "Pure-O" describes exactly what I've experienced with my OCD. The worst of my "Pure-O" obsessional themes centered themselves on my relationship or standing with Christ. I will be going into greater detail about my struggle with this type of OCD in the chapter that bears the title of this book; "Strivings Within".

The bottom line here is that the experience of living with an Anxiety Disorder is nothing like the common experience that all humans have, where we might worry or fret about a legitimate stressful circumstance that happens to crop up in our lives. Rather than the activity of worry being the *cause* of an Anxiety Disorder, it's actually the disorder itself that will cause a person to experience extreme emotional terror that is inappropriate or disproportionate to a thought or idea. In an Anxiety Disorder if the *feeling* of anxiety was a chicken and the specific obsession was an egg, then the correct answer to the question; "which comes first the chicken or the egg?"; Would be "the chicken". The obsession would not become such a huge problem if it were not for the misfiring in the anxiety center of the brain.

Anxiety disorders can range from mild as in when they are nothing but a minor nuisance to severe as in when they are overwhelming, consuming and debilitating. They are afflictions and should be treated as such *and* thankfully there are successful treatment methods that are available.

For the Christian, there are also lessons to be learned and growth to be gained from living with these disorders. God's grace is sufficient for even this, but I'll be getting into that later on. For now, my hope is that the things I've shared in this chapter may have opened up a door of knowledge and understanding concerning the validity as well as the impact of Anxiety Disorders in the lives of those who are afflicted with them.

Notes:

1. "Letters to Malcolm, Chiefly on Prayer," By: CS Lewis, Harcourt Inc., Chapter 3, Page 41, and Paragraph 3.
2. "The Anxiety and Phobia Workbook – Third Edition," By Edmund J. Bourne, Ph.D., New Harbinger Publications Inc., Page 5, Paragraph 1.
3. "Brain Lock," By Jeffrey M. Schwartz, Regan Books, Introduction – pages xvii & xviii.
4. http://www.ocdonline.com "Rethinking the Unthinkable" By Dr. Stephen Phillipson.

CHAPTER 2

Misguided Counsel and Stinging Blame

CS Lewis: "The act of cowardice is all that matters; the emotion of fear is, in itself no sin." 1.

HE MEANT WELL – to encourage her and strengthen her faith, but his words only deepened her mental torture. They placed the blame squarely on her shoulders and the hideous weight of it all drove her into even greater depths of despondency. In an attempt to ease her into his assessment of her problem he had said; "this is not *completely* your fault. It also sounds like you are oppressed by an evil spirit of doubt and guilt, shame and embarrassment, self-hatred and self-condemnation." *Wow*, she thought, *I must be a complete spiritual basket case!*

Then he instructed her to pray a prayer that he had composed for her that she could use to rebuke the "evil spirits to come out of her." After that, he told her to pray this additional prayer. "Lord Jesus I release myself to you and repent of and refuse to let my past sins define or control me. And give me a better and deeper relationship with you - in your name, Lord Jesus, amen."

His instructions made her feel as if she was still a baby Christian, like someone who didn't even understand the basics of repentance and forgiveness. But she *wasn't* a baby Christian and his condescending words hurt and offended her. Furthermore, she'd already prayed a multitude of times for forgiveness and deliverance from this fear. But what made her feel worse was his suggestion that maybe, just maybe her anxiety was rooted in something far more ominous and disturbing – an evil spirit – a demon! *What if he's right?* She pondered the accusation; *How could someone who is a Christian be indwelt by or controlled by a demonic presence?*

All of her Biblical knowledge told her that this wasn't possible and yet the *suggestion* of it – the accusation, stood out in her mind as a ghastly menacing doubt. She tried to turn her thoughts from it but then another accusation popped into her consciousness; *Haven't you been struggling for all these months with the possibility – the relentless nagging doubt that you might not really be saved after all?*

With that, she felt the familiar rise of nausea in her gut. The tears began to flow uncontrollably. She had sought the comfort of Christian counsel and it had slapped her right back into that same dark place of excruciating doubts, shame, and isolation. *Perhaps,* she despaired, *I'm a hopeless case.*

The above scenario is based upon actual advice that was offered up by a well-meaning Christian to a person who was afflicted with Religious OCD. The response to the advice is, however, my own and is based on what my reaction would have been if it had been offered up to me when I was in a bad flare of my Religious OCD. I've shared this scenario in an attempt to demonstrate just how damaging, hurtful and counterproductive uneducated and ill-informed advice can be to a Christian, who is suffering from OCD.

Whenever well-meaning but misinformed Christians attempt to diagnose the cause of any type of mental disorder as a spiritual problem they are risking doing great harm to the very person they are attempting to help. Yet this happens on a regular basis. There seems to be this bizarre notion within a large portion of the Christian community that a Christian cannot be afflicted with a mental illness or that mental illnesses are nothing more than bad or sinful attitudes. It's as if a Christian's skull contains nothing more than a spirit like vapor rather than a brain that's made of flesh and blood. Or if they'll admit a flesh and blood brain they believe that it's somehow immune to any sort of malfunction. It would appear, however, that a malfunction in any other organ within a Christian's body is considered legitimate. I'm sorry to have to say it, but that's just bad science and it's also a mar on the testimony of the Christian community to dismiss mental disorders as either invalid or the fault of the individual sufferer.

I recall a conversation I had about my Panic Disorder with a Christian lady. She too meant well – to encourage me and more than that to "cure" me of my panic attacks with just a few words of advice. She shared with me concerning a *one-time* incident that had occurred in her first week of starting college. She had moved into a dorm far away from home and family. Basically, she was very homesick, well out of her comfort zone and had begun to question her decision to go away to college. She said that she'd gotten herself so worked up emotionally over this that she believed she'd experienced a panic attack. It is very possible that the stress of starting college, lack of sleep and moving away from home contributed to her possibly having an actual panic attack. But, having just one panic attack, if it really was one, especially in response to engaging in normal worrisome thoughts does not mean that a person has Panic Disorder. She then went on to tell me that she suddenly realized that she was getting herself all worked up when she should just give the whole situation over to the Lord. So she bowed her head and prayed, laying all her concerns at Christ's feet, got up and had perfect peace from that moment forward.

My inner reaction to this mini counseling session went like this; (Big sigh) – then Duh?! Then; (inside sarcastic tone) *I wish I'd thought of this years ago. If only I'd had the forethought to just pray and turn everything over to the Lord, then, just like my friend here, I'd have been free from panic attacks all this time! Oh well – go figure, I am quite blonde and she being a brunette is obviously a lot smarter than I am.*

Even though the little counseling session that I'd had with this lady seems innocuous and innocent, the underlying accusation is that of choosing worry over faith or fear over trust. Therefore, it causes the person with an Anxiety Disorder to feel as if it's entirely their fault. The misconception that a person with an Anxiety Disorder just doesn't understand how to have faith or doesn't grasp even the most basic things about salvation and forgiveness will often lead to these types of condescending conversations.

I recall hearing from one young man about his experience in a counseling session at his church. He had bravely opened up about having OCD and how, due to that, he experienced relentless thoughts which centered on the theme of doubting his salvation. The counselor, completing ignoring the fact that he had just told her he had OCD, proceeded to give him an overview of how to be saved in the most basic and simplistic way as if he were a small child who was just hearing it for the very first time. This young man was highly intelligent and very well studied in the scriptures so the counsel that she offered up wasn't at all what he needed. What he needed was for her to empathize with him in his suffering and to encourage him that God would not just carry him through his ordeal of OCD but that God's grace was sufficient for it. She could have prayed for him, that God would provide the proper medical help that he so needed.

This scenario demonstrates how Christians with religious OCD can often be viewed by a Pastor or church counselor as being Biblically illiterate or somehow stunted in their spiritual growth. This can happen because many Pastor's or spiritual counselors haven't a clue as to what OCD is or how it affects a person.

It's very hard for people with Anxiety Disorders which are often accompanied by clinical depression not to indulge in self-loathing in response to their disorder. There is often a feeling of shame over how weak they feel in not being able to rid themselves of the disorder. Therefore, when anyone else dares to suggest that if they'd just change their attitude they could feel better it's like adding fuel to a fire.

Sadly, there are also times when people can be downright mean, mocking and offensive in their reactions to people with Anxiety disorders. I experienced this just after I had shared my public testimony concerning God's provision and grace toward me in my own experiences of living with Panic Disorder. Afterward, my youngest son witnessed a young woman doing a humorous performance of me out in the foyer of our church. She was pretending to be me as she mockingly blurted out, "I'm having a panic attack - I'm having a panic attack!" It really hurt my feelings to be mocked and made fun of because I had dared to share about my disorder in the hope that it might encourage others. In the end, I chose to focus on the positive rather than the negative. Some folk came up to me afterward and told me that they'd been encouraged by my sharing in that they too had been afflicted with Panic Disorder. So rather than to continue to dwell on the fact that I'd been mocked or become angry or bitter about it, I decided that I would just accept and expect that there will always be someone who doesn't understand my anxiety disorder or who just flatly refuses to believe that it's a legitimate affliction.

Some mistaken attitudes about Anxiety Disorders are due to the fact that most people have very little education about them. It's not that these people are choosing to be mean or judgmental it's rather that they really have a sincere desire to try and help.

Awhile back I was listening to a sermon on the topic of worry which was being given by a Pastor for whom I have the highest regard. I was very disappointed when he chose, as a backdrop for his sermon, an account of a woman who was afflicted with Panic Disorder and Agoraphobia. He was using her, as an illustration, to warn his congregation as to how the sin of worry if left unchecked could lead to such consequences. I know the motivation behind his sermon was well intended, but he was mistaken in his assessment as to why this woman had these disorders. Excessive worry isn't the thing that causes these disorders to develop but rather a malfunctioning of the fight or flight center in the brain.

The most blatantly intentional case that I've ever encountered of people heaping shame and blame on an individual with a mental disorder came through the airways of a Christian radio talk program. The focus of this particular program's discussion happened to be Clinical Depression. Since I had experienced Clinical Depression as a co-morbid condition arising out of my Anxiety Disorder, I was very curious as to what these fine Christian leaders would have to say on the topic. A few minutes later I found myself sitting there in jaw-dropping disbelief and horror as I heard them spewing out harmful words borne out of ignorance. During one segment of the program, they spent a great deal of time defending the irresponsible actions of a pastor who had taken it upon himself to give medical advice to a young man who was suffering from Clinical Depression. The pastor had advised the teenager to stop taking his medication and just trust in Christ to heal his "sadness." The horrific consequence of this was that after following the pastor's advice the young man ended up committing suicide. His devastated parents were suing the pastor for his irresponsible actions. Even if the motivation behind this pastor's advice had been prompted by compassion, his lack of education about mental disorders and his blatant disregard for the medical treatment this young man had been receiving was unbelievably negligent.

This pastor obviously had no regard for the legitimacy of mental disorders and, therefore, took it upon himself to usurp the role of the young man's parents as well as his physician. I was astonished that rather than warning pastors not to overstep their roles by trying to diagnose or treat medical conditions these radio hosts were defending the actions of this pastor while not offering up one word of compassion or empathy for the family of this young man.

On yet another day, I turned on my radio to find them still undeterred in sharing their ignorance about Clinical Depression. The focus of discussion on that day was regarding an article they'd picked up about a police officer's personal experience of living with depression. This courageous civil servant had willingly opened up about his depression and how it impacted his life in an effort to offer up encouragement and hope to others in the field of law enforcement who shared his disorder. As the radio hosts discussed his story which included the negative impact the depression had caused to his quality of life, they began to mock his statements. They read out loud from the article about how the depression had interfered with his normal sleep cycle. After that, they spent some time joshing around with one another and making snide and mocking remarks like; "well if he'd quit taking naps in the middle of the day he might have been able to sleep at night – duh!" Then when they read the part about how the depression had robbed him of his ability to enjoy things like his former hobby of collecting antique toys, they responded by poking fun at him by saying; "what use would anyone have for a police officer who still likes to play with toys. That's a real *manly* hobby." These remarks were followed by even more laughter. They really seemed to be getting quite a lot of enjoyment out of mocking his suffering.

After a short commercial break, these wonderfully compassionate Christian men made a weak and halfhearted attempt to try and undo the damage. They said, "we don't want anyone to think that we don't care about this man's pain or that we're poking fun at his suffering, but really all he needs to do is to turn his life over to Christ and then he won't have to deal with depression anymore."

All I could think was; *why would he want to turn his life over to Christ if being a Christian means that you not only deny the validity of someone's affliction but that while you're at it, you mock and poke fun at them?* If I'd been that police officer and had heard these cruel remarks, I would have made the decision to avoid Christians like the plague.

Although these radio hosts refused to admit it, they really *were* poking fun at this man and they should have fully apologized for it. I feel that the reason they didn't was because they really believed that it was his fault that he was depressed. I wondered if they'd of dared to offer up that same sort of counsel to someone like the great preacher Charles Haddon Spurgeon, who also suffered from debilitating bouts of depression. I couldn't help but imagine how if any unbelievers who held *real* degrees in the field of psychology had heard this radio program that they'd be sure to tell most or all of their patients to steer clear of Christians during their treatment program. But mostly I thought about how the Enemy had found something to gloat about as a result of this. I could almost hear him chuckling to himself, "well looks as if we have no need to fight against the Christians in *this* arena, these guys are doing a pretty darn good job of it themselves."

Having an Anxiety Disorder is not the result of unchecked worry or sinful choices anymore so than any other type of illness is. It is, however, always a struggle for the person who is afflicted to be able to divorce the disorder and its symptoms from their actual inner character and motives. For that reason, any suggestion that their illness is their fault will generally lead to a worsening of their condition.

Having said all of this, I think it's very important for the person with an Anxiety Disorder to consider that in most cases of misguided counsel, that the people offering up, the counsel really *do* intend to help rather than to hurt. The sting and hurt that arises from these kinds of incidents can often lead to anger if we let it. Instead, we need to ask God to help us use these instances as teachable moments where we may have an opportunity to educate one more person about the real cause of our disorder. This can be done in a loving and respectful way.

For example, you can ask questions that go something like this; "I'm curious to know why you think that my disorder is caused by a lack of faith, bondage to sin, or a spiritual stronghold? Could you please explain how you came to this conclusion as I'm very interested in understanding your point of view?" This will put them in the position of having to defend their own position without you coming across as accusatory. Then, after listening to their explanation you can offer up the knowledge that you have about your disorder by continuing the conversation with; "Did you ever consider that - _____?" (You fill in the blank.)

Surprisingly even fellow sufferers will often misjudge one another's experiences with their disorders. For instance, in the case of OCD one person's obsession may seem entirely absurd when compared to another person's obsession. One person with OCD might suffer tremendously with obsessing about germs while another might not even be slightly bothered by the thought of germs being on their skin. The other person might struggle tremendously with horrid harmful or aggressive thoughts and think that their OCD is more valid or more painful than the person who is obsessed about germ contamination. It's important in these instances to point out that just because you don't share another person's specific obsession doesn't mean that they aren't suffering just as much as you are with their disorder. *All* experiences of OCD are painful and distressing so it's important for fellow sufferers to show compassion toward one another by acknowledging this.

There will always be times in our lives when we just know what we know because of having experienced it. As far as other people believing in or understanding just how real and excruciating Anxiety Disorders can be it's important to not only accept that some folk will never get to that place, but also to let go of the need to prove to them that you are right and they are wrong.

There was an incident in our family which taught me the value of being able to let go of the need to prove myself to be correct. I call it the "yellow boat incident." I was a young teen at the time and our family was dining out while on vacation. The restaurant had a lovely view that overlooked the Keweenaw Waterway.

I can't remember just *why* all of us had taken note of a certain boat that was docked by the restaurant, but when we did we had, each and every one of us, seen it as being a green boat. My younger brother and I having finished eating first asked to be excused so we could take a walk down by the water. When we got out to the dock, we walked out to the place where the green boat was tied up.

Once we got there, we were both surprised to see that the boat we had all thought to be green was actually yellow. After discussing this interesting phenomenon, we decided that it must have been the combination of the tinted restaurant windows combined with the reflection of the water that had made it look green to us while we were sitting in the restaurant.

When our parents and older brother finished dining and stepped outside both of us felt it important to inform them that the boat was actually yellow. When we did, all three of them said; "No it's not, its green." We then invited them to go around to the back of the restaurant and take a look at it from the dock. We wanted them to see it from a different perspective so that they would agree with us that the boat was indeed yellow rather than green. They flatly refused and insisted, while walking to the car, that the boat was still green. It really angered us that they wouldn't bother to walk out on that dock so we could be proven right.

On the drive back to the cottage, we began to argue rather heatedly with them about why we knew that the boat was yellow. They thought we were silly and our older brother really seemed to be enjoying his favored position of siding against us with our folks. The anger that we felt at not getting them to believe us or not being able to prove that we were right built up to a point that we became indignant and mouthy and I was even starting to cry about the whole thing. My younger brother and I went to bed feeling mad and hurt.

The next morning it was decided by our parents that there would be no further discussion on the matter. There would never be an opportunity to prove the matter, never a chance for them to see the boat from the close-up perspective that we had experienced.

Although the pride in the both of us had wanted so badly for them to know that we were right, it was an important lesson for me to learn to let go of needing to convince people to understand or see things from my perspective.

It was important for me to see that although I may know what I know that doesn't mean that everyone must agree with me. But greater than these lessons were the lessons of my being willing to give other's the benefit of the doubt. I needed to learn to let go of all my preconceived assumptions about things for which I have neither the education nor personal experience. I needed to learn to not be so quick to jump to conclusions before knowing – I mean *really* knowing all the facts.

"*He that answereth a matter before he heareth it, it is folly and shame unto him.*"2.

It became necessary for me to realize that some facts, like just how painful an Anxiety Disorder can be, will only be understood experientially. Therefore, the lessons from my "yellow boat" illustration are as follows: Firstly, expect and accept that not everyone will believe that your disorder is real and secondly be willing to let go of needing to prove to others that your disorder is valid. Finally, be teachable and open toward learning about other's experiences rather than jumping to conclusions which are not based on fact or experience.

With more knowledge comes more understanding and with more understanding comes more compassion and that is one of my goals in writing this book. There is certainly a need for education within the Christian community, most especially for those in leadership roles, about the causes and sadly even the reality of psychological illnesses. Much undeserved judgment and misguided counsel, which can be both harmful and counterproductive, could then be avoided. Where previous attitudes of blame and the consequential despair they provoke have existed, there could instead be attitudes of understanding, compassion, empathy and hope.

Notes:

1. "Screwtape Letters," By C.S. Lewis, Broadman and Holman Publishers, page 105, Paragraph 2
2. Proverbs 18:13 KJV

CHAPTER 3

Causes of Anxiety Disorders

IN THIS CHAPTER, I will be addressing a few of the known causes for individuals to develop Anxiety Disorders. But before I do that, I want to touch on some of the most common misconceptions as to why people develop these disorders.

I would venture a guess that most people who haven't had the experience of living with an Anxiety Disorder or haven't been educated as to *why* they develop might be quick to point to excessive worry as the most likely cause. Others might surmise that irresponsible living, sinful life choices or spiritual strongholds could be at the root of the problem. There will likely even be a few individuals, as demonstrated in the last chapter, who attempt to blame the presence of an Anxiety Disorder on supernatural or demonic activity. I've encountered all of these errant views in response to my own Anxiety Disorder. Hearing such things used to really shake me up and make me feel inadequate, weak or guilty about my disorder.

Now, after years of educating myself about the causes of and treatments for my disorder, I am able to hear these things without detriment to my being able to manage it. A clearer understanding of what causes these disorders aids the sufferer in their effort to treat them properly without a bunch of faulty information throwing confusion into the mix.

Chemistry

In order to understand the cause of these disorders, one must first be willing to admit that the organ in our skulls which we call the brain is made up of flesh and blood and, therefore, is subject to illness and or malfunctioning just as any other organ in our body might be. Imagine how ridiculous it would be for anyone to approach a diabetic and insist that their disease is due to a lack of faith or sin when medicine has uncovered that diabetes is caused by the lack of or absence of the chemical, insulin in the organ called the pancreas. Yet for some reason it's hard for people to understand that the brain is also dependent on a specific chemical balance to function normally. Physicians who specialize in treating these disorders have done a plethora of scientific studies which demonstrate that Anxiety Disorders are associated with biological and neurological changes in the brain.

Dr. Jeffrey Schwartz states that; "Together along with many other brain scientists our UCLA team believes that OCD is a brain disease, in essence, a neurological problem…primarily a biological problem, tied to faulty chemical wiring in the brain." 1.

Dr. Archibald D. Hart in his book titled, "The Anxiety Cure" states that; "we now know that a lot of anxiety is biologically based." He goes on to say that; "the form of anxiety that I am discussing in this book can best be described as 'endogenous anxiety,' meaning that it is 'from within' the brain. This form of anxiety is essentially biological and not psychological, at least in its symptoms." 2.

Furthermore, Dr. Mark Crawford reveals the scientific evidence for abnormal brain activity on MRI and PET scans of patients with OCD in the following excerpt from his book, "The Obsessive Compulsive Trap." "The findings of these types of studies have shown that two areas of the brain seem clearly implicated in OCD: the basal ganglia and the orbital frontal region of the brain. These areas of the brain seem to be overstimulated in people who suffer from OCD even when they are at rest. These areas of the brain are also intensely active when a person with OCD is engaged in a compulsive ritual. Further evidence for the role of these regions comes from the fact that these areas of the brain show "normal" functioning when the person is treated for OCD with medication or behavior therapy." 3.

The functioning of a human brain is amazingly complex. It relies on blood flow, electrical impulses, neurotransmitters and chemical messengers. I'm not a brain scientist and, therefore, my knowledge of these functions is certainly minimal. What I *have* learned from reading books by physicians who specialize in treating brain disorders is that the deficiency of one or more chemicals in the brain of a person with an Anxiety Disorder is often implicated as playing a huge role as to causation. Those chemicals are serotonin and nor-epinephrine.

Dr. Edmund J. Bourne confirms this by stating that; "Researchers believe that deficiencies of neurotransmitters such as serotonin and nor-epinephrine may contribute to insufficient inhibition of the amygdala and associated structures that make up this fear system. He goes on to say; "that is why SSRI or tricyclic antidepressant medications, which increase the amounts of serotonin and norepinephrine throughout your brain, can diminish panic attacks." 4.

In light of all this scientific evidence, a person who suffers from an Anxiety Disorder will need to take the very first big step in learning to manage it by admitting that it's a real disorder. It's not something that they brought upon themselves or something that they should be ashamed of. It's a real affliction, but thankfully it's also a very treatable one.

INHERITANCE

There is a great deal of evidence which points to genetic inheritance as one of the predisposing elements which sets some of us up for the possible development of these disorders. Dr. Bourne, writing about the role of genetics in Anxiety Disorders states that; "It is estimated that 15 to 25 percent of children growing up with at least one agoraphobic parent become agoraphobic themselves, while the rate of agoraphobia in the general population is only 5 percent." He goes on to say that; "more compelling evidence comes from studies of identical twins, who of course, have exactly the same genetic makeup. If one identical twin has an anxiety disorder, the probability of the other identical twin having an anxiety disorder ranges from 31 to 88 percent, depending on the study you're looking at." 5.

I'm living proof of the legitimacy of genetic predisposition. Sometime after I developed Panic Disorder, I learned of others in my extended family who struggled with various types of Anxiety Disorders which ranged from mild to severe. Many disorders are inherited genetically so it shouldn't be surprising that disorders which afflict the brain are also inheritable. These genetic tendencies are inborn. Therefore, the person afflicted with them should not be blamed for their development any more than other individuals should be blamed for the development of their specific disorders. For instance, when I was pregnant with my third child I had abnormally high blood sugars and ended up delivering a nine-pound fourteen-ounce baby boy. My doctor told me that because diabetes ran in my family that the blood sugar problems combined with the size of my baby could be indicators that I was predisposed to developing diabetes and should watch out for that possibility later on in my life. It was suggested that I try to maintain a healthy weight, avoid eating too much sugar and get regular exercise to ward off the development of diabetes. So far I've been able to avoid the disease but it remains to be seen whether or not I will be able to prevent the disease as I continue to age. On the other hand, my genetic predisposition for hypertension and high cholesterol is so strong that even though I don't really eat much meat or high fatty foods I still have to be treated for high cholesterol and I developed hypertension at the age of twenty-five when I was still very thin and fit. There are things, however that I can do to manage both these disorders, just as there are things that I can do to manage my Anxiety Disorders.

The point I'm trying to make, is that folk who don't happen to suffer from any sort of mental disorder shouldn't be proud of the fact that they don't. Rather, they should be thankful that they haven't inherited a tendency to develop them. Just because I haven't as of yet developed Diabetes doesn't mean I should admonish those who already have it as if I am somehow better than they are.

Sadly, it's not uncommon for a person with an Anxiety Disorder to be admonished by others, most especially their Christian friends. Those doing the admonishing tend to pat themselves on the back for their "great faith" and will often get rather preachy toward a person who is afflicted with an Anxiety Disorder.

I encountered this unpleasant circumstance while attending a class on depression which was being taught through a video series by a highly respected individual. He actually made statements to the effect that he was better qualified to teach a class on how to overcome depression because he had never suffered from it. I remember wanting to stand up at that very moment and give him a sarcastic round of applause. The underlying implication of his statement was that his attitudes and outlook on life were far superior to those of us in the class who had been afflicted with depression. It seems that he was very confident that he had it all figured out while the rest of us were stuck in our negative attitudes or "spiritual strongholds." This, to me, meant that he was still blaming us for our condition. Though he may not have been able to see it as such, that is exactly how it came across to me.

Yet I wasn't alone in my assessment of his statements. There were several other people who had attended the class who had revealed that they weren't there because they had depression but were there to learn how they might be able to help a friend or acquaintance of theirs who had it. After the pastor had made those statements concerning his "qualification" to teach the rest of us how not to be depressed, one of these individuals approached a person in the class who suffered from depression and offered to help them.

The "lesson" that I came away with was, if you are depressed, it's your fault and those who aren't depressed are that way because they have the right attitude. The end result of this conversation was that the person with the depression dropped out of the class – and so did I.

Even though this individual's statements concerning his *amazing* ability to avoid depression were insulting to me, they weren't the only reason I dropped the class. The thing that really irked me was that he had at one point suggested that if your depression was a chemically based disorder that there was "less hope for you." Talk about a sucker punch to the gut for a person who is suffering from depression. I finally couldn't hold my frustration in any longer and decided to speak up. I took the opportunity to remind everyone, including myself, that God had said, *"His grace was sufficient for us and that His strength could be made perfect in our weaknesses."* 6. I pointed out that no matter what the thorn or affliction was, His strength would not only carry us through it but that He could and would use it to make us better equipped to serve Him.

The lesson that I'm driving at in relating such unsettling encounters is that being human means that we all live under the effects of the fall. There is something in every one of us that isn't as it should be. This encompasses every part of our being from our flesh to our character. At the same time, there is something in every one of us that shows forth the creative goodness of God. He's given us gifts and abilities, not because we deserve them, but because He is a good and gracious Father. We may wrongfully beat ourselves up about things that are part and parcel of living within a creation which, *"groans under the weight of sin".* 7 We may also wrongfully pat ourselves on the back for those things in our being which are not of our own doing but rather undeserved gifts bestowed on us by a loving God.

When we finally step into eternity, we'll likely see these things with a clarity that we haven't had while we live within this realm. I imagine that there will be many healed blemishes that we always figured were our fault, which were, in reality, afflictions. I also imagine that there will be many beauty marks for which we praised ourselves that will, in the end, be revealed to us as the creative work of our loving Father in and through us.

The apostle Paul in his letter to the Corinthians had related to this subject; *"Learn from us the meaning of the saying; 'Do not go beyond what is written.' Then you will not take pride in one man over another. For who makes you different from anyone else? What do you have that you did not receive? And if you did receive it, why do you boast as though you did not?"* 8.

So in the end, we must acknowledge that when it comes to gifts and weaknesses or blessings and afflictions that although we may differ, *that* difference should not ever be viewed through the lens of pride as if we were the ones who created us to be the unique individuals that we are.

When it comes to our physical/mental health, we mustn't point the finger at anyone else because they aren't as healthy as we might be. There will always be differences in this area. Just as there are some folk who can indulge in fatty foods without gaining weight or ever developing high cholesterol or high blood pressure, there will also be some folk who don't over indulge but still suffer from those disorders. Some folk might be able to go through lengthy periods of high stress, health problems or hormonal shifts without ever developing an Anxiety Disorder whereas these events in the life of a person who is pre-disposed to an Anxiety Disorder will serve as a trigger for its development. God didn't make us all the same. He made us different and *that* difference extends to all areas of our being. Whether or not a person suffers from a particular disorder shouldn't be something to either take pride in or to beat oneself up about. What's important is that we make sure we don't beat up on one another regarding these things. A better choice is to acknowledge our differences even regarding weakness and affliction and to look to the One, who has promised to not only sustain us in and through them but to accomplish good on our behalf in and through them.

Triggering Factors

Just as many disorders can lie dormant until something happens to trigger them, the same is often true of Anxiety disorders. One of the major triggers implicated as a cause for a person to develop these disorders is stress. This phenomenon isn't exclusive to mental disorders as it is well documented that stress is a huge contributing factor in many other illnesses. Going through lengthy periods of stress will often create the fertile soil conditions whereby a person who is genetically predisposed to an Anxiety Disorder will have it suddenly crop up.

Dr. Bourne acknowledges the role of stress in triggering panic attacks in the following quote; "A first panic attack is often preceded by a stressful event or situation. In my experience with people already vulnerable to Panic Disorder……, I have found that the following types of stressors often preceded their first panic attack." His list includes; "significant personal loss, significant life changes and the use of stimulants or recreational drugs." 9.

This brief list of stressors is just a small portion of a much larger list of subcategories too long and extensive for me to cover in this book. What I *am* able to say, in looking back upon my own experience is that stress, both good and bad was definitely the forerunner to every big flare of my disorder.

Hormonal Shifts

Another stressor or trigger for women who are predisposed to these disorders is the hormonal shifts that occur during the menstrual cycle, postpartum pregnancy or in menopause. This has also proved to be true in my own life. I experienced a worsening of my symptoms after childbirth as well as in and through the hormonal changes of my surgical menopause. In an online article titled; "Hormones Can Affect Mental Health", Dr. Vivien K. Burt, a UCLA psychiatrist confirms this assertion by stating that; "Although the precise reasons are unclear research has shown an association between times of dramatic hormonal changes and vulnerability to psychiatric conditions."10.

Medical Conditions Associated With Anxiety Disorders

There are some medical conditions that can be associated with or even be the underlying cause of some types Anxiety Disorders. Some of these conditions may include, hypoglycemia, Mitral Valve Prolapse, and Thyroid Disorders. This short list doesn't cover all of the medical conditions that can contribute to Anxiety Disorders but includes some of the most common ones. The conditions that I've chosen to list are those that I've had either firsthand experience with or firsthand knowledge of and, therefore, can speak about them with some measure of understanding.

A. HYPOGLYCEMIA

Hypoglycemia affected me as far back as junior high school. I began to have horrible feelings of anxiety associated with attacks of nearly fainting. These attacks would often come on at the end of a Sunday service at my church. In retrospect, it eventually became clear to me that the reason for these attacks was that I hadn't eaten enough food in the morning, before church, to keep my blood sugar up long enough to sustain me through the hours between breakfast and lunch which happened to be lengthier on Sundays. That drop in my blood sugar would often hit me as I stood up during the final hymn and invitation at the end of service. It was a very frightening feeling and I became concerned that I might be dying when the attacks would come or that I had some scary medical condition that was making me feel that way. In general hypoglycemia causes a person to feel weak and shaky and can even cause fainting in some individuals. It's very important for a person who is afflicted with Anxiety Disorders to keep their blood sugars as stable as possible. Eating small frequent meals is recommended and is also easier to manage if the loss of appetite is a part of your overall symptoms.

A. MITRAL VALVE PROLAPSE

I've also been diagnosed, undiagnosed and re-diagnosed as having Mitral Valve Prolapse. (Doctors don't always agree which can be a hard thing to live with for those of us with OCD who always want to have absolute certainty in these matters.) The seemingly erratic behavior of my heart that I experience from time to time feels incredibly disconcerting. I experience a weird change in rhythm that can feel like a big butterfly flapping about in my chest. Or it can feel as if my heart skips a beat which can often prompt me to cough. Sometimes I even have a sensation that my heart is trembling or vibrating in a painless manner. I will often wake up from a sound sleep with my heart racing and beating so hard that it feels as if it could burst out of my chest. I've been reassured by a Cardiologist, that my Mitral Valve prolapse is a normal, abnormality and nothing to be concerned about. Realizing that doesn't really change the effect that this seemingly bizarre heart activity has on my brain.

Dr. Bourne states that; "For reasons that are unclear, mitral valve prolapse occurs more frequently in people with panic disorder than in the population at large." 11.

One thing that I've learned about my symptoms of Mitral Valve Prolapse is that they improve greatly as my level of physical fitness improves in the same way that my Anxiety level improves with increased levels of fitness. Therefore, I'm a huge advocate of regular exercise as a powerful tool to manage these disorders.

B. THYROID DISORDERS

My knowledge about the effects of Thyroid disease on mental disorders comes from having a son with Grave's disease – a form of hyperthyroidism where the thyroid is putting out an excessive amount of thyroid hormone throughout the body. The opposite of Grave's disease is another disorder referred to as either Hashimoto's or hypothyroidism. I have several close acquaintances who suffer from this type of thyroid disorder and it too has had a negative impact on their mental health.

Our son, Lindsey's Grave's disease is a perfect example of how the thyroid affects mental health. Lindsey had intense anxiety, a rapid pulse, sweating and trembling and weight loss. His weight loss was different from my own, in that he was eating plenty of food but still losing weight. The other symptom that differed from me was that he had very frequent, large bowel movements. In the beginning I thought he had surely inherited an Anxiety Disorder through me, especially since all of this was occurring in his late teens. After he had his thyroid irradiated to prevent the disease from progressing, he was put on thyroid supplementation which he would need to take for the rest of his life. As his labs returned to normal levels, his anxiety disappeared.

Sadly, for him, the battle wasn't yet over as months later he began to develop the symptoms of severe hypothyroidism despite being on thyroid medication. His symptoms at this point were the exact opposite of when he was hyperthyroid due to the Grave's disease. He was tired and listless. His face became puffy and his speech became very slow. He had a lot of difficulties concentrating. His basal body temperature dropped to the point where he felt cold all the time. The worst symptom of all was the effect it had on his mental health. He became clinically depressed. And, as previously mentioned we went through a very long and frustrating period of trying to get him help because most of his doctors were depending on his blood work to diagnose whether or not he was hypothyroid rather than looking at any of his clinical symptoms. They diagnosed him with depression but rather than thinking that his thyroid function might be implicated as the cause they diagnosed him as having a serotonin deficiency and put him on an antidepressant medication called an SSRI. (Selective Serotonin reuptake inhibitor.) This medication, though he was on it for quite some time had absolutely zero effect on his depressive symptoms.

We had to go through quite a few doctors until we found Dr. Walter Woodhouse. Dr. Woodhouse was in a unique position to understand what Lindsey was going through as he also suffers from Grave's disease. He was able to confirm that even though our son's labs looked normal he was quite obviously, severely hypothyroid.

You will remember that this was because he needed two kinds of thyroid supplementation instead of just the one which was the T4 that his doctors had prescribed for him.

Dr. Woodhouse placed him on a new medication called Armour Thyroid which contains both T4 and T3 thyroid hormones. Within twenty-four hours of going on Armour all of his hypothyroid symptoms began to improve, most especially the depression.

Since that time, we've encountered several other people that had the same thing happen to them. They had all the symptoms of hypothyroidism with normal lab results. Both of them experienced the intense misery of clinical depression and both of them were able to get better after finding a doctor who recognized that they needed to incorporate T3 supplementation into their thyroid treatment program in order to feel better. For more information on how the Thyroid impacts mental health I would advise a Google search on the following topics; "Dr.Mirkin.com" and the "Use of T3 Thyroid Hormone to Treat Depression," "Stop the Thyroid Madness" and the "Psychiatric, Psychological and Emotional Aspects of Thyroid Disease."

I wanted to share these stories because it demonstrates that medicine is not an exact science. We often have to keep up the search until we find a doctor who will listen to us and be willing to take into account all of our clinical history as one of the biggest tools they can use in an effort to obtain a correct diagnosis. There is currently a great deal of controversy about how Thyroid disorders are diagnosed and treated.

Several questions that I used as a screening tool to find a doctor who could help my son were; a. "Do you base a good deal of your diagnosis and treatment on clinical history and observations or do you base it only on lab results?" b. "Do you prescribe T3 supplementation to any of your patients?" If the answer to the first question was that they relied more heavily on lab tests than on clinical observation, then I crossed them off my list. If the answer to the second question was that they *never* prescribed T3 to any of their Thyroid patients, they were also crossed off my list.

So if you suffer from anxiety or depression that is unresponsive to antidepressants and you have quite a few of the symptoms of Thyroid disease you might want to take the time to learn all you can about the function of the thyroid gland. Then, try to find a doctor who will take all of your symptoms into account in order to discover whether or not you need T3 supplementation in order to feel better.

The things that I've shared in this chapter on the causes of Anxiety disorders are extremely limited, but they are meant to demonstrate that they are indeed real disorders that are treated by real doctors. It was an important first step in my own life toward managing my disorder to be willing to make the following statement without any reservations; "My name is Mitzi VanCleve. I'm a believer and follower of Jesus Christ and I have Panic Disorder and OCD." Many people have trouble reconciling those statements with one another. My hope is that this book will go a long way toward helping them through that process.

Notes:

1. "Brain Lock," By Dr. Jeffery Schwartz, 1196 Regan Books, Introduction – Page XXX, Paragraph 3
2. "The Anxiety Cure," By Dr. Archibald Hart, Word Publishing, Preface, Page 4, Paragraph 3
3. "The Obsessive Compulsive Trap," By Dr. Mark Crawford, Regal Books, Page 46, Paragraph 2
4. "The Anxiety and Phobia Workbook – Third Edition," By Dr. Edmund J. Bourne, Ph.D., New Harbinger Publications, Inc., Page 38, Paragraph 2

5. "The Anxiety and Phobia Workbook – Third Edition," By Dr. Edmund J. Bourne, Ph.D., New Harbinger Publication, Inc., Page 29, Paragraph 3, Page 30, Paragraph 1
6. 2 Corinthians 12:9 (KJV)
7. Romans 8:22 (KJV)
8. 1 Corinthians 4:6b – 7 KJV
9. "The Anxiety and Phobia Workbook – Third Edition," Dr. Edmund J. Bourne, Ph.D., New Harbinger Publications, Inc., Page 42, Paragraph 4
10. HTTP:// www.uclahealth.org
11. "The Anxiety and Phobia Workbook – Third Edition," By Edmund J. Bourne, Ph.D., New Harbinger Publications Inc., Page 40, Paragraph 2, Page 41, Paragraph 1

CHAPTER 4

Strivings Within - OCD

> "The soul that has once been waked, or stung, or uplifted by the desire for God, will inevitably (I think) awake to the fear of losing Him."
>
> CS Lewis 1.

OCD HAS CERTAINLY proved itself to be the most confusing and diabolical of all my Anxiety Disorder experiences. It still shocks me to think of all the years I lived with this disorder without a clue that I had it. I'm not alone, though.

Dr. Mark Crawford writing about OCD statistics states that; "the average person sees three to four doctors and spends over nine years seeking treatment before receiving a correct diagnosis." He goes on to say that; "some studies have found that it takes an average of seventeen years from the time OCD begins for people to obtain appropriate treatment." 2.

This makes perfect sense to me because the symptoms of my type of OCD are not manifested by outwardly observable signs but are well hidden deep within the mental activity of my brain. For those of us with this type of OCD, it's very difficult to verbalize the content of our mental obsessions for fear of being labeled a "nutcase." So we can go many years suffering in silence and that self-imposed silence often prevents us from obtaining the help we need.

As mentioned in an earlier chapter, for the most part, my type of OCD is what's referred to as "Pure O" or purely obsessional. In looking back over my life, I can identify the presence of OCD as far back as my early childhood. I remember not wanting to use blankets because I feared they might stop me from being able to get out of bed as fast as I needed to in case of a monster in my room or in case I suddenly had to go to the bathroom. I would lie in bed uncovered in the dead of winter rather than risk getting trapped or wound up in my covers. Some other long-held themes were: A fear of being flushed down the toilet, a fear of swallowing my tongue, a fear of hearing my own heartbeat, (afraid that it might stop), a fear of poking my eye out in my sleep and a fear that I'd have a brain aneurysm if I got too mad.

One year my entire summer vacation was ruined by my obsessing that my Dad might die of a heart attack if he ate too much. I remember trying to monitor what he put in his mouth and spending a great deal of time trying to convince him that he shouldn't eat too much food or he might die. My dad wasn't even overweight, but I'd heard somewhere about the connection between overeating and heart disease and I was terrified that his enjoyment of good food might kill him and take him away from my family and me. I remember being unable to sleep at night because of this obsession. It faded away in time and I'm happy to report that my Dad is still with us, still enjoys eating and is doing great at the age of eighty-three.

While I'm well aware that we all have childhood fears, the difference between normal childhood fears and the ones I've mentioned are that my fears caused me a great deal of physical and emotional distress and plagued me for a very long time. Yet, even as a child I knew they had a certain degree of absurdity. I mean *really*, how could a five-year-old girl fit through that small hole at the bottom of the toilet? That's the nature of OCD. There's a place of knowing deep down inside that its threats aren't really valid, but the intense anxiety that accompanies the threats overrules *that* knowing and tricks us into believing that they are. Some examples of my more normal or common childhood fears would be that I'd drown because I couldn't swim or that my uncle's unruly cattle with their long sharp horns might actually get ticked off and charge me when I was asked to help herd them back into a field from which they'd escaped. I wonder if there's such a thing as feral cattle. If there are, my uncle's beasts seemed to fall into that classification.

Despite the fact that I had obsessional fears, in many other ways, as mentioned before, I was a pretty brave little girl or should I say tom-boy – even a daredevil at times. I preferred to eat my summer lunches in a high tree fort which I'd constructed with my own hands. I preferred to ride my bike without using my hands to steer. My favorite sledding hill happened to be the steepest and most treacherous hill in my home town which was referred to as "the flying angel". I preferred tackle football to flag football. In enjoyed riding my brother's minibike as fast as I could through a field of high weeds behind our house. My favorite books were those that had a scary or spooky theme.

It's not unusual for a person with OCD to be uncommonly brave or daring in other aspects of their life. I remember watching a movie about Howard Hughes, who was known to have been horribly afflicted with severe OCD and being astonished at how he could climb into an airplane and actually feel delight in flying solo and yet the idea of the slightest contamination from a tiny little germ could lay him lower than dirt.

While it's true that my episodic themes of OCD in childhood were definitely unpleasant, they couldn't hold a candle to the blows that OCD delivered to me once I reached adulthood. My first bad bout was after the birth of our first child – a precious little girl. Dennis and I had moved away from our hometown in order for him to better his career in a new position. I quit working after the baby came to be a stay at home mom. Dennis's work kept him away from me for fifty to sixty hours a week. I was lonely beyond belief and unsure of my role as a new mom. During that time, I struggled on and off with bizarre and frightening thoughts and graphic images of me harming my baby girl. I remember holding her and sobbing at the horror of how I could even think such thoughts about someone that I'd gladly die for to protect. I told no one of my terror.

I also went through a miserable period of fearing that I'd become demon possessed. This obsession was triggered by a sermon from a missionary at our church who spent an entire hour talking about his experiences in another country where the occult was very active. He even went so far as to suggest that a Christian could become demon possessed. I totally disagreed with him on that point, but I still ended up having to call my Pastor from the church I'd grown up in just to have him confirm through scripture that I was right. Even after his reassurance I still couldn't let go of it. I just kept on asking myself over and over, "what if that guy was right and what if it's a demon that put those terrible thoughts about my baby in my head?" I spent countless hours fighting against that obsession, only to feel worse after each mental battle.

This period of OCD was short-lived in comparison to the bout I went through after the birth of our eldest son. That one which started with Panic attacks and moved on to the OCD harming themes that I shared about earlier lasted about two years in total. I'm not implying that OCD hasn't pestered me at all other than during these periods, but it was during these periods that I was most debilitated by it.

Then my third big flare, the most recent, was briefly described at the end of part one of this book. It's that episode of "Religious OCD" that I'd like to focus on for the remainder of this chapter.

My discussion of this disorder will be limited to "Religious OCD" as it relates to the Christian. What I mean by the word "Christian" is a person who believes in Jesus Christ as their personal Savior and who has committed their life to serving and following Him as their only Lord. Religious OCD can certainly attack other types of faith as it tends to latch on to anything that is of extreme importance to the sufferer. However, I am only able to share how it affects the Christian from relating my own experiences with it.

From my perspective, Religious OCD is very similar to another form of OCD that psychologists refer to as "Relationship OCD." Typical Relationship OCD is experienced by the sufferer as questioning or trying to ascertain whether their love for their spouse or another close relationship is real or not. In Relationship OCD, common episodes such as a disagreement can be tremendously upsetting as they are blown up and exaggerated into dire or ominous events or signs that the relationship is doomed to failure. Although there is far more to Relationship OCD than this simple description, it is, at its root, an intense fear of the loss of a very close relationship. The fear at the root of Religious OCD for a Christian is also a failure or loss of their relationship with God through the person of Jesus Christ.

I say all of this because Christianity is not based in a religious ceremony or ritual observances, but rather on a personal and individual relationship with Jesus Christ. Indeed, Christ himself referred to His followers in relational terms. *"Greater love has no one than this; that he lay down his life for his friends. You are my friends if you do what I command. I no longer call you servants; because a servant does not know his master's business. Instead, I have called you friends."* 3. It is in regard to *this* friendship - *this* relationship that religious OCD attacks and threatens. To the Christian, this relationship is the most vital one of their entire existence. The possibility of either losing it or of never having had it to start with wreaks havoc in the lives of those who have had their OCD latch onto it. The threat of losing this relationship also carries with it the fear of eternal separation from God in the afterlife. This, for the Christian, is the very essence of hell.

Another way Religious OCD is described is called, "Scrupulosity." Dr. Jeffrey M. Schwartz describes this as; troublesome blasphemous or sacrilegious thoughts" and "excessive concerns about morality and right or wrong." 4. My OCD has definitely caused me to experience blasphemous thoughts that get stuck in my head. One example of this occurred years ago when an "artist" got national attention by doing a disgusting painting of a cross in a container of urine. When I heard about this on the news, I was completely revolted by it. A day or so later the title of this supposed work of art kept popping into my head over and over. When I was unable to get it out of my head, I began to obsess that this might mean I was evil or hated Jesus. It seemed as if I actually wanted to think that thought or that I was doing it on purpose because I couldn't get it out of my head. I found myself asking God over and over to forgive me for thinking it. Instead of that wiping the thought away it only made me think about it all the more. The more freaked out I became about the presence of the thought the more it seemed to plague me. It's one thing to get a song or tune stuck in your head but to have something utterly vile yelling out a blasphemous obscenity over and over in your head is not only disturbing it's downright torture.

These types of thoughts are in no way desired by the person with Pure O. They are unwanted, undesired trespassers. Having them pop into your head is not something that you can control. What you *can* control is how you react to them. Now that I've learned and am practicing how to handle their presence I can sit here typing this account and hear the title of that hideous painting reverberating in my head but can tolerate its presence without overreacting to it. I can choose to ignore it as irrelevant. I can say to it and more importantly to my OCD. "This is no big deal. I'm not getting on that hamster wheel again so blab on all you want." This is also much easier for me to do at this moment because I don't happen to be experiencing what I like to refer to as "free-floating anxiety." Free floating anxiety, in my own case, is often experienced as a precursor to my OCD, which is basically due to a lack of circulating serotonin. For now, my serotonin levels are good and I'm not experiencing that kind of anxiety so it's much easier for me to have that thought floating about in my mind and be able to just turn away from it or ignore it. This is because my brain isn't sending me an inappropriate burst of adrenaline in response to it.

I often describe my OCD as latching on to a particular thought or theme. For me, this seems to only happen when my brain is already primed to do so. This, from my past experience with the disorder, is when my fight or flight system isn't operating properly. I like to use analogies to help myself understand how my disorder operates and one that has helped me is based on my experiences with fishing.

When I go fishing for Northern Pike, I will often use a lure that resembles an eight-inch-long fish. This lure has three triple hooks hanging from the bottom of it. I toss the lure into the water and then troll around hoping that it will attract a fish. That is its *proper* purpose – to catch or hook a fish. But if I happen to unwittingly drag it through a tall patch of underwater weeds, its hooks will latch onto those weeds and they will become entangled in the lure. When this happens, I can actually be tricked into setting the hook by yanking on my rod really hard. This is because I think that the lure has actually hooked a real fish. But as I reel in my line, I'm disappointed by the discovery that I've only caught a bunch of useless and annoying weeds. I can't continue to use the lure for its proper purpose, (which is to catch a *real* fish) until I remove all those weeds.

Now for the analogy; my brain has an area which is referred to as the "fight or flight center". Its purpose is to respond to real or valid emergencies like the real fish in my story. When it's working properly, like the lure, to catch and react to a real emergency it's very useful for getting me to respond properly by causing me to either flee from a dangerous situation or to take action to protect myself. If, however, it's not working properly it will flood my brain with an inordinate amount of fight or flight chemicals. In this way, it puts out way too many hooks and goes into overdrive. Then when an unwanted or trespassing thought, which can be described by my analogy of the weeds, pops into my brain, that thought gets all tangled and stuck in there because my brain has latched onto it just like the fishing lure latched onto the weeds. But instead of my being able to just toss the weeds out, my brain begins to send me all these faulty signals which are manifested by a huge surge of anxiety. This anxiety tricks me into feeling that the thought is more threatening than it truly is. This is just like when I thought the weeds were a real fish. I am tricked into feeling that the unwanted thoughts are real threats so I "set the hook" so to speak by over reacting to them as if they really *were* true or valid. I will then begin to obsess about them and engage in a tremendous amount of mental effort to detangle or remove them from my mind. But you can't un-think a thought in the way you can remove a bunch of weeds from a fishing lure. With the way the OCD brain works, the harder you try to detangle the "weeds", or intrusive thoughts from the brain the more entangled and enmeshed they become in the mind.

My fishing analogy was confirmed to me when I read an article written by Dr. Stephen Phillipson about Pure "O" OCD where he described the OCD patient as having "faulty wiring" in the brain which is the igniting factor which drives the OCD machine. He explained that apart from this false signal in the brain, a person would be able to just pass over such a thought, to realize that the thought wasn't in any way true or valid and then be able to put it out of their mind and move on. Therefore, he suggests that just "shedding light" on the irrational nature of the thoughts doesn't help the person with OCD. (I can attest to that.) He goes on to state that; "those with OCD might suggest that in order for psychologists to fully understand what they experience; their amygdala's could be stimulated to the point of feeling that the world is ending." Further on in this article he states that; "therefore it is crucial for the patient to understand that OCD involves faulty wiring, not an irrational belief system."5.

Some of what I share in this portion of this book will have been mentioned before, but my experience with OCD has taught me that I must often go back and review the things that have been truly beneficial toward training me to manage my OCD. As mentioned in the forward of this book, OCD is a redundant disorder in that it comes back at you over and over with the same scare tactics. Yet each new theme is experienced as terribly frightening and urgent. Therefore, I believe that OCD requires a redundant approach in learning how to manage it. You may have to go back to square one with a new OCD theme, but the more you review and practice using what you've learned the quicker you'll be able to appropriate those things each time the disorder rears its head. I often have to read a helpful section in a book or article three or four times for it to really begin to click in such a way that I can actually put it into practice.

I will also be sharing some passages that parallel my own experiences with religious OCD with that of John Bunyan, which he related in his book, "Grace Abounding to the Chief of Sinners." This book has been a tremendous source of blessing and encouragement to me as it revealed to me that my struggles with this disorder were not unique. To think that so great a servant of God as Mr. Bunyan has traversed the same painful road of OCD as me and that God still used Him has been incredibly heartening to me. This wonderful little book should, in my opinion, be required reading for any Christian, who is afflicted with Religious OCD.

Just before my last big flare of OCD I was well aware that I'd been experiencing the symptoms of anxiety. In the beginning, I only had a constant feeling of impending doom that was accompanied by the physical symptoms of anxiety. As the disorder progressed, those feelings eventually latched onto a few obsessional themes as all that excess adrenaline needed something to chew on.

Just as undesired blasphemous thoughts can plague a person with OCD as to whether or not those thoughts are indicators of a broken relationship with Christ, so too can persistent doubts and questions. I found it easier to shove past a random blasphemous thought than to shove through the doubts or questions about whether or not I was truly saved. This is because Pure "O" OCD demands certainty and it will continue to throw "what ifs?" at you for as long as you are willing to entertain its insatiable questions.

As mentioned before in an earlier chapter, Dr. Phillipson describes it in this way; "In 'Pure O,' the anxiety emerges in response to an unwanted, intrusive thought or question; what I call a 'spike.'" 6. I appreciated his descriptive term, "spike," because that is exactly how an OCD thought feels when it crops up. It's rather like a knife to the gut when it shoves into your mind. In my case the first spike I had in relation to this obsessional theme was; "how can I be sure that I'm still saved" which then morphed into; "how can I be sure if I ever really was saved to begin with?" I remembered the fictional character who was a pastor in the Tim LaHaye and Jerry Jenkins novel, "Left Behind." This character was portrayed as someone who had lived his entire life as a fake Christian. *What If I was just like him?* The threat of my not being able to prove the answer to that question with one hundred percent certainty was that in the end, I might end up eternally separated from God. How is one supposed to press on and just live their life with that kind of threat hanging over their head? Mr. Bunyan could relate; "I could not rest content until I did now come to some certain knowledge whether I had faith or no; this always running in my mind, 'but how if you want faith indeed? But how can you tell you have faith?' And besides, I saw for certain, if I had not, I was sure to perish forever." 7.

As my anxiety heightened with each new question, the compulsive side of my disorder began to kick in. I was driven or compelled to mull these questions over and over in my head. The accusations that I might not really be saved after all demanded that I obtain proof that I was. I would spend a great deal of time trying to recall and remember the exact details about how I became a Christian. I would go over things in my past that seemed to confirm the likeliness that I was a real Christian. And as I would do these things I would often experience a brief period of relief. But then a seemingly fresh or new doubt would crop up very quickly which seemed to force me into searching for even more proof. I would recall verses that had comforted me about my salvation in the past and look up even more verses to reinforce the others. Yet as I flipped through the pages of my Bible I would often alight upon a particular verse that would cause me to question the authenticity of my salvation even more intensely than I had before. *Was this the very voice of God condemning me through His Word?* I was in terrible anguish that this notion might actually be true. I recoiled in horror at the accusation. Mr. Bunyan relates a similar experience: "That which made me sick, was that of Christ, in Mark, 'He went up into a mountain, and called to him whom he would, and they came unto him.' (Mark 3:13) This scripture made me faint and fear, yet it kindled a fire in my soul. That which made me fear was this, lest Christ should have no liking to me, for he called whom he would." 8.

This is a perfect place to stop and review Dr. Phillipson's description of the activity of Pure "O" OCD: "The ritual or compulsion with this form of OCD involves the non-observable, mental 'pushing away' of the thought, avoiding the recurrence of the thought, or attempting to solve the question or undo the threat that the thought presents." 9.

My 'pushing away' of these thoughts was manifested by an internal argument in my head that went something like this; *you probably really aren't saved and then, yes I am, I have to be, I must be, I reject that idea!* The "avoidance" factor began to be manifested by my not wanting to read my Bible at all because it forced me to think about my salvation. If I found even one verse to reassure me, I would find ten more which seemed to leap off the page and strike a fresh terror within me as to the uncertainty of my condition.

Even the great hymns which had strengthened and comforted me in the past now seemed to mock and torment me. Dennis had purchased a CD of hymns that were performed on a majestic pipe organ. He would play this often during my season of torment. The power and resonance of the chords behind the words of those hymns became to me like the background music in a horror movie. I didn't want to hear it. I wanted to shut it out because it stirred up fears and threats within me that seemed wholly unbearable. The music made me feel like a vampire in a horror movie who cowers at the sight of a cross. My OCD began to twist my emotional response to this music into a dire "sign" that I might in reality be an actual enemy of the Cross.

Although I still forced myself to attend church, it was, at that time, an extremely stressful and exhausting experience rather than a source of encouragement. It took tremendous willpower to sit through a service. Certain phrases from the sermon or passages that we studied in the Bible would stand out and seem to shout accusations at me; *you are still dead in your sins, you have never truly believed, you're a hypocrite, a phony!*

So although I still went to church, it would have been far easier to give into the compulsion to avoid it.

Above all else the "solving" activity was what I spent the majority of my time on. There was a continual and seemingly inexhaustible debate going on in my head with endless argumentation for and against the reality of my salvation. All this time I wondered how I could have gone so many years feeling confident and at peace about my standing with Christ but now literally everything that related to Him seemed to make me feel lost, cast off and condemned. These things included prayer, Bible study, worship and listening to other's share about their faith in Him.

I could picture His sheepfold in my mind's eye with the whole of His flock safely sheltered within and me on the outside of the fence bleating with desperation to get in. Yet the more I struggled to somehow find that one perfect reassurance that would get me through a gap in the fence the more anxious I became that I'd never find a way to be certain that Christ had already or would eventually give me access. All those family members and acquaintances who I knew to be Christians now stood in stark contrast to my own condition. I would look at them with a mixture of admiration and envy. Their faces seemed to shine with the blessed joy and peace of their salvation. When I would watch Dennis as he worked about the house, he might as well have been wearing a halo because that's how I envisioned him in comparison to me.

Again, dear Mr. Bunyan could relate to my pain: "How lovely now was everyone in my eyes, that I thought to be converted men and women! They shone, they walked like a people that carried the broad seal of heaven about them. O I saw the lot was fallen to them in pleasant places, and they had a goodly heritage. (Pss. 16)" 10.

The next wave of assault came upon me through the fear of atheism that I mentioned before. One of the triggers for this piercing "spike" occurred one day as I was feverishly trying to sort out what was true from what was false about my salvation. It was then that I had this thought crop up suddenly. *What if the reason you're having these doubts isn't at all related to whether you've ever trusted in Christ but rather your logic trying to get you to acknowledge that God might not be real after all?* At that very moment the word, **"atheist"** bellowed in my brain in such a way that I felt as if the wind had been knocked out of me. My ears rang, my heart raced and I felt the familiar rise of a panic attack in response to the mental enunciation of that seemingly horrific word.

Though my previous thoughts had created quite a storm in my soul, these thoughts were more like a tornado in the violent way they struck at me. Mr. Bunyan knew well what this kind of storm felt like when he related the following experience. "A very great storm came down on upon me, which handled me twenty times worse than all I had met with before; it came stealing upon me, now by one piece, then by another, first all my comfort was taken from me, then darkness seized upon me; after which whole floods of blasphemies, both against God, Christ, and the Scriptures, was poured upon my spirit, to my great confusion and astonishment. These blasphemous thoughts were such as also stirred up questions in me against the very being of God, and of His only beloved Son, as whether there were in truth a God or Christ or no? And whether the Holy Scriptures were not rather a fable and cunning story, than the holy and pure Word of God"" 11.

Horrid statements would shove in and intrude upon my mind that seemed to confirm this new fear such as; *you'll be much happier as an atheist, this is what you've wanted all along. Wouldn't it be much easier to just walk away and forget the whole notion of God?* Then; *why or how could you think such a thing? A true Christian would never have thoughts like these. Is this some kind of sign or confirmation that you're a child of Satan?*

Every effort to shove or throw these thoughts out of my mind seemed to stir them up to haunt me in ever more menacing and cruel ways. Then nausea would rise up again as terror bore down ever more heavily upon me. I would tremble uncontrollably under the weight of this to the point where I ached in all my joints.

With this event, I began to tread a seemingly new and excruciating trail that wound round and round twisted turns of unending questioning and debate over whether or not I was becoming an atheist. It seemed as if these doubts were somehow different and unrelated to the others which had caused me to question my salvation, but in actuality their root was fixed within a familiar theme. The branch had only appeared to be different but was merely just another path in a maze which didn't lead to an answer but rather to even more trails of doubt which never lead me to the certain answer that I wanted. The driving force behind my desperate meanderings in this maze was the root fear of eternal separation from my God.

I remember one particular day where I experienced a few moments of clear-headed thinking when it occurred to me that if I were actually a *true* atheist then I'd have no real cause to be upset by that fact. *After all, how could a person who calls themselves an atheist be tortured by a fear of separation from God? The whole concept of or even the term "God" should carry no meaning or significance to them whatsoever.* When I would ponder these thoughts, I would at times be amazed at how easily confounded I could be over this. Then I'd enjoy a very brief period of comfort. But the doubt would somehow manage to creep back in upon me and keep me questioning if it might not still be possible for me to become an atheist, maybe not right at that moment but maybe later on at a future date.

Then for quite some time I fixated on the word "unbelief". This word brought an unpleasant leap in my gut, was *I still in a state of unbelief? Was God trying to get me to acknowledge this and repent? Was that the real reason for this nightmare?* As these questions began to endlessly pound upon my heart and drone on and on in my mind, I began a desperate attempt to scrutinize my faith in an effort to see if I could test whether it was legitimate and genuine, or if, God forbid it was fake. That desperate question also plagued poor Mr. Bunyan; "But how if you want faith indeed? But how can you tell you have faith?" 12.

Yet the more I attempted to examine my faith the more frightened I became because I couldn't muster up one ounce of comfort or confidence that I had it. The result of this was an intensifying of my anxiety to the point where I found it hard to sort anything out in my mind. It was like trying to navigate my way through some kind of dense mental fog. It was like a puzzle had been strewn about in my head and I could not make one piece link up with another in a way that would clearly and finally solve all my questions. What kind of test or proof could I grab ahold of to answer this question as to whether or not I had real faith? I couldn't figure this one out. All the proofs that I could come up with left room for a measure of uncertainty. This was unacceptable to me. I wanted one hundred percent proof that I had faith. How could I ever rest without it? How could I go on in this life without having it?

Sometime later in the course of my recovery I came upon the following quote from C.S. Lewis regarding the activity of faith in the life of a Christian.

Lewis: "Yes, yes, I know. The moment one asks oneself 'Do I believe?' all belief seems to go. I think this is because one is trying to turn round and look at something which is there to be used and worked from – trying to take one's eyes out instead of keeping them in the right place and seeing with them. I find that it happens about other matters as well as faith. In my experience only very robust pleasures will stand the question, 'Am I really enjoying this?' Or attention – the moment I begin thinking about my attention (to a book or a lecture) I have ipso facto ceased attending. St Paul speaks of 'Faith actualized in love.' And the heart is deceitful; you know better than I how very unreliable introspection is. I should be more alarmed about your progress if you wrote claiming to be overflowing with Faith, Hope, and Charity." 13.

This quote demonstrates just how futile it is to try and examine or scrutinize whether our faith is present or operational in our lives. It also explains how the very activity of doing so will interrupt the natural flow and activity of faith. Instead of allowing the faith that is in us to flow out naturally in the volitional exercise of it, we can instead get stuck, distracted and sidelined by trying to obtain evidence of it by using our inner feelings to try and detect its presence. This is very similar to what Religious OCD does to its victims. Now I can see that, but I seriously doubt that this quote would have provided any lasting consolation to me while I was in the midst of this horrible flare. This is because I hadn't yet learned how to tame or manage my OCD. It was, instead, managing me.

I could have written enough of my experiences with Religious OCD to crowd every page in this book, but the redundancy of it all would have bored my readers to tears. What I *have* written is enough for anyone who suffers from this kind of OCD to recognize its tactics. If this chapter has too much of a ring of familiarity, if it's as if I have been writing a good bit of your own story, then it's highly likely that you are now or have in the past experienced Religious OCD. You can find that out for sure by seeking a professional opinion to confirm this suspicion. Although, trust me, OCD can still cause you to doubt even the professional diagnosis of a physician. Don't be surprised if even after being diagnosed you still find yourself wondering things like: *What if the doctor is wrong and all of this has nothing to do with OCD? What if it turns out that it's really me doubting, really me disbelieving, blaspheming, turning away from Christ?* And - on and on it goes. That's how the disorder operates and that's why learning how to properly respond to those accusations is key to managing it. Is that an easy task? No, it's not! It feels very much like a risky business. So if you dare, go ahead and turn the page because, "Risky Business" is the title of the next chapter. It's time to tackle the monster of OCD on its own turf? So buck up, take courage and let's press on!

Notes:

1. "Letters to Malcolm, Chiefly on Prayer," C.S. Lewis, Harcourt, Inc., Chapter Fourteen, Page 76, Paragraph 4.
2. "The Obsessive Compulsive Trap," Dr. Mark Crawford, Regal Books, Introduction: Page 10, Quotes - #5 & #6.
3. John 15: 13-15a (NIV)
4. "Brain Lock," Jeffery M. Schwartz, Regan Books, Introduction – Page xvii.

5. http://www.ocdonline.com, "Rethinking The Unthinkable", Dr. Steven Phillipson, Center For Cognitive Behavior Psychotherapy, Page 4, Paragraph 3.
6. http://www.ocdonline.com, "Rethinking The Unthinkable", Dr. Steven Phillipson, Center For Cognitive Behavior Psychotherapy, Page 1, Paragraph 2.
7. "Grace Abounding to the Chief of Sinners," John Bunyan, Penguin Books, Page 17 - #49.
8. "Grace Abounding to the Chief of Sinners," John Bunyan, Penguin Books, Page 22 - #74, #75.
9. http://www.ocdonline.com, "Rethinking The Unthinkable", Dr. Steven Phillipson, Center For Cognitive Behavior Psychotherapy, Page 1, Paragraph 2.
10. "Grace Abounding to the Chief of Sinners," John Bunyan, Penguin Books, Page 22 - #74.
11. "Grace Abounding to the Chief of Sinners," John Bunyan, Penguin Books, Page 27 - #96.
12. "Grace Abounding to the Chief of Sinners," John Bunyan, Penguin Books, Page 17 - #49.
13. "The Collected Letters of C.S. Lewis", Volume 2, Harper Collins, Page 983, "To Mrs. Lockley (L):27 September 1949.

CHAPTER 5

Risky Business

John Bunyan; "I am for going on, and venturing my eternal state with Christ, whether I have comfort here or no." 1.

THE VAST MAJORITY of this chapter will be devoted to the management of Religious OCD. To that end, I will be dissecting some of my own OCD themes which I wrote about in the last chapter in order to categorize and define the typical components of an OCD episode. Next, my aim will be to clarify how the *wrong* response to those components will rev up the OCD engine in comparison to how the *right* response will train a person to manage their OCD instead of having it manage them. Alongside these things I will, again, be paralleling John Bunyan's OCD themes with mine to demonstrate that the manifestations of OCD are shockingly similar no matter how many centuries separate the lives of those who are afflicted. Although the focus will be on Religious OCD and even more specifically, the purely obsessional type of OCD, the basic tactics for managing the disorder are the same. This is true whether the obsessions have latched onto our faith, our health, or the welfare of our loved ones.

The title of this chapter, "Risky Business", reflects how a person with Religious OCD will feel when they finally make the decision to take the advice of a professional therapist in learning how to manage their obsessions. The only behavioral therapy that has been helpful to me is, "Exposure and Response Prevention". Therefore, that's what I'll be describing throughout this chapter. It's important for the person with Religious OCD to expect and acknowledge that this type of therapy will feel wrong to them. It will feel as if they are taking an enormous risk. But before they can get to that place they will have to first be willing to run another risk of choosing to label their problem as OCD rather than attributing it to a character flaw, or a sickly spiritual condition. For many of us we will only arrive at this place out of sheer desperation. We may have traveled the OCD path for months or years by trying over and over to obtain that perfect reassurance that we think will finally lay it all to rest. We will have to realize and admit that these tactics have not been working. That rather than making us feel better, we've only become more deeply mired in the quicksand of our OCD. The pain may have become so intense that we will finally decide that it's time to run the risk of abandoning our old tactics by learning to treat our OCD as a real disorder. Every aspect of this will feel like *risky business*. The very things that we've felt compelled to do in response to our obsessions will be the very things that we must abandon. Even when our emotions refuse to line up in confirmation with this decision, we will have to admit that our continual search for reassurance has actually been the hammer that has increased our pain. This has pounded our obsessions deeper and deeper into our consciousness in such a way that we can't seem to pull out those painful nails. Although it feels as if they are embedded too deeply for us to ever stop experiencing this pain, this is untrue. It's only the blows of the hammer that have made them so painful to us and in therapy we will be learning how to lay that hammer down and resist picking it up even when we feel intensely compelled to do so. That sounds like it should be easy, but it isn't. The emotions that compel us are very strong.

At one point in my recovery process, I remember thinking about the doctor on an old TV show called "Hee Haw" whose patients would come to him for help and say something like; "Doctor, when I do such and such it *really* hurts." Then he'd give them a swat upside the head and declare emphatically; "then don't do that!"

I knew that in order to feel better I had to stop engaging in the compulsive side of my disorder, but that was no easy task. I needed a plan of action. First I needed to understand just how to recognize an OCD obsession. Then I needed to take note of my inappropriate anxiety response to the obsession. After that, I needed to grasp just how it was that I was engaging in a compulsive response to it. Without that knowledge, I wouldn't be able to interrupt the cycle of the OCD. In order to do that, I had to take a step back from my feelings and look at my OCD episodes in a very clinical manner. I needed to separate and define the components of each of my OCD episodes.

The Components Of An OCD Cycle

There are two main things that occur with an OCD episode. One is the originating thought and two is the inappropriate response to that thought. These two things are common to all types of OCD, it's just that the second thing will manifest itself in differing ways depending upon whether the person has purely obsessional OCD, (Pure "O"), or the kind of OCD that causes them to perform outwardly observable rituals or compulsive behaviors. I have Pure "O" and, therefore, my compulsive activities are carried out by engaging in repetitive and exhausting mental activity. In both types of OCD, the compulsive activity is what must be stopped in order to effectively manage the disorder.

As mentioned in an earlier chapter, Dr. Phillipson's description of the cycle of 'Pure O" helped me tremendously in being able to identify the two components of my Religious OCD. He classified them in this way; "The 'Pure O' has two parts; the originating unwanted thought, (spike), and the mental activity in which the sufferer attempts to escape, solve, or undo the spike. This is called 'rumination.'" 2.

Dr. Mark Crawford describes the components in this way; "Obsessive Compulsive disorder is characterized by two main categories of symptoms; obsessive thoughts and compulsive behaviors." He goes on to say that; "in OCD, obsessions refer to intense thoughts, worries, or images that are experienced as intrusive and unwanted." 3 While Dr. Crawford's use of the word "intense" is certainly accurate, it still falls short of actually being able to relate the overwhelming emotional terror that accompanies such intrusive thoughts. It's *that* terror that drives the compulsive machine of the disorder. This terror or anxiety response is the event that occurs in between the occurrence of the thought and the compulsion. This "in between" event is way out of the realm of what would be considered normal in that it's outrageously exaggerated in comparison to an appropriate emotional response to the thought.

What follows is an example of how I would categorize the components of one of my OCD themes which I borrowed from a previous chapter. Following that, is a categorization of a similar theme that plagued John Bunyan.

1. THE OBSESSIONAL THEME
   (Remember that this will generally appear in the form of an intrusive/unwanted thought or image, or in the form of a doubt or question.)
   A. QUESTION/DOUBT – "What if the reason you're having these doubts isn't at all related to whether you've ever trusted in Christ, but instead, it's your logic trying to get you to acknowledge that God might not be real after all?"
   B. INTRUSIVE/UNWANTED THOUGHTS - "At that very moment the word – "Atheist!" bellowed in my brain. Horrid statements would shove in and intrude upon my mind that seemed to confirm this new fear such as; 'you'll be much happier as an atheist. This is what you've wanted all along. Wouldn't it be much easier to just walk away and forget the whole notion of God?"
2. ANXIETY RESPONSE - "It felt as if the wind had been knocked out of me. My ears rang, my heart raced and I felt the familiar rise of a panic attack in response to the mental enunciation of that seemingly horrific word – "atheist!
3. COMPULSION – (In Pure "O" OCD this is referred to as "rumination"). - "Why or how could you think such a thing? A

true Christian would never have thoughts like these. Is this some kind of sign or confirmation that you're a child of Satan? Every effort to throw these thoughts out of my mind seemed to stir them up to haunt me in ever more menacing and cruel ways. I began to tread a seemingly new and excruciating trail that wound round and round twisted turns of unending questioning and debate over whether or not I was becoming an atheist

Mr. Bunyans Ocd Cycle:

1. THE OBSESSIONAL THEME
   A. INTRUSIVE/UNWANTED THOUGHTS - "Whole floods of blasphemies, both against God, Christ, and the Scriptures, was poured upon my spirit."
   B. QUESTIONS/DOUBTS – "As also stirred up questions in me against the very being of God, and of His only beloved Son; as whether there were in truth a God of Christ or no? And whether the Holy Scriptures were not rather a fable and cunning story, than the holy and pure Word of God?" 4.
2. ANXIETY RESPONSE – "A very great storm came down upon me, which handled me twenty times worse than all I had met with before. First all my comfort was taken from me. Then darkness seized upon me. These suggestions... did make such a seizure upon my spirit, and did so over-weigh my heart, both with their number, continuance and fiery force that I felt as if there were nothing else but these from morning to night within me." 5.
3. COMPULSION = RUMINATION – "Sometimes I have endeavored to argue against these suggestions, and to set some of the sentences of blessed Paul against them; but alas? I quickly felt when I thus did, such arguing's as these would return again. Only by the distaste that they gave unto my spirit, I felt there was something in me that refused to embrace them.... So that

whether, *(in the process of rumination)*, I did think that God was, or again did think there were no such thing; no love, nor peace, nor gracious disposition could I feel within me." 6. (Italics mine.)

It's important to understand that once an OCD theme has taken hold that the components of the disorder overlap in such a way that one component leads to the next component. For instance, you can be right in the midst of ruminating when another unwanted thought or "spike" can occur which then leads directly to the anxiety response which in turn leads to more rumination. It can all seem to blur together in such a way that it seems as if the obsessions and compulsions are one in the same. It can be very difficult to apply the brakes before engaging in the compulsive activity if you can't figure out just when and where to do so. This is most especially true of Pure "O" because a person usually won't understand that the rumination they've been engaging in is *actually* the compulsion.

I remember an online conversation I had with an individual who was suffering tremendously from Pure "O" – Religious OCD. In an effort to try and help this individual categorize the components of a particular OCD episode, I asked if they would mind telling me about the compulsive activity they engaged in as a response to the fearful obsession. Their answer to my request was to state that they didn't engage in any sort of compulsive behaviors at all. My reply to this was to ask them the following questions; "Do you ever ask the Lord to save you repeatedly during the day? Do you repeatedly ask His forgiveness for the same thing? Do you ever counter a blasphemous thought or a doubt filled question with opposite or undoing statements in order to try and cancel them out? Do you ever spend any time trying to figure out why you are having these disturbing thoughts or what they might mean? Do you ever engage in mental debate against them by trying to gain some sort of logical proof or reassurance that they just couldn't be true of you? Do you ever ask a close Christian friend if they think that you are saved?" The answer that I got back from this individual in response to these questions was just three little words; **"All – the - time!"** This individual was engaging in the compulsive side of their disorder every waking minute of the day. This is the nature of the Pure "O" beast. It's a relentless slave-driver that keeps you in an exhausting mental battle. But you never win the war.

Rumination means to bring something back up over and over or to mull it over like a cow chewing its cud. The longer and more intense the focus is on the thoughts the more stuck they become in the brain until we find that they are with us every waking moment. I used to dread going to bed at night because I knew that once my eyes opened up in the morning that the thoughts would be there to greet me.

After having learned and practiced how to categorize the components of an OCD episode the next step is to practice applying the brakes. The point at which an individual with OCD needs to apply the brakes is that "in between" event which is just after the "Anxiety Response." This is where a person has a choice in what they do. The reason being is that the first two components of the OCD cycle do not fall within the realm of our control. A person with OCD doesn't choose to think their intrusive thoughts any more than someone would open up the door of their house to a malicious intruder. Nor are they able to control the inappropriate surge of anxiety which is caused by the misfiring in their brain. What they *can* control is how they respond to the presence of the thoughts.

At this juncture, I want to address a common misunderstanding about how OCD operates by contrasting how an unwanted or intrusive thought affects a person *without* OCD in comparison to how it affects those of us *with* OCD.

If I was to ask a large crowd of people by a show of hands, just how many of them ever had a thought pop into their heads that was strange or bizarre in that it was the complete opposite of how they really felt or what they really desired, it is quite likely that nearly every hand in the crowd would go up. This is because our brains have incredible memory and storage capabilities. A brain can take in and store up all sorts of information whether that information is acceptable or pleasant to a person or not. Therefore, thoughts can float up to the surface of our consciousness from time to time that have nothing to do with our true desires, our belief system or our character. We might be standing near the edge of a cliff when suddenly the thought, "jump!" pops into our heads. Our brain has the knowledge that sometimes people really *do* jump off very high places. Or, we might be driving along quite peacefully when a thought crops up that says something like; "Drive into that big tree." Our brain has the knowledge that sometimes people really *do* drive into trees. Sometimes a very unpleasant profane word or phrase might just suddenly intrude into our thoughts. Our brain has heard vulgar speech before and it's stored up those phrases in its memory banks. These types of random and bizarre thoughts can happen to just about anyone.

The difference is that people who aren't afflicted with OCD can just shrug them off. They can have unwanted thoughts pop into their brain but when their logic kicks in to inform them that they don't agree with the thoughts, they are able to easily dismiss them as unimportant or meaningless. But for the person with OCD the brain is already primed to overreact to the thoughts by flooding the body with a huge surge of anxiety. This anxiety is what ignites the obsessive-compulsive cycle. Without this inappropriate anxiety response, OCD could not develop. Folk who don't understand how OCD operates, usually have this whole process turned around. They believe the person with OCD is purposely encouraging or choosing to think the bad thoughts which, in turn causes them to become overly worried. They have the whole thing backward because it is actually that "overly worried" feeling, which precedes a thought, and then attaches itself to *that* thought in such a way, that it then, becomes an obsession. Therefore, the flare of intense anxiety in response to a random or unwanted thought is something for which the sufferer has no control. The anxiety of OCD is nothing more than an inappropriate instinctive fear response.

While it is true that everyone's brain is prepared to respond to a *real* or valid emergency by sending out alarm signals, the brain of a person with OCD is *overly* prepared. Therefore, it responds inappropriately to random unwanted thoughts.

If the fight or flight chemistry of the brain could be represented by gasoline which was released only when needed to rev up our engine to enable us to flee or protect ourselves in the event of *real* danger, we would be right in saying that the system was functioning properly. But the malfunction of OCD is like having a big gas leak that has already flooded the engine of the brain in such a way that just the slightest spark as represented by an unwanted/intrusive thought will cause a flash fire of intense anxiety.

So now, having established that the first two components of an OCD cycle fall outside of the realm of a person's control, what can be done about that consequential flash fire of anxiety that has been ignited?

This is where "response", becomes a key word in learning to manage OCD. When I first read about "Exposure and Response Prevention" (ERP) therapy, I didn't pay too much attention to the word "response." But as I began to understand the therapy it began to click with me that my usual response to the anxiety was what was fueling the engine of my OCD. I needed to learn how to prevent that response. I knew that I needed to learn how to train myself to have a different response to both the thoughts and the flash fire of anxiety. And the really tough thing about it was that it felt very *wrong* to apply that knowledge. These are the two main things that I would need to learn to apply;

1. NOT RESPONDING TO THE THOUGHT OR THE ANXIETY
2. RESPONDING THROUGH VOLUNTARY/ACTIVE EXPOSURE. (Opening the door to the intruder.)

What follows is the knowledge that I've gained which has helped me to apply these techniques.

1. *NOT* RESPONDING OR RESPONSE PREVENTION

"Leave it alone!" That statement must be applied to all the invalid obsessions that we experience with OCD. The anxiety that drives OCD, when combined with the inability to obtain absolute certainty in response to a doubt or question, drives a person with OCD to keep up the search or continue checking in a vain attempt to wipe out every possible "what if" that crops up.

In the case of outwardly observable OCD compulsions where a person might have an obsession like; "what if the door is still unlocked?" that person will have difficulty leaving off checking that lock over and over. The only way they can begin to invalidate this obsession is to stop checking the lock. When the thought pops into their brain; "what if I didn't lock it right?", they have to just leave it alone and ride out the uncertain and anxious feelings that remain while refusing to go back and check it, "just one more time." My favorite quote regarding this "leave it alone" strategy as it relates to Religious OCD came from a guy who had made great strides in learning to manage it. He said he finally had learned to *stop checking* to see if his faith was still locked." That quote has been enormously helpful to me.

Every time a person with OCD engages in any type of reassurance-seeking behavior they validate the obsession by making it seem weighty or important. It's just as if they had picked up a big yellow marker and highlighted the obsession in their brain in such a way that it stands out amongst all other thoughts as being the one that they should give top priority.

What follows are several analogies that I've employed to assist me in my efforts to "leave it alone" when an OCD thought is plaguing me.

Analogy # 1. – "Put The Fly Swatter Down!"

I've always figured that the reason bugs are called bugs is because they really *bug* us. They fly in our faces, land on our skin, bite us and buzz in our ears. When thinking about some of my OCD obsessions I've come to view them as "bugs." Some of those "bugs" are like small annoying gnats' others are kind of like flies – disgusting and dirty critters. Then there are mosquitos whose visit upon my person leaves an itching reminder that keeps me scratching for days while still others come at me like angry bees that have the potential to harm and sting me. What influences the kind of "bug" they are, depends upon my response to them. One weapon that I've used against many *real* bugs is the fly swatter. I've conquered many flies and annihilated quite a large number of bees with this simple weapon. But using that sort of tactic against the "bugs" of my OCD is not only ineffective, it actually stirs those bugs up to plague me even more.

Another interesting thing about my OCD bugs is that they have the ability to morph and grow. If, when they make their first appearance, I would just choose to leave them alone they would eventually be nothing more than an irritating gnat that dies a natural death. But if I begin to swat at them through the activity of rumination they will, over time, turn into threatening bees. For instance; when that first notion that maybe my belief in God wasn't quite good enough popped into my brain, even though it fired off an uncomfortable anxiety response in my gut I still needed to leave it alone instead of "swatting at it". I made the wrong choice *and* as I began to swat at it by trying to ascertain whether it was true or not it quickly morphed into a fly which seemed to buzz incessantly in my head. The "buzzing" made me feel even more anxious so I swatted at it all the more. The fly swatter was employed through argumentation and logical countering statements. Yet I just couldn't kill off that fly and from there it morphed into a mosquito. Now it not only buzzed it actually bit me and those bites itched so badly that I felt compelled to scratch at them. So now I'm not only swatting, but I'm also scratching and everyone knows that the more you scratch mosquito bites, the more they itch. At this point, I'm finding it nearly impossible to ignore my OCD "bug." I want it gone! It's making me miserable. So I step up my warfare. I simply must solve this. I must find the perfect reassurance to make all this dreaded uncertainty disappear. So now I'm swatting and scratching nearly constantly through the compulsive activity of rumination. As I do this, the mosquito begins to morph. Now it's become a bee – a bug that has the potential to do me great harm. The more I swat at it, the angrier it gets. It stings me multiple times and each sting seems more painful than the last. I am, at this point in incredible mental pain and anguish and I feel very strongly that I have to kill that bee or I'll never know a moment's peace again. So I swat and swat through continual mental rumination and reassurance seeking and as I do, the pain of its sting intensifies. On and on this painful cycle goes right up until I am willing to run the risk of putting down the fly swatter so that my OCD "bug" can die a natural death.

Here's the formula that I use:

A. The obsession = the bug. (Uncontrolled event)
B. The anxiety = the buzzing, the itching, and the stinging. (Uncontrolled event)
   ERP: Applying the brakes: "Put the fly swatter down!"
C. The Compulsion = Employing the fly swatter through any activity which seeks to provide temporary reassurance. In the above case, this equates to mental rumination. This is the chosen behavior that must be stopped.

Therefore, if I want to break this cycle I have to "put the fly swatter down" and leave it alone no, matter how big and scary that OCD bug has become.

Analogy #2 "No More Ghost Busting."

My favorite ghost story is also a true one. (Just here, you might want to shut off the lights and fire up a few candles for effect and then brace yourself!)

One night many years ago I was awakened by the eeriest sound I'd ever heard. As first I thought I was dreaming as I became aware of a strange high pitched moaning that seemed to undulate in pitch in an almost melodic way. Within a few moments, I was fully awake and made the rather unsettling discovery that the sound was actually real and also seemed to be quite near. Mere seconds later I was relieved to discover that the sound was actually coming from the other side of the bed and more specifically from my husband, Dennis, who was lying on his side curled up into a tight ball. I sat up, leaned over to watch him for a couple moments of entertainment, but then becoming more and more aware of the cartoon-like quality of the sound coming out of him, I started cracking up. He sounded just like a ghost from a Scooby Doo episode. My laughter woke him up and as he turned over he too began to laugh hysterically.

It took quite some time before we were finally able to compose ourselves enough to talk about it. Finally, I was able to ask him what he'd been dreaming that prompted him to make those strange noises. He told me that he'd been dreaming that a ghost was floating above the bed and howling at him. But when he woke up he realized that *he* was the one making the sound effects in his own dream, which was hilarious to him. Basically, he'd spooked himself. We had a really hard time getting back to sleep afterward because just as one of us would gain some measure of composure and finally quit laughing the other one would start up again. We even woke up the kids who wanted to know the following morning; "just what the heck was so funny last night?"

Years later when thinking about my OCD I came to view my unwanted obsessions in a similar way. They seemed like ghosts or phantoms of my own making which, just like my husband's dream, had been created by my own brain. The difference was that there was nothing funny about them and rather than being able to laugh at them I had cowered in fear and viewed each and every one of them as serious concerns. As I learned more and more about ERP, it dawned on me that I needed to learn to treat them, in the same way, we'd treated my husband's ghostly experience all those years ago. The difficulty in doing this with OCD obsessions is that they *feel* horribly scary and threatening. Never the less I had to learn to treat them as if they weren't, even while I was in the midst of experiencing intense anxiety. From then on when an intrusive thought would begin to plague me, I started to practice treating it like a silly cartoon ghost. Instead of hiding from it through avoidance or employing ghost busting techniques through rumination, I would instead visualize allowing the thought/ghost into my brain and offering it a seat while doing my level best to ignore it. I could imagine my intrusive thought as an actual ghost sitting there and doing everything imaginable to try and get me to freak out. There might be all sorts of howling threats, each one creepier than the last. But no matter how much it tried to spook me I would refuse to flinch or give it any attention what so ever. If its main goal was to scare me, then I wouldn't give it any satisfaction. No matter what tactics it employed, I'd just smile at it and say; "Whatever!......... I really don't have time for your shenanigans right now."

The Formula For The Ghost Analogy

A. The Obsession = The appearance of the ghost. (Uncontrolled event)
B. The Anxiety = The fear response to the haunting nature of the obsession. (Uncontrolled event)
ERP: Applying the brakes = "No ghost busting allowed!"
C. The Compulsion = Applying any ghost-busting tactics through mental rumination, argumentation, avoidance or any reassurance seeking behaviors or rituals.

So in order to apply this analogy we have to learn that when our OCD ghosts say "Boo" we must stand firm and refuse to flinch and make room for them in our consciousness even though to do so feels horribly wrong.

The Key Of Uncertainty

There is a key that has to be appropriated whenever a person begins to apply the techniques of ERP, with the intent to manage their OCD. This key opens up a door to a place where the person with OCD doesn't wish to go. That place is where they must choose to make room for the feelings of uncertainty that accompany their obsessions. They must be willing to stay there for as long as it takes for their brain to become accustomed to the presence of their obsessions. It doesn't matter what theme those feelings are attached to, as all OCD themes carry with them weighty and distressing feelings of anxious uncertainty.

The disorder has a nasty habit of dangling the possibility of gaining absolute certainty and complete reassurance like a carrot just out of the reach of the sufferer. The sufferer is then enticed to keep on jumping for it even though every attempt to do so leaves them feeling even more desperate than they felt before. There are certainly many things in our lives for which we can't obtain absolute certainty. Some of those things are part and parcel of the joy of being human; things such as the love of our parents toward us as children or the love of our spouse toward us or vice versa. We can't prove these things with one hundred percent certainty, but we can observe things about our parents or our spouse which then lead us to choose to place our faith in them. But in so far as obtaining one hundred percent proof or certainty of another's love for us, well there will always be room for doubt if we choose to contemplate all the "what if's." It's important to remember that faith isn't just a feeling it's a choice. I'll delve into this further on.

With OCD themes, there will always be room for doubt and uncertainty regarding themes such as these: "What if my hands are still contaminated? What if I really *did* hit someone with my car? What if I only *think* I unplugged the iron but I really didn't? What if I don't really love my spouse? What if thinking that thought means that I want to do that thing? What if the doctor is wrong? What if I'm only fooling myself by thinking that God has forgiven me when I might really be on my way to hell?" Learning to live with the feelings of uncertainty that attach themselves to these type of obsessions while refusing to engage in any compulsive activity is without a doubt the most important key to managing OCD. Therefore, the person with OCD must expect and accept the feelings of uncertainty to flare up just as they begin to employ some of the tactics of ERP.

As I began to understand how ERP worked, I was astonished to discover that John Bunyan had learned to manage his "Religious OCD" by using it even without the knowledge that such a therapy would exist in the future and that it would turn out to be the best weapon in our arsenal against the disorder. Below is one example of how he unwittingly employed the techniques of ERP as he made the choice to accept and live with his feelings of uncertainty.

A. BUNYAN'S OBSESSIONAL THEME;
"But whither must you go when you die? What will become of you? Where will you be found in another world? What evidence *(certainty)* do you have for heaven and glory and an inheritance among them that are sanctified? 7.

B. ERP = Choosing to remain in the presence of the obsessions and accepting the feelings of uncertainty that they produce while refusing to fight against them.

Bunyan; "Twas my duty to stand to his Word, whether he would ever look upon me or no, or save me at the last: wherefore, thought I, the point being thus, I am for going on, and venturing my eternal state with Christ, whether I have comfort here or no; *(the "comfort" equates to feelings of reassurance or certainty)*, If God doth not come in, thought I, I will leap off the ladder even blindfolded into eternity, sink or swim, come heaven, come hell; Lord Jesus, if thou wilt catch me, do; if not, I will venture all for thy name." 8.

John Bunyan did not come to this place quickly or easily. It was only after a very long and tortured struggle with his OCD obsessions that he finally came to the place where he realized that he needed to just let go of demanding certainty. His willingness to run the risk of not being able to gain absolute certainty in the face of his obsessions was the beginning of his being able to move past them and focus on his fruitful and productive ministry for the gospel of Jesus Christ. His courageous example has bolstered me time and time again in my own efforts to manage my Religious OCD.

The information covered thus far, included examples of ways to apply *the ignoring* or *passive* practice of ERP. The next level of ERP is different in that it involves choosing to voluntarily engage with the obsessions via exposure in an effort to force the brain to become accustomed to their presence.

2. RESPONDING THROUGH VOLUNTARY/ACTIVE EXPOSURE (Opening the door to the intruder.)

Why on earth would anyone want to encourage their obsessions? Wouldn't this serve to just make them worse or get them more stuck in our heads? These were the questions that bothered me as I began to consider whether or not I should employ the technique of active exposure.

Understanding why this type of therapy works can be demonstrated through the illustration of how allergy shots desensitize a person's body to an allergen. The goal of active exposure is to cause the brain to become so accustomed to the presence of an obsessional theme that it no longer overreacts to it. Just as an allergist will expose the allergic individual to ever increasing doses of the allergen through the use of injections, the person with OCD can expose themselves to doses of their obsession in ever increasing amounts in order to desensitize the brain to its presence. Also, just as the person who is exposed to their allergens will, in the beginning, react to them by sneezing or itching, the person with OCD must expect and accept that, in the beginning, this type of ERP therapy will cause a temporary increase in their anxiety level.

Exposure works with all types of OCD obsessions as well as specific phobias. If a person is obsessed about their hands being contaminated with germs, they have to refrain from washing their hands in increasing increments of time in order for them to become accustomed to living with the uncertainty of whether or not germs are on their hands. If a person is terrified of riding in elevators, then the only way for them to get over that phobia is to gradually expose themselves to elevators until they are able to ride them without experiencing the phobic response.

Voluntary exposure should, at first, be a scheduled event – a period of time that is specifically set aside to engage with the obsession. Rather than having OCD run the show, the person decides when and for how long they will voluntarily engage with the obsession. The rest of the day the obsessions are to be ignored as illustrated by the preceding examples and ruminating about them should be put off until later on. After one becomes adept at the practices of active exposure they can employ its techniques to take the punch out of any obsession that may crop up throughout their day. So when is the best time to do this? The answer to that question isn't a welcome one. The best time to engage in active exposure to the obsessions is when you are actually feeling fairly calm. I know you're probably thinking; "Oh joy! Just when I finally catch a break from my anxiety she's asking me to stir it up again?" What I've discovered is that the more willing I am to engage with my obsessions, to even encourage them to the level of absurdity; to take whatever they want to dish out and stand up to them by swallowing all the anxiety they dish out, that over time, they lose their punch. Standing firm in the face of the obsession with a; "Bring it on baby!" attitude or even a; "Seriously – is that the best you can do?" stance, will eventually weaken its power over me and train my brain to stop overreacting to it.

What follows are some more analogies that have been helpful to me in understanding why this form of ERP is effective. These are the practical strategies which have helped me to apply exposure techniques to several of my obsessional themes.

Analogy #1 Fighting Fire With Fire

In order to stop a wildfire from advancing firemen will often use the technique of setting another line of fire in its path. This is referred to as "back burning". The goal of a back burn is to reduce the amount of flammable material in front of the fire. This usually stops the wildfire from an uncontrolled advance as there is nothing left over for it to burn. This method will often keep the wildfire contained in such a way that it can eventually be extinguished.

I like to imagine that the use of active exposure is similar to a back burn. When I become aware that an OCD obsession has lit a big wildfire of anxiety in my mind, rather than running from the obsession or attempting to douse it by engaging in the compulsive reassurance-seeking behavior, I can, instead, choose to light my own fire of obsessional "what if's" against it. In this way, I am not giving it any ground to advance in my mind. I've already chosen to deliberately ponder the worst and scariest outcomes that the obsession has been threatening me with. I must refuse to douse those flames of anxiety that will certainly crop up when I do this. In doing so, I am using up all the fuel which feeds the obsessional theme. There's nothing left over for it to suggest to me as I've already lit all those frightening fires of my own volition. And, I am willing to let the fire of anxiety that they create burn for as long as it takes for the whole firestorm to settle down into a harmless smoldering pile of ash. This will eventually happen as my brain becomes more and more accustomed to the presence of the obsession and finally stops reacting to it as if it were a real or valid emergency.

Here's an example of how I would use this analogy/technique in response to one of my obsessional themes:

The Obsession – "What if I'm becoming an atheist?"
Before I understood ERP, my reaction to this distressing question was to spend hours and hours trying to douse the flames of anxiety it created in me through compulsive rumination. This type of rumination included logical counterstatements as to why I wouldn't or couldn't become an atheist. I was attempting to prove my belief in God by trying to measure my feelings, pouring over scriptures that had reinforced my faith in the past, constant praying where I would ask forgiveness for even thinking such an awful thought and pleading with God to please keep me from becoming an atheist. None of these things brought relief to me. Instead, they only seemed to give the obsession more weight and validity. In doing all of these things I was, in getting back to my analogy - running from the fire. Once I understood why ERP works and how to do it, this is how I began to use the; "fighting fire with fire" technique.

A. Obsession – "What if I'm becoming an atheist?"
B. Anxiety Response – "Ok, this is really uncomfortable but now I know that I feel this way just because the anxiety center in my brain isn't functioning properly. I realize that it's misfiring and overreacting to this thought.

(Please take note here that acknowledging the anxiety response does not make it go away. It only helps the sufferer to expect and accept it rather than to be blindsided by it or fight against it.)

C. ERP – Lighting the back burn.

(OK, fasten your seatbelts – here goes!)
"That's right Mitzi; you probably really *are* going to become an atheist. It's just a matter of time. The more you read your Bible,

the more you'll begin to really see that maybe it's not true after all. Maybe the whole thing has just been a sham all along. Maybe that will make you so mad that you won't just be a closet atheist but a militant one. You might even become one of those people who fight against religious freedom and protests Christianity openly out in the streets in front of the media. Everyone in your family *and* in your church will see you on the news and be utterly shocked and dismayed. Then as you go on in your aggressive and militant march against the Gospel, you will eventually become a bitter old wretch. You'll look back on your life and struggle to find any purpose or meaning in it. You'll grow weak and sick and die a miserable and lonely death apart from anyone and everyone who ever loved you. It's then that you'll find out that you've made the wrong choice because you'll end up in hell where you'll be separated forever from the only One who ever offered life and hope – the Savior, Lord Jesus." (Big defeated sigh just here.) Then - letting go of it; "I suppose there's nothing to be done for it. Guess I might as well finish cleaning the house."

That's how exposure is done. For those of us with OCD the idea of encouraging these kinds of thoughts to this level not only seems wrong but it also *feels* very wrong because in doing so we are purposely allowing the fire of our anxiety to flare up. The goal of being willing to light the "back burn", (to imagine the worst possible outcome), is that in doing so we flood the brain over and over with the obsessional content until it gets so used to it that it no longer responds by pulling the fire alarm.

ANALOGY #2 WELCOMING THE GHOST

For this analogy, we'll need to revisit my ghost story. This time, however, instead of just ignoring the "ghost" of my OCD obsession I decided that to do active exposure I'd have to invite it in and even encourage all its spooky howls and threats. I had this imaginary scenario in my mind about a university named; "Casper's Academy of Studies in the Art of Spectral Haunting".

I imagined that as part of the general requirements at this college, each student would have to pass a final test by being assigned to a human. In order to pass the test, they'd have to illicit an obvious terror response from their human victim that would be outwardly observable by the human either screaming in terror, hiding or attempting to drive the ghost away through "ghost busting" tactics. For my analogy purposes, the ghost assigned to me would be represented by my obsession. But in applying ERP I was determined to not only cause him fail the test, but I was also going to humiliate him in the process.

Here is how I applied this analogy to yet another of my obsessions:

A. Obsession – "What if I stay clinically depressed for the rest of my life?"
B. Anxiety Response – "OK... I'm aware that my brain has just latched onto this right now because of the excess adrenaline in my system. I know this is due to the chemical imbalance in my brain and, therefore, my brain needs something to be upset about in order to expend all that excess energy on. That's the reason this thought is making me feel so uncomfortable."

(Again, being mindful of why the anxiety is there does not make it go away, it just helps to acknowledge its presence as part and parcel of the disorder. Expect and accept it.)

C. ERP – Welcoming the "ghost" in and mocking its haunting efforts:

So in floats my OCD ghost with horrid howls and threats of how I might have to spend the rest of my life in a state of hopeless despair and depression. Every time he howls out the word, "DEPRESSION!" it feels like a knife in my gut. But I'm determined not to let him know that I find him even the slightest bit frightening. As he rises up and spreads himself out over the top of me, baring his ugly decayed teeth, I take a step toward him. Then I take a step to the side and gesture for him to come on in and have a seat in the house of my mind. Then I pull up a chair right next to him, pat him on the shoulder and say, (with a condescending tone), "really is that the best you can do? Why it's such a shame that you obviously haven't gained much expertise in the art of haunting, even with all that college behind you. You poor, pitiful excuse of a ghost! Please allow me to offer up some suggestions. You might have tried spooking me in the following ways; "Mitzi...(using my cartoon ghost voice), this depression is going to become so unbearable that you'll have no choice but to kill yourself! But you will fail in your attempt. Then you'll have to be committed to a mental institution to keep you from harming yourself. While you're there, you'll be required to undergo intensive psychotherapy, none of which will bring relief. Nothing and I mean nothing; will make the depression go away, not even electroshock therapy. Every drug in the arsenal against depression will be tried, but none of them will work. You'll have to live in a padded cell for your own safety. So there you'll sit in misery day after day with no relief in sight. Isn't that the most horrific thing you can imagine?"

So what's the point of being a ghost if you can't scare anybody or to put it another way, how can my OCD obsession continue to terrorize me if I'm willing to contemplate the very worst outcomes that it's been threatening me with? In practicing this type of ERP, I'm howling even louder that the ghost of my obsession. I drown it out and in doing so I eventually rob it of its ability to terrorize me.

As I've had the opportunity to hear from others who are afflicted with OCD I've found out that the vast majority of them are deep thinking, imaginative and creative individuals. These are wonderful qualities that can be employed in learning to manage OCD. This means that they can come up with their own helpful analogies and catch phrases to assist them in their effort to "apply the brakes" before an OCD obsession gets the best of them. When I've been mindful enough to catch myself in any sort of compulsive rumination in response to a fearful obsession, I remind myself what to do by using my own catch phrases such as; "put the fly swatter down – now!", "Stop the ghost busting tactics right now!" or, "quit running from that fire!" These catch phrases often provide the nudge that I need to help me get back on the right track.

At this point, you may be wondering; "so did John Bunyan ever do this type of voluntary ERP in response to his obsessions?" Yes, he did. It's clear that he was willing to ponder the most frightening outcomes of his obsessions. He was willing to accept the feelings of uncertainty that they created and to leave off trying to gain that perfect reassurance in an effort to make them go away.

The following statements are evidence of his willingness to let the obsessions "do their worst" without trying to obtain reassurance; Bunyan: "…Whether He would ever look on me, *or no*… whether I have comfort here, *or no*…*if God doth not come in*…*sink* or swim…come heaven, ***come hell***…Lord Jesus, *if* thou wilt catch me, do; *if not*…"9.

The words marked by bold italics demonstrate that Mr. Bunyan was willingly exposing himself to such things as; "Maybe God won't ever look upon me as his child. Maybe He will never give me feelings of comfort or reassurance concerning my eternal state with him while I live on the earth. Maybe He'll never come into my life and save me. Maybe in the end, I'll sink. Maybe I'll end up in hell. Maybe He won't pluck me from death's grip."

Those of us with OCD will certainly understand that the willing consideration of such horrible outcomes had to have been extremely hard and painful for John Bunyan. But in doing so, he was finally able to walk away from the exhausting and fruitless search for one hundred percent reassurance. Then, having done that he was *finally* able to get back to the task of actively serving his Lord.

Bunyan: "…Wherefore thought I, the point being thus, I am for going on and venturing my eternal state with Christ. I will venture all for thy name."

To that, I can only say; "I'm with you John, Amen!"

A Word On Avoidance

This chapter wouldn't be complete without addressing the side of OCD referred to as avoidance. Avoidance still falls into the category of compulsive behavior because the person with OCD will often feel compelled to avoid anything that triggers their obsession. I will once again be using my own experiences to illustrate what avoidance behavior looks like by sharing how I've reacted with avoidance in response to several of my OCD obsessions.

One of my milder avoidance compulsions is about using public restrooms. This obsession has been with me on and off since I was school age. It usually bothers me the most during the winter months when many folks are sick with flu viruses and stomach bugs. The obsessional fear is that of being contaminated by viruses in public restrooms because of the large volume of people that use them. I have more of a phobia about stomach bugs than the flu, even though the flu is far more serious. This is because I have an intense fear of vomiting. (I wonder if there's a class I can take that might be titled; "Vomiting 101.)

What I do in response to this fear is to avoid using public restrooms. This can be a bit tricky as I have to take a diuretic drug for my high blood pressure. I can't begin to tell you how many times I've left Wal-Mart with a full bladder and had to race home to use the bathroom. Yet when I avoid public restrooms, it causes me to be even more anxious over the possibility that I might get sick. This is because I'm giving the fear more validity by engaging in the avoidance behavior. Then if I'm not being mindful of the fact that I'm giving in to my OCD I might also begin to avoid other activities like; fulfilling my once a month nursery duty at church, or using bathrooms in other people's houses, or shaking someone's hand, etc.

The reason that this behavior is labeled as a compulsion is that it falls into the category of reassurance-seeking behavior. It I don't use the public bathroom I will feel *temporarily* reassured that I might not get sick. The reassurance will, however, be short-lived because my OCD will come up with yet another possibility of how I might still come in contact with the germs of a stomach bug.

With my Religious OCD, I went through a period where I avoided reading my Bible. The reason for this was two-fold. One was that in reading it my OCD would often latch onto a phrase, twist it out of context and use it to make me feel even more afraid that I might not really be saved after all. The other reason is that in reading my Bible I was forced to contemplate my relationship with God and this also caused me to feel extremely anxious. Avoiding reading my Bible made the fearful obsessions about my salvation seem even more valid and threatening. I was in effect, running from them. Although it was far more comfortable to avoid reading my Bible, than to willingly stay in the presence of my obsessions, in doing so, I was cooperating with my OCD and giving it a measure of validity that it didn't deserve.

Another ugly consequence of this avoidance behavior was that instead of it removing the obsession it just gave my OCD one more accusation to fling at me; "maybe you not wanting to read your Bible is a sign that you really don't have any desire for God. This might mean that you aren't a Christian after all." So there I was stuck between a rock and a hard place. I could either read my Bible and be forced to think about my obsessions and feel all that anxiety welling up in me, or I could avoid my Bible, which was then turned into self-condemning evidence to back up my original obsession. This too caused me tremendous anxiety.

Eventually, I learned that I needed to go on with reading my Bible because to do otherwise would be engaging in the compulsive avoidance behavior of my OCD. I had to read it and allow the doubt-filled thoughts and accusations to just be in my head without attending to them. If I chose avoidance, I would be perpetuating the vicious cycle of my OCD.

OCD is a complex and confusing disorder. This brief glimpse into my Religious OCD cannot possibly begin to cover the many twists and turns it can take. My hope is that what it *has* accomplished is to give just enough information to encourage others who have the disorder to look into obtaining help for it. At the back of this book, I've included some reading resources that have greatly assisted me in my own efforts to manage my OCD.

Anyone who is severely debilitated or distressed by their OCD in such a way that it has a big impact on the quality and functioning of their daily life should seriously consider getting professional help. I would recommend finding a psychologist who specializes in treating OCD through the Cognitive Behavioral approach of Exposure and Response Prevention. When OCD has had its way with any of us for a long period of time, we will usually need the help of a seasoned coach to help us stay the course in putting the knowledge that we've gained into practice.

1. "Grace Abounding to The Chief of Sinners," John Bunyan, Penguin Books, page 82, #337.
2. http://www.ocdonline.com, "Rethinking the Unthinkable", Stephen Phillipson.
3. "The Obsessive Compulsive Trap," Mark Crawford, PH.D., Regal Books, Chapter One, Page 13.
4. "Grace Abounding to The Chief of Sinners," John Bunyan, Penguin Books, Page 27 - #96.
5. "Grace Abounding to The Chief of Sinners," John Bunyan, Penguin Books, Pages; 27 - #96 & 28 - #99.
6. "Grace Abounding to The Chief of Sinners," John Bunyan, Penguin Books, Pages: 27 - #98, 28 - #100 & 28 - #101.
7. "Grace Abounding to The Chief of Sinners," John Bunyan, Penguin Books, Page 82 - #336
8. "Grace Abounding to The Chief of Sinners," John Bunyan, Penguin Books, Page 82 - #337

CHAPTER 6

Common OCD Questions

"We have seen the enemy and he is us." Walt Kelley – Pogo

My Original intent was to place this chapter at the end of the book. Then I remembered how my own OCD brain operates. I envisioned myself reading the preceding chapter as if it had been written by someone else. I knew that upon finishing it, I would have been very adept at coming up with all sorts of "what if's" or "what about this or that" questions in response to it. Therefore, I figured any reader who is afflicted with OCD would likely do the exact same thing.

It is, of course, impossible for me to predict *all* the questions that can crop up with OCD. Anyone who is afflicted with this disorder is quite aware of its capability to keep them in a state of continual questioning. There are, however, some fairly common questions that are likely to plague most folk who do battle with it. What follows are some examples of typical questions that might crop up and how I recommend handling them.

1. What if this isn't OCD after all, but instead it's really me, actually wanting to think these things? I mean - how can I know for sure?

This kind of question will usually crop up just as soon as someone is daring to believe that they might indeed be afflicted with OCD. It's really a rather common phenomenon. In fact, with me it was one of the things that initially made me afraid to seek help. I was terrified that I would hear from a professional that I didn't meet the criteria for a diagnosis of OCD or any sort of Anxiety Disorder and, therefore, I would have to accept that I might really be a very warped individual – a deviant or something worse.

It might at first glance appear that this type of question is unrelated to one's original obsession, but if you begin to chase it around you will quickly discover that it leads you right back to your original or root obsession. OCD can almost seem crafty at times with the way it keeps us ruminating. If I'm questioning whether it's OCD or not, I will inevitably begin to ruminate about my original theme again as I can't be certain whether or not it's caused by the disorder or whether it's a valid concern. My experience was, that when this question cropped up and I felt I couldn't obtain an answer to it which left no room for uncertainty, that I once again found myself ruminating about my original theme; "I might not be saved after all, because all of this might have absolutely nothing to do with OCD."

One day when I was thinking about all of this I started to realize how my OCD uses so many variations to get me back to ruminating, but that if I really stop to think about them, I'll discover they are all variations on a *familiar* theme.

It's like when our son Denny was first learning to play the violin. His first song was "Twinkle, Twinkle Little Star". Once he had that down the teacher added a few minor variations to it. Then as he became adept at that she added even more. But underneath all those variations you could still hear the original theme of "Twinkle." It may have seemed to him that he was playing something new or different, but it was just a variation of his original song.

The *telling* thing about OCD themes is that they are generally going to be accompanied by an intense feeling of anxiety. Then, if you react to that by attending to them, you will quickly discover that you will be right back to treading that same old misery-laden trail of obsession, anxiety and compulsion. *All* OCD themes carry a weighty feeling of uncertainty. The question – "is this OCD or me?" is no exception and it must be left alone.

2. Wouldn't the decision to use medication or to go and see a Psychologist be an indicator that I'm not really trusting God to heal me from this disorder? Could this be a sign that my faith isn't genuine?

Amazing, isn't it, how OCD questions lead to more OCD questions as demonstrated in the example above. They seem to build off one another or morph into another question. Every action must be scrutinized and every thought analyzed in an effort to *check* whether or not the obsessional theme is true or not. There will always be another; "yeah, but what about this?" that crops up just when the person with OCD thinks they've attained a fairly high degree of certainty.

This kind of question can seem valid and yet if you think about it in light of the fact that OCD is a *real* disorder with proven treatment strategies it would be absurd to suggest that taking advantage of those strategies demonstrates a lack of faith. If a person with OCD had a friend who developed Lupus would they suppose that their friend was demonstrating a lack of faith by seeing a Rheumatologist to treat their Lupus? I think not! It's really not the case that the person with OCD really believes that seeking the help of a physician reveals a lack of faith it's rather that they are caught up in scrutinizing their every thought and action to try and ascertain some measure of certainty regarding their obsessional theme. If there is an anxious feeling of uncertainty that attaches itself to any thought or activity, (such as seeing a Psychologist), then the person will often respond by trying to avoid that thought or activity – "just to be safe." The sad thing about responding to the questions posed above in this manner is that it can prevent them from getting the help they need.

One thing that helped me over this hurdle was to consider that I was actually trying to force God to help me out on my own terms as some kind of proof that I was still His child. I wanted to choose the method of healing. When I dug deeper into this consideration, I had to admit that it would have been more comfortable for me to have God just miraculously heal me rather than being willing to consider that seeing a doctor might actually be the way He chose to help me. I needed to give Him that choice instead of expecting Him to follow my own agenda, even if it frightened me to take that step.

Another thing that I had to admit was that whatever healing I received would still be from Him whether it came through a doctor or not. After all, it's God that has gifted doctors with the knowledge to treat and heal all kinds of sicknesses. He is still the "great physician" who has made all healing possible. All that is good is derived solely from Him.

> 3. "If I allow the thoughts to be there without fighting them won't that mean that I really *want* to think them or might be in agreement with them?"

This question will usually come up just when a person first begins to employ the "not attending" techniques of ERP in regard to any of their unwanted or intrusive thoughts.

Of course, one wouldn't even think to pose this question if they truly desired the presence of the thoughts or actually agreed with them. Therefore, the *real* reason this question is being asked is because, in OCD, anxiety trumps logic. The OCD'er would say; "it makes me feel anxious to ignore the thoughts and I find it extremely hard to accept that *this* level of anxiety should be ignored."

A person can be logically or rationally well aware that their OCD theme is most likely not true but the anxiety that accompanies it is so intense that it causes them to feel very strongly that it must be attended to. *Not* attending to it feels like taking an enormous risk. But, to be able to move forward a person must will themselves to take that risk and refuse to give these questions any attention.

4. I haven't been feeling very upset about my obsession lately. Does this mean that I really *agree* with my obsession or actually *want* to think it?

This question usually pops up at the beginning of ERP just when a person may start to experience a few hours of peace from the intense anxiety of their obsession. The brain is finally starting to let go of it and this should be viewed as a good thing, but if there is still free floating anxiety, then the brain will continue to search for something to be upset about. So what would normally be seen as progress will instead, become a reason to continue obsessing.

In revisiting my earlier "bug" analogy, one way to move past this question is to picture my OCD as if it's a Venus fly trap. The fly trap is starting to grow weak as the anxiety to the obsession begins to wane. But this doesn't mean that the flytrap isn't hungry. It still wants food because there yet remains an overabundance of flight or fight chemistry. This is like the hunger stimulant to the OCD and, therefore, it still wants food to chew on. So when this question wanders into my consciousness, it's like a buzzing fly. This is a huge temptation to the fly trap/OCD. The good news is that I'm still in charge of whether or not to spring the trap. If I close the jaws of my fly trap down on this fly/question by attending to it, I'll be feeding my OCD. If I do the exact opposite and just let the fly buzz by letting the question just hang there unanswered, then it will die a natural death and the fly trap of my OCD will continue to grow weaker. This is one of those times where I remind myself to "put the fly swatter down!"

The important thing is not to make a big deal about whether or not you've made the wrong choice in these instances as if there's no turning back. Managing OCD is a learning process and it takes quite some time to become adept at it. Once you realize you've been attending to any obsession you still have the choice to open up the jaws of your mind and release the thought by saying… "go ahead and buzz all you want. I'm not going to chew on you any more or I'll have to live with the taste of you in my brain for a long time."

5. Why should I encourage the thoughts? Doesn't that go against the whole idea of getting rid of them? After all, why should I bother to do that when they're already in my head 24/7?

In thinking about these types of questions, these are some of the things that should be considered. First of all, are these questions being asked because there is a great deal of fear associated with the idea of encouraging the thoughts? In other words, am I giving in to the avoidance compulsion of my OCD by refusing to willingly stay in the presence of the thoughts? I know *my* answer to this would have been a sarcastic; "of course I want to avoid them. They terrify me – duh!" Yet if I'm avoiding active exposure to my thoughts, I am in effect giving them a huge measure of validity. It's like my OCD is a schoolyard bully who I'm either hiding from or handing over my lunch money, just to appease him. When I do that, I'm letting the bully know that I'm terrified of him and he'll get all bloated up with smug confidence. When that happens, the bully perceives me as being weak and will continue to pick on me and see me as an easy target. If I stand up to the bully, even though I know he might punch me in the face, I'm showing him that he's not as tough as he thinks he is. It is no longer satisfying to pick on me because I'm not feeding his ego.

The next thing to consider is that in asking these questions it's very likely that I'm completely missing the point as well as the goal of active exposure. There is a huge difference between having thoughts stuck in my head because I'm trying so hard *not* to think of them and choosing to stand up to my thoughts by daring them to punch me as hard as they want to. The attitudes of these two positions are totally opposite. The first attitude seeks to push away or hide from the thoughts. The second attitude stands up to them with a "bring it on and do your worse" stance. The first attitude feeds OCD. The second attitude starves it. The first attitude validates the obsession the second attitude invalidates it. So the answer as to why you should choose to encourage the thoughts is; in order to beat the bully of your OCD.

6. Will therapy make the thoughts go away and never come back?

I don't think I've talked to anyone who suffers from OCD, who hasn't wished that they could somehow erase the obsessions from their mind. One thing I've come to accept about my OCD obsessions is that I cannot unthink them and that every effort to do so will only make me think about them all the more. So it's important to completely let go of this desire. This does not mean, however, that my response to the obsessions cannot become milder and milder over time or that I'll never get to a place where I'm no longer bothered by them.

Using ERP and/or medication to manage OCD will, in the end, allow for the obsessions to pop into my mind from time to time without having that horrible anxiety reaction to them. As I write this book, I am experiencing a very long period of relief from the severe form of my OCD. My brain chemistry is comfortably balanced and I'm actively engaged in the daily management of my disorder. Basically what I'm saying is that I feel pretty darn good right now. Therefore, on most days I am able to willingly ponder the obsessional themes of my past and feel fairly calm about them. In fact, this level of calmness reveals just how abnormal my emotional response to them was while my brain chemistry was severely imbalanced. But "doing great" for me still means that I will have an occasional brief period or an "off" day where I might begin to feel a bit of anxiety when I think of an obsession. When that happens, I acknowledge the anxiety and wait for it to pass while refusing to engage in any sort of compulsive activity in response to it. If I fall off the wagon, so to speak and find myself ruminating about them, I just acknowledge that I'm doing the wrong thing and do my best to apply the brakes by ignoring the obsession, even though at first, it makes me feel anxious to do so.

Living with OCD means expecting and accepting that it's going to try and trip us up from time to time. One way it trips us up is when we allow these kinds of questions to stop us from either getting the help we need or keeps us from applying the therapy of ERP to manage our disorder. When we do this, we cooperate with the OCD and in effect we become our worse enemy. So while OCD may throw branches across our paths, put rocks in the way for us to stumble on, or even dig holes in the road for us to fall in, we just have to be willing to say; "so what!" In all of these experiences, our free will remains intact. Therefore, we can choose to climb over the branches, walk around the rocks and climb up out of the holes. Is this annoying, exhausting, irritating and sometimes even painful? Yes, it is. But really when you think about it, is there any affliction that doesn't carry with it a certain level of discomfort? Why should OCD be any different? At the same time, we should acknowledge that nearly all afflictions can also build positive character traits in those who suffer from them and this includes OCD. But I'm getting ahead of myself. I'll be delving into *that* in greater detail in the last chapter of this book. So read on!

CHAPTER 7

PRACTICAL MATTERS

Albert Einstein: on the definition of insanity; "Doing the same thing over and over and expecting different results." 1.

BEFORE DELVING INTO this section of the book, I thought it might be best to consider whether or not the information in it will be beneficial to those who read it. Gaining knowledge about something is useless unless we act upon it. The things that I've covered thus far in this book are not just meant to console the reader with the knowledge that someone else understands their pain. They are meant to help bring about change. Not just a change in attitude, but a change in *behavior* regarding their disorder. It's really not a matter of stubbornness that keeps most of us from appropriating the things that will manage our disorder, but rather it's a matter of how willing we are to choose courage and perseverance in order to *act* upon the knowledge that we've gained. Therefore, regarding whether or not this book is going to be helpful, it's imperative to hold in mind that the difference in knowing what to do and actually doing it is what will determine the outcome.

Most chronic disorders will require that a person make certain modifications in their life in order to maximize the benefits of treatment. Anxiety disorders are no different.

One of the biggest hurdles that most of us need to get over is letting go of the notion that these disorders are somehow our fault instead of regarding them as legitimate afflictions. We may have been stuck in this mode of thinking for a very long time, but it's never too late to turn the page and take a new approach. It should be evident that the things we've been doing in response to the anxiety not only haven't been working but have actually been making our disorder worse. OCD certainly compounds this problem, because there is a tremendous urge to tread the same path over and over. Yet once an individual begins to understand how detrimental that path has been to their recovery it becomes clear to them that they must take a different route.

In this chapter, I will share some of the practical measures that I've applied in treating my own Anxiety Disorder that have proven to be beneficial to me. When I employ them in a consistent manner, I become more convinced of their effectiveness in managing my disorder. When I'm in the midst of a lengthy flare up of anxiety, I will generally employ *all* of them in order to speed up the balancing of my brain chemistry. For other periods, when my disorder has waned, I still keep up some of the practices which I've found to be the most beneficial. This requires a disciplined and determined effort. What helps me to keep at it is that I've actually experienced the positive benefits of these things and *that* provides enough motivation to continue incorporating them into my daily routine.

The need for consistency is something that I've had to learn the hard way. Experience has taught me that when I've backed off in the routine practice of these things, the consequence, is that I experience an increase in the symptoms of anxiety.

It is my opinion, *and* I think it's shared by many physicians, that Anxiety Disorders are generally lifelong conditions that wax and wane over time. There have been times when my symptoms have been so minimal that it really seemed as if I might have been completely cured of my disorder. Then there have been other times where life events and physical problems have come together in such a way to create the perfect soil conditions for my disorder to crop up once again and take me by surprise. This can be horribly discouraging when you've felt certain that you'd never have to deal with it again.

Learning to be proactive in the management of Anxiety Disorders in practical ways will serve a person well in getting a leg up on minimizing or even preventing those excruciating flares. What follows are the practical measures which have greatly bolstered and assisted me as I live with this chronic condition. My prayer, for those of you who suffer from these disorders, is that you will make the choice to apply some or all of these things in managing your own condition and that in doing so, you will reap many benefits from them. I also hope that you will take the time to research some of the recommended reading materials listed at the back of this book. In doing so, you will be able to increase your arsenal in the management of your condition. The goal is to manage it, rather than having it manage you.

It seems absurd to think that someone who is suffering wouldn't want to take the medicine that will make them feel better, but the problem isn't so much that they don't *want* to take the medicine but rather that the medicine itself can often seem just as unpleasant as the illness. I remember when my daughter was about five years old and came down with the flu which was complicated by a double ear infection. Her fever was very high and she was one miserable little girl. Therefore, per her doctor's orders I was diligently giving her children's chewable acetaminophen every four hours. As the day wore on I became increasingly concerned as every time I checked her temperature it was still way too high. She felt awful and I felt awful too, wanting so badly for her fever to settle down and for her pain to go away. I was just at the point of calling her pediatrician after taking her temperature just one more time and finding it to still be hovering at about 103 degrees, when I had a sudden intuition that maybe, just maybe she hadn't been taking the pills. This was because I usually just handed her one with a glass of water and then left the room without actually witnessing her swallowing it. She usually minded me very well so it just hadn't occurred to me that she wouldn't take the pill. So I went to her and asked her; "Honey, have you been chewing up and swallowing those pills that Mommy's been giving you?" There was a pause, then her lower lip started to quiver and then the tears started falling. I was down on my knees in a flash and looking under her bed, I spotted a little pile of pretty pink pills. Apparently she didn't like the way they tasted so she'd made the decision to reject them. A short lecture later with an explanation as to why she absolutely had to take the pills combined with me standing there to be certain that she actually swallowed them put everything right within an hour. Her fever went right down and she began to feel good enough to sit up in bed and play with her dolls.

The reason I chose to relate this little story was to illustrate the fact that those of us with Anxiety Disorders will tend to resist the very things that can help us get better. This is especially true of the first practical measure that I am going to recommend, which is medication. There are so many reasons that we can come up with as to why we don't think we need medication even though a physician may have advised us to take it, but most of those *reasons* aren't legitimate. They may *feel* legitimate but in most cases those feelings must be set aside in order for us to really make good progress toward getting well. So I've decided to address some of the typical reasons that cause a person with an Anxiety Disorder to resist using medication as the first practical measure in the management of it.

Practical Measure One – Medication

This is undoubtedly one of the highest hurdles that I struggled to climb over regarding the management of my OCD and Panic Disorder. What follows, are some examples of the "reasons" I came up with as to why I felt I couldn't choose medication as a part of my management plan. I'm sure many of them sound familiar to those who suffer from OCD.

You will notice as you begin to read these reasons that many of them carry with them a big element of uncertainty or doubt. This is because I have OCD and when it's bad, it latches on to anything and everything it can to keep me in that unrelenting cycle of obsession, doubt, anxiety and checking behaviors.

> A. I don't need medication. I'm not like other people. I'm strong enough to handle this on my own without the aid of drugs.

This reason was based purely in stubborn pride. I didn't want to admit that I might actually need the help of medication. I felt that using medication was a sign of weakness, even though I would never dare to criticize anyone else for making that choice. Not me, though, I was too tough for that. I was going to win the bragging rights of defeating this monster all on my own. Now why on earth would I go through needless suffering when there was a medication that could alleviate some of it? Here's why; "What if someone found out that I needed to take one of these drugs? What would they think of me?" And that, right there, is the evidence of pride at work in my heart.

It was a blessed day when I actually admitted that I was no different or better than anyone else who was afflicted with an Anxiety Disorder. I was finally able to acknowledge that it wasn't just *okay* to use medication to assist me in managing my disorder it was actually a wise and good choice. This is because the level of my distress had become so high that I found it hard to function, eat, sleep or even gather up enough strength to be able to focus in such a way that I could employ any sort of behavioral modification therapy.

Dr. Archibald Hart in his book, "The Anxiety Cure", points out that the answer to the following question should help a person determine whether or not they need to use medication to assist them in their efforts to get better. He asks; "Is your anxiety so debilitating that you can make no progress in therapy without medication?" Then he goes on to say; "if so, medication is necessary." 1. Such was the case with me.

Another thing that really pressed me to consider incorporating medication into my treatment regimen was that in doing so I would be showing my husband Dennis that I loved him and also respected his counsel. He was extremely concerned about me and wanted very badly for me to give the medication a try. Basically, he just wanted his wife back and I don't blame him for that. I had become an uncommunicative, unproductive, paralyzed lump. He had been so gentle, compassionate and sweet to me throughout all of it, that it just hit me one day that if our roles were reversed I'd also be doing everything in my power to convince him to take the medication which would lessen his pain and bring back his wonderful personality. So in light of these considerations, I made the choice to put my pride in my pocket and give the medication a try.

I have never regretted that choice and can now say that I'm thankful to God for these drugs and for His helping me to get past all that nonsense and do the right thing for my husband and for me. To love someone is to be concerned for them. So, if your family loves you, they will be in distress when you are in distress. It's important to acknowledge this.

B. I don't want to be dependent on a drug for the rest of my life.

This reason also had an element of pride attached to it in that it seemed to me that having to take an anxiety medication for the rest of my life was somehow an indication of failure. This is an illegitimate notion because there are many disorders that require a person to be on medication for the rest of their lives. I already had two disorders that fell into that category; high blood pressure and high cholesterol. Yet I felt no shame or fear about swallowing *those* pills every single day. That's because I understood *those* disorders to be legitimate whereas I struggled tremendously with accepting the fact that my Anxiety Disorder was also a legitimate affliction. I needed to learn to take advantage of the medications and therapy that had proven to be beneficial to others who shared my disorder.

Yet there still remained other errant ideas connected to this reason. While there certainly are some people who will need to be on medication for the rest of their lives to keep their Anxiety Disorder at bay, this is not the case for every individual. I fell into the second category, but it would have been all right if I'd fallen into the first. I was already aware that I'd experienced many years where my Anxiety Disorders affected me in such a minimal way that I didn't need medication to function normally. Still I was very afraid that if I started the medication that I'd never be able to get off it. Wrong again! Most often medication can be beneficial at the beginning of learning to manage these disorders when they are at their worse. Later on, when a person is consistently practicing the proper therapy and employing other practical measures, it is very probable that they might be able to gradually decrease their medication and in some cases even be able to go off it entirely. This has been the case with me. I have, at this point been able to completely quit one of the most potent of my two medications and have done very well on half of the smallest dosage of the less potent one.

What I found encouraging was that in choosing to take the medication I was able to see that it really *was* a serotonin imbalance all along that had ignited my disorder. If that hadn't been the case, then the medication would not have benefitted me at all. The other really comforting thing is that I now know what kind of medication is the most helpful to me and now I have the option of incorporating it into my treatment regimen should I ever experience another debilitating flare. So the choice to use medication is not an all or nothing scenario. If, however, a person has been stuck for a very long time in pain filled obsessional cycles or unrelenting panic attacks without using any medication, it would be prudent for them to go and see a doctor. They can then inquire whether a medication could assist them in breaking free from the hold the disorder has on them. After all, if the Queen of Pride can do it, anyone can.

C. What if I become addicted to the drug?

Most of the medications that are used to treat Anxiety Disorders are not at all addictive. They don't make a person feel *high* or provide some sort of euphoric pleasure which they might crave more and more of. Instead, they bring the person's emotional responses back into the realm of what I would refer to as "normal". This is because they bring the brain chemistry back into its proper balance.

Some of the more common of these drugs are Selective Serotonin Reuptake Inhibitors and Tricyclic antidepressants. There is a wide range of medications for Anxiety Disorders which are available and a person has to be willing to try another if one doesn't work, in order to find the right fit. There are some drugs that have the potential to create dependency if not used properly, under a doctor's supervision. These medications are called Benzodiazepines. These are usually used in a short term manner or intermittently.

I'm not going to go into great detail about medications since I'm obviously not a physician. It is a good idea, however, to educate yourself about the different types of medications that are available and to bring up all your concerns about them to your physician. The only thing that I would advise is that it's best to start these medications at a very low dosage and work up gradually to a therapeutic dosage. Some people will experience a thing called, "paradoxical anxiety" when starting some of these medications and much of that can be avoided or minimized by building up the dosage very gradually. If you experience an increase in anxiety, you can try cutting the dosage back until you feel better, then go up in incremental baby steps from there. This same principle applies to weaning off these medications. The dosage needs to be decreased very gradually over at least several months. If you begin to experience severe anxiety, you might need to go back up a step and taper even more gradually. Again, your physician is the best source of information when you have questions or concerns about which type of medication might be good for you and how to introduce it into your daily regimen.

    D. What if it changes my personality or I have horrible side effects from it or I'm allergic to it?

I can actually grin about these "reasons" in retrospect but at the time when they first cropped up they seemed incredibly scary. The obviously logical answer to these questions would be that I would try a different medication if any of these things became an issue. But when you have OCD your emotions will trump your logic. Therefore, because I have OCD these questions were actually offshoots of the former question; "What if I get addicted to the drug?" OCD doubts and uncertainties tend to feed off one another so I had this image of myself addicted to a medication that made me act strange, feel horrible and also gave me hives to the point of causing my throat to swell shut.

There is truly no end to the "horrifying" possibilities that an OCD afflicted mind can come up with. So – "what to do, what to do?" If you've learned anything from the previous chapter you will know that the right thing to do is to run the risk, live with the uncomfortable feelings of uncertainty that are attached to these questions and go ahead and take the plunge. Or, if you want to prolong your suffering *and* your recovery you can keep on looking for proof or certainty that these things won't happen to you. (Remember that knowing what to do won't help you a bit. Doing what you know, you should do, will.) Besides all that, if you stay on *that* path of questioning and debating about whether or not to try medication for too long the fear will intensify. This is because the constant attending to it will make it all seem eerily valid.

E. If I take one of these drugs won't that be an indication that I'm not trusting God to heal me?

This is round two of the redundancy that I was referring to earlier. I am revisiting this question on purpose because people with OCD revisit the same questions over and over again.

Now here's my response to it; "Yes, that's *exactly* what it means *and* if you do not trust God then that might also mean that you don't have *real* faith and if you don't have real faith that might mean you're on your way to hell after all! (Big sigh!) Oh well – looks like you'll just have to run that risk because I know you really, really want to feel better."

That was an example of how to apply active exposure to this question. Instead of arguing with an insistent and redundant question you need to switch tactics and just let it do its worse by taking its threats up to the level of absurdity. Then after that, just let it be.

I can't emphasize this enough. You cannot defeat OCD by debating with its questions. If you keep on trying to do that the questions that it poses will become ever more threatening and valid than when they first appeared. You will find yourself arguing the same subject over and over again and instead of feeling relief you will only feel worse. It might be a good idea, just here to turn back and take a look at the Einstein quote at the head of the chapter.

Honestly, deep down my logic did tell me that this question was completely invalid. Yet because my root fear with this obsession was that I'd be eternally separated from God, my OCD latched onto to it, which in turn threw me right back into the rumination cycle. Therefore, it was far easier for me to avoid doing certain things than to run the risk that doing them might be a thing that might "seal my doom." To engage in the feared activity felt to me as if I could be spiritually contaminated by it. But if I cooperated with the OCD by avoiding the very thing that could help me, I would be legitimizing its threats. I didn't want to do that so I made the choice to run the risk and take the medication plunge. In doing so, I dealt my OCD a double blow. I was using ERP therapy against it and also using the medication that would help bring my serotonin levels back into a normal range. Score: OCD = 0, Me = 2 points!!!!!

I certainly don't wish to give the impression that the use of medication to treat OCD or any type of Anxiety Disorder is, in all cases, a necessary thing. In my own past, I was able to come through a pretty long and excruciating flare of Panic Disorder and OCD without the aid of medication. It *is* possible to do so, but this should be decided on a case by case basis with the advice of a physician. Several things will likely be considered when deciding on whether or not to use medication. Here are just a few of them.

1. Will the person be able to appropriate the therapy without medication?
2. Is there a depression component that is so severe that the person is too paralyzed to do anything?
3. Is the person's quality of life so greatly impaired that they are very debilitated by the disorder and unable to engage in their everyday routines or activities?

If the answer to *any* of these questions is yes, then I would advise you to seek the advice of a physician concerning the use of medication to help manage your disorder. Don't put it off.

Practical Measure Two - Panic Attack Strategies

I've lived with panic attacks for most of my adult life. My first encounter with them was incredibly distressing. Now, after many years of living to tell about it yet another day, they don't pack quite the punch that they used to. The biggest challenge that my panic attacks cause to me is the avoidance of triggering factors. For some folk, the avoidance of triggering events can become so severe that it leads to Agoraphobia, which can become so bad that it means the avoidance of going anywhere outside the confines of their home.

I have struggled on and off throughout my life with driving because it has been a trigger for my panic attacks and it's very difficult for me to keep on driving when riding out a panic attack. What I've learned about this is that the more I engage in the triggering activity, the more accustomed my brain becomes to it. Therefore, it eventually stops reacting to it by giving me a panic attack. I find that I have to drive a route over and over in order for my brain to relax about it. This truth that exposure to the triggering event will in the end stop the brain from overreacting was proven to me by my being able to ride across, (ride, *not* drive) the Mackinaw Bridge without experiencing a panic attack. We used to travel over that enormous five-mile suspension bridge once a year. Every time we did I would have such bad panic attacks that I wanted to dive under the seat. I couldn't look up or out or down without experiencing a panic attack. Then our living situation changed which required us to drive across that bridge far more often. The increase in exposure to this triggering factor totally resolved the problem of my having a panic attack when I ride across that bridge. Now I can look up, out and down and feel perfectly calm when we make that journey. Perhaps someday

I'll even be able to drive across it. The knowledge that I've gained about the benefits of exposure encourages me that this is indeed very possible.

A huge part of managing panic attacks will mean being willing to purposely engage in active exposure to the very activities which are the triggering factors for having a panic attack. It takes a lot of grit and a willingness to experience temporary distress which is something that I battle with myself. It's very hard to choose to put yourself in a situation that you know will bring on a panic attack when avoidance is so much easier. The key lies in perseverance. Set goals for yourself starting with small periods of exposure and work up gradually to longer and longer periods of exposure. Right now I can only drive in familiar areas and at speeds under 40 miles per hour without experiencing a panic attack. This is actually quite amazing given the fact that my Anxiety Disorder used to have such a grip on me that I couldn't even ride as a passenger in a car without a panic attack let alone drive. Over time, my goal is to train my brain to accept highway driving so I can make longer trips without having to depend on my husband to do all the driving. Some of my other triggers are gazing up at tall buildings or the sky, thinking about or pondering infinite things like space and eternity and watching movies with fast and furious driving or flying scenes, most especially in an IMAX theater. Then there are just those times when I'm overly tired or stressed which can cause a panic attack to crop up at any time, even when I'm drifting off to sleep.

If you have Panic Disorder, you are going to have to learn to live with and ride out panic attacks that will come from time to time.

The first thing you need to think about is why the attack is happening. It's happening because your brain is misfiring at an inappropriate time. All that adrenaline which is supposed to be released in the event of real emergency floods your body when it's just not needed. So you feel intense anxiety without a reason. It's good to think in this clinical way as to what is happening in your brain when a panic attack crops up. You can say something to yourself like; *Here we go again. This is nothing more than a big meaningless and useless adrenaline surge. It feels awful, but if I just ride it out, it will pass.* Secondly you need to learn to recognize the early warning signs that often precipitate an attack. Your heart may start beating faster, you might feel sweaty or find it hard to sit still and just have an overall sense of being ill at ease. When this happens, you need to begin practicing deep breathing techniques which will often help to ward off a full blown attack or at least shorten its duration. I have to employ these breathing techniques quite often when I'm driving and feel an attack coming on. What I do is to forcibly slow my breathing down. I breathe from my abdomen and inhale slowly counting to eight until my lungs are filled. Then at the top of the breath I hold my breath for a count of eight. After that, I slowly exhale counting to ten or even higher to gradually empty my lungs. Then I take two regular breaths and start the sequence all over again until the panic subsides.

This sounds very easy, but the physical symptoms of a panic attack will often cause a person to either hold their breath or to breathe very rapidly and shallow which only serves to exacerbate the anxiety. Learning to take note of your breathing patterns and making this correction during a panic attack will help it to subside and give you a great tool to aid you in your effort to just ride it out. It's a very good idea to practice deep breathing techniques even when you aren't experiencing a panic attack so that you'll be adept at them when you need to use them.

Panic attacks are miserable events, but they are meaningless and pose no real threat to your health. They are usually brief in duration and it is entirely possible that when you become adept at riding them out that you can actually experience one in a public setting without anyone, but you knowing it. I've been at dinner parties, sitting in church, or a doctor's office and have been able to ride out these attacks without having to get up and leave. That wasn't always the case, but over the years I've had so much practice in riding out panic attacks that I rarely see them as much of a big deal. Driving is my biggest issue because I find the attacks to be distracting and I know that driving demands my full attention. Therefore, I have to do my driving exposure in baby steps. I'm very hopeful and confident that one day I will drive completely free of panic attacks; maybe even on a highway or better yet, over the Mackinaw Bridge.

Practical Measure Three – Exercise

I can honestly say that I can't think of one time of when I knew I needed to exercise that I didn't whine about it. I whine because it takes up so much of my time, because it's really hard work, because I get all sweaty and dirty and then afterward I have to take a shower and re-do my makeup and hair. "Sigh!" So why bother? The answer is just this, if you suffer from an Anxiety Disorder, regular exercise can be just as beneficial in managing the disorder as medication. Dr. Edmund Bourne in his book on the treatment of Anxiety Disorders, states that; "One of the most powerful and effective methods for reducing generalized anxiety and overcoming a predisposition to panic attacks is a program of regular, vigorous exercise." 2. There are actual physiological factors that ignite Anxiety Disorders and regular exercise is very effective in correcting many of these physiological problems.

 The exercise that I'm referring to is aerobic. It's the kind that causes you to breathe deeply and increases your heart rate. It should also cause, at the very least, mild perspiration. The two types of exercise that I practice most consistently are kickboxing and speed walking. I prefer speed walking to kickboxing because I am able to pray or meditate while walking. I usually start out by praying and then move into meditation speaking out the words of a hymn or verse in my mind with the rhythm of my breathing. This is a form of moving meditation and it's very beneficial in alleviating anxiety. There are lots of other options available which are appropriate for a person's age or level of physical fitness, such as running, biking, aerobic dance, swimming and yoga. I don't engage in the traditional form of yoga due to personal convictions but prefer to use a program which teaches the beneficial postures, stretches, and deep breathing while meditating on scripture passages. The DVD program that I use is called "Praise Moves" by Laurette Willis. 3.

Regular exercise is an essential component of my overall approach to managing my Anxiety Disorder. The benefits of this discipline have been proven over and over to me in my own life. Whenever I slack off or make excuses for not getting regular exercise my level of stress and tension begin to increase dramatically. The muscles in my neck and shoulders become chronically tense and painful. I begin to struggle with falling asleep as well as staying asleep at night. My heart acts up and I experience more palpitations, especially when I lie down at night. I have more headaches and my TMJ becomes bothersome. Panic attacks begin to creep back in and become more frequent and intense. Whenever I've made it a habit to incorporate consistent, vigorous exercise four to five times a week for at least thirty to sixty minutes, all of these things either go away entirely or improve to the degree that I would classify them as mildly annoying.

Before choosing to engage in a regular exercise program, it's always best to check, (that's just *once* for you OCD'ers), with your doctor as to whether there are any physical limitations as to what type of exercise you can safely engage in.

I would like to add a little word of caution concerning exercise for the person with OCD. There are some people with OCD, who use exercise in the wrong way. Exercise can be perverted by the disorder in that it becomes a compulsion that they engage in, to gain temporary reassurance from certain types of fearful obsessions regarding their health. It might also become something that they feel they must engage in to undo or cancel a certain fearful thought or image that has been plaguing them. Many of these obsessions will have a health-related theme. A person who suffers from this type of OCD will exercise in a compulsive and extremely excessive way to the degree that it takes up a huge allotment of time out of their day. They will do so because they fear that if they don't, the fearful consequences of their obsession might come true. The exercise sessions will usually be every day for hours at a time with increasing frequency and intensity. If they can't exercise, they will experience tremendous anxiety for not being able to engage in their compulsion. What needs to happen in this case is for them to learn to use exercise in the correct way. Not as a compulsive reassurance seeking activity but rather as a healthy lifestyle choice that is disconnected from the content of their obsession. ERP is just as effective in managing this type of OCD as it is in any other type. These folk would need to seek professional help from a doctor who is trained in the application of ERP in order to be able to apply it correctly to this consuming OCD behavior.

Practical Measure Four – Proper Nutrition

What I've chosen to share concerning the role that diet plays in either exacerbating or alleviating anxiety is based on the observations that I've been able to make about how my own eating habits affect my disorder. There is more and more evidence coming to light on the positive and negative effects that certain foods have on anxiety.

Dr. Bourne states that; "In the last twenty years the relationship between diet, stress, and mood has been well documented. It's known that certain foods and substances tend to create additional stress and anxiety while others produce a calmer and steadier mood." 4.

The other thing that I've noticed about how my eating impacts my disorder pertains to whether or not I'm keeping my blood sugar levels as stable as possible. This is affected not just by the kind of food that I choose to eat but when and how often I eat.

I'll admit that this is a tough discipline for me. I have a hard time eating correctly when I'm experiencing a flare of my disorder because of a lack of appetite and nausea and I also have a tough time when I'm feeling better because I'm so often tempted to choose foods which cause my blood sugar to spike and then drop dramatically.

When I'm having a really bad bout with OCD and/or Panic Disorder food is absolutely revolting to me. Yet the knowledge I've gained about how important it is to keep my blood sugar levels stable has bolstered me in my effort to eat whether I feel like it or not. Learning how to graze on beneficial foods throughout the day is well worth the effort. During these times, I concentrate on making sure that I eat protein with every small meal. Here is an example of what a successful day of eating looks like for me when I'm in a flare of bad anxiety. (Please keep in mind that eating is a huge challenge for me during a flare of my disorder and, therefore, it takes a great deal of effort to get even *this* much food down.)

Breakfast: Half a cup of yogurt, half a banana and one slice of cheese.

Mid-morning snack: One protein drink, such Ensure or Boost.

Lunch: One-half cup of cottage cheese, a slice of low-fat lunch meat, half an apple and water.

Mid afternoon snack: String cheese, a few crackers and a small glass of V8 juice.

Dinner: A few small baby carrots or a piece of celery with peanut butter, half a sandwich made with some type of healthy meat, half a piece of fruit, half a small yogurt and water.

Evening snack: Ensure or Boost.

Eating in this way helps to keep my blood sugar levels stable and prevents me from experiencing episodes of weakness or faintness which only serves to increase my level of anxiety. I also cut out all caffeine during a flare because it exacerbates my anxiety.

When I'm not in a flare, I still choose to eat in a grazing manner at the same times of day as listed above. The difference is that I'm actually able to enjoy *all* kinds of food as my appetite returns and I'm also able to eat larger portions. I strive to include protein with every meal, especially if I'm having any type of sugary or starchy food. I eat more vegetables and fruits when I'm not in a flare because I don't have to struggle to get them down. I strictly limit my caffeine intake to one cup of coffee first thing in the morning. I do my level best to eat in moderation. I eat slowly and try to avoid eating chocolate in the evening. I try to avoid second helpings so that I don't experience gastrointestinal distress. I also avoid those things which tend to upset my stomach. For me, these things would be certain kinds of dairy products or any type of artificial sweetener.

Eating balanced meals at regular intervals is a good health practice for all people, but it's especially important for those of us who are afflicted with Anxiety Disorders.

Practical Measure Five – Adequate Sleep

One of most common symptoms of anxiety is an inability to get enough sleep which can also include abnormal sleep patterns. Even when my disorder is managed to the point where it's only mildly annoying, if I don't get adequate rest I will experience more panic attacks as well as a tendency to feel generally anxious.

Dr. Archibald Hart refers to this problem as a "two-way street." He says that; "disturbed sleep is both a symptom and a cause" when it comes to the role it plays in anxiety. He goes on to say that disturbed sleep is "a symptom of too much stress as well as anxiety *and* the *cause* of excessive stress and anxiety." 5. In other words, a lack of good sleep can create a vicious cycle for the person who is afflicted with Anxiety Disorders. I can remember my own thoughts on this; "I feel so anxious that I can't sleep" *and* "the fact that I can't sleep makes me feel even more anxious."

Over the years, I've learned to make use of several tactics to enhance my ability to get the rest that my body needs. Probably the most important thing that I do is to try and go to bed at the same time every night and get up at the same time every morning. I'm not *super* rigid about this, but as a general rule I try not to vary my bedtime and waking time by more than forty-five minutes to an hour. My body is so accustomed to going to sleep and waking up at the same time that it seems to have developed an internal clock which causes me to feel sleepy around the same time every night and to wake up at the same time every morning. If I push myself to stay up too long past that window of sleepiness, I can actually lose that sleepy feeling and be very awake and alert into the middle of the night. If I stay in bed even after my body wakes me up and try to catch up on more shut-eye, then, when I finally *do* get out of bed I feel pretty sluggish as well as down in the dumps mentally. So even if I end up getting only four hours of sleep, I refuse to try and "catch up" on sleep in the morning. I find that I'm better off just getting up at my usual time and then going to bed on time the following evening.

I've also learned to avoid engaging in activities which are too mentally stimulating as bedtime approaches.

Just recently, our youngest son and his family were staying with us for a week. One evening I decided to teach my daughter in law how to make a beaded bracelet. We sat on the couch from ten p.m. until way past midnight absorbed in our beading. We were both so absorbed by the creativity and fun of our project that neither of us got sleepy like we normally would. We finally hit the sack at about one a.m. and both of us were still wide awake and had a great deal of trouble getting to sleep.

Although this wasn't a big deal, it just reinforced to me that as a practice, I shouldn't allow my mental activity to be so engrossing that my brain gets overstimulated to the point where I might be lying awake for hours past my normal sleep time. I even have to be careful about what I might read. It' can't be too thought-provoking, mysterious, funny or exciting to the point that I get so swept up in it that I find it hard to sleep long after I've put the book down. It's the same with television. If I watch something on TV that's *really* entertaining, I won't get sleepy. I usually choose mentally relaxing shows that might not even have a story line. If I watch something like Antiques Road Show or a documentary, I will generally fall asleep within minutes of tuning in if it's near my sleep window time. My husband Dennis, the night owl, knows that if he waits just a little while that I'll drop off to sleep and he can switch the channel to something else that he finds entertaining.

While it may be true that many people are able to go to bed before they actually *get* sleepy and still fall asleep quite easily, this is just not the case with me. If I try to go to bed before I feel sleepy, the mental effort of *trying* to sleep will generally keep me wide awake. I can become so obsessed and upset with the fact that I'm not yet sleeping that I end up looking at the clock at regular intervals. I then begin to count the hours I have left to sleep in the hope that I can squeeze in an adequate amount before morning arrives. This generally gets me too anxious and worked up to be able to fall asleep.

Awhile back, I was reading a letter that CS Lewis had written to friend on this topic and found that he obviously could relate to my own experience. He wrote; "About sleep: do you find that the great secret (if one can do it) is not to *care* whether you sleep? Sleep is a jade who scorns her suitors but woos her scorners." 7.

So for me to get around this obstacle to my sleep, I will usually stay up until I notice that I'm actually getting sleepy and then head off to bed. Now, if I'm really disciplined about my evening hours, I will usually be all ready for bed before I actually get sleepy. This means that I have my nightwear on, my face is washed, my contacts are off, my teeth are brushed and my bite splint in my mouth. (I'm sure this paints a pretty unattractive picture, but thankfully Dennis's love for me sees past all that.) If I put off doing these things until I begin to get sleepy, then the time and effort that it takes to do them will often snap me out of that sleep mode to the point that sometimes I have to go back to the living room and wait to get sleepy again.

I try to have all of my bedtime preparation done by at least ten thirty p.m., so that when that sleepy feeling comes I can just give Dennis, who happens to be rather nocturnal, a goodnight kiss and then stagger off into the bedroom and fall into bed. Oh, the bliss of falling asleep the moment your head hits the pillow! For me, this is nothing short of miraculous in comparison to the misery of all the sleepless nights I'd experienced in the past while in the throes of my disorder. Even so, I can still experience the occasional night where sleep is elusive. Maybe I ate too late or got swept up into an engaging late night phone conversation with a friend. Whatever the reason, I've learned that making a big hairy deal out of not being able to sleep only serves to make matters worse. Instead, I choose to accept the fact that I'm not yet asleep and try to adopt an ambivalent attitude about it. During those times, I might pick up a book and read for a while or I might decide to pray or practice progressive muscle relaxation exercises. When I choose to accept that I'm not sleeping instead of allowing myself to get upset about it, I stand a better chance of eventually getting to sleep.

Practical Measure Six - R & R

The two "R's" that I want to touch on are relaxation and recreation.

Children have no qualms about engaging in activities which are both pleasurable and relaxing to them. Recess tends to be the highlight of the day for most grade school aged kids. I can remember coming home from school with one goal in mind; to get outside and play as soon as possible. Most days I had some chore or task to complete before I was allowed to go outside which was clearly important to my learning to be responsible and to set priorities. As a matter of fact, "responsibility" was one of my Mom's favorite words. Indeed, irresponsibility will certainly lead to stress but conversely the absence of play and relaxation in the life of a responsible individual creates a scenario where stress can build up to such a degree that the person might break under too much pressure. As adults, we tend to view ourselves, our time, our goals and our work so seriously that we devote all our attention to high achievement in each of these categories. Meanwhile, we forget to play.

Have you ever been around folk who from the first moment of conversing with you say something like; "I'm just exhausted! I've just been so incredibly busy! When will this end!" Then you get to listen to them launch into a list of all the things they've been doing and when they finally finish with an exasperated sigh you just want to put a hand on their shoulder and say something like; "It sounds as if doing all of that is making you pretty miserable. So why don't you make it a point to find out what you can let go of?" To be honest, I can think of times when I've been guilty of the exact same thing. It's almost like I have an addiction to excessive busyness. It makes me miserable, but I can't seem to stop.

Sadly, as grown ups we become so absorbed in the activities of our life that we forget to stop and enjoy the blessings which God has given us. In stepping back to observe my own behavior I've discovered that I have a bad habit of biting off more than I can chew. I think maybe this is because I have a tendency to "think of myself more highly than *I* ought." 7. It's as if I think I'm some sort of superwoman who can handle an inordinate amount of work without it having a negative effect on me. What I mean by this is that I over stuff my life by trying to be heavily involved in too many activities at one time. When I do this, I choke out any opportunity for relaxation and recreation.

For instance, I might be working on painting the interior of our house, gardening, harvesting, canning and freezing vegetables, helping my husband with the rest of the yard work while sticking to a regular exercise program. All of this would include, bi-weekly exercise classes, going to a weekly Bible study course, working on a writing project, designing and making jewelry to sell at the City Market on the weekends as well as keeping in touch with and being available to all my friends and family. I would attempt to do all of these activities right alongside my usual daily tasks of cooking, cleaning, paying bills, laundry, etc. Then when it appears that I'm not doing an adequate job in any one of these areas I instantly feel like an incompetent failure.

I know that this illustration of the level of my activity is likely the norm for most of us. What's terribly frustrating is that we have a hard time sorting out what we can let go of as we will usually feel that most of our activities have value. The need lies in being able to prioritize and attend to these things in the proper order as well as in learning to pace ourselves as to how much time we will devote to each of these things on any given day. In this way, we will limit ourselves so that we can set aside some time to relax and unwind.

This can be especially hard for the homemaker. When you are the supervisor as well as the employee, the boss in you will push you to "keep at it" and, therefore, the employee never gets to punch out. It's only when I let go of some stuff and then prioritize and pace myself for the rest of it that I can find the time to be able to punch out. It's so hard to ignore the boss in me who might argue; "But I planned to clean the whole house today and now I won't be able to do it." The proper reply to that might be; "That's OK, just pace yourself and finish it gradually over the next few days." The boss might pipe up again; "But then I won't be able to finish turning the garden and it's going to snow tomorrow! Employee: "So what! It's not like the State Journal is going to show up in your back yard with a camera crew and take pictures of your garden for a story titled; 'Lansing's Laziest Gardener'. Good grief, lighten up! You can turn the rest of it next spring when you plant if need be. Now go run a warm bath, get a cup of cocoa, lock the cats out of the bathroom and soak until you feel relaxed."

I find that it's not only important for me to rest my body but that it's equally important for me to rest my mind. I can generally tell when I've been pushing my brain too hard. I will have the sensation and the thought, "I feel like my head is going to explode!" That's when I need to stop and take a break from all my frenzied busyness as well as my mental gymnastics.

Relaxation, for me, doesn't mean switching to another job which I consider less stressful. It means dropping everything and taking the time to do something very enjoyable or even just crashing on the couch with a cup of cocoa or a bowl of popcorn and watching a funny sit-com. The ability to laugh is such a blessing and when we make the time to enjoy the blessing of humor we feel rejuvenated by it.

When I was a kid, my folks used to have my Aunt and Uncle come over and play cards with them after we kids had gone to bed. My bedroom was just down the hall from the kitchen and I used to lay there and eavesdrop on their conversations. My dad is one of the funniest people I know and when his brother and sister were over he seemed to really be in fine form in the humor department. I would lay there cracking up at some of the hilarious stories he'd be telling often having to bury my face in the pillow as I laughed so my folks wouldn't know I was still awake. Eventually, I'd drop off to sleep with a contented grin on my face. Those memories are so precious to me but more than that they demonstrate just how valuable the gift of laughter is.

Whatever you choose to do to unwind just be sure that's it's really fun or relaxing to you and not just a less pressing duty.

The other aspect of relaxation involves teaching our bodies how to relax. The pain of an Anxiety Disorder isn't just limited to our mental state it also affects our bodies. Large muscle groups are often held tense for hours on end without the sufferer being aware that they are doing it.

During my first really long battle with Panic Disorder and OCD I happened to pass by the full-length mirror one day after bathing and actually took a moment to look at my body. I was startled to see that I'd developed what is commonly referred to as six pack abs. I could count every one of my abdominal muscles. I never did a single sit up during those dreadful months, but my muscles were always held in such a state of tension that it looked as if I'd been going to the gym every day. I also had a tremendous amount of shoulder, neck, jaw and head pain during that time due to my inability to relax my body. Accompanying this muscle tension was the tendency to breathe abnormally that I mentioned earlier in this chapter. So I would like to re-emphasize the importance of practicing those breathing techniques to teach the body how to relax.

The other method that I've used to teach my body how to relax is the progressive muscle relaxation technique that I mentioned in the section on sleep. This practice has helped me to be in tune with my body in such a way that I'm very aware of when I'm tense and can learn to relax and release those muscle groups when I notice it. What I do is to lie down in a comfortable place flat on my back making sure that my head is at a comfortable angle so my neck isn't strained. Then I begin to single out every muscle group in my body starting with my arms/shoulders and moving from there to my face, neck, chest, abdomen/back, hips, thighs, calves, and feet. I will hold each one of these muscles groups very tense while relaxing all the others and breathing deeply from my abdomen. I generally count to fifteen while tensing each muscle group then completely release it and lie limp and relaxed while continuing to breathe deeply for a count of twenty. Then I move on to the next group. This method of relaxation is so effective that if I try and do it when I'm having a wakeful night, I generally don't manage to get through all the muscle groups before falling asleep. Therefore, if you want it to be an effective tool for managing anxiety it has to be practiced during the day when you're not as likely to fall asleep. I currently only use it to fall asleep when I'm having a bad night but when I'm going through a flare of my disorder, I practice it on a regular basis as a proven tactic against the anxiety response in my body. Detailed instructions for progressive muscle relaxation can be found by doing an internet search as well as in Dr. Edmund J. Bourne's book – "The Anxiety and Phobia Workshop – Edition 3."

The body and the mind need relaxation in order to recover from the stresses of everyday life so it's unwise for any of us to ignore this necessity. But for those of us who are afflicted with Anxiety Disorders it's imperative that we incorporate it into our lives as a practical part of our recovery plan.

Practical Measure Seven – Distraction

The mind absorbing nature of Anxiety Disorders will usually keep the sufferer from focusing on anything else except their fear, their physical symptoms or the mental pain and anguish that OCD obsessions create. It's important to learn how to use the tool of distraction no matter how much the disorder tries to insert itself into your every waking hour. It's hard to imagine that it's even possible to be distracted from the symptoms of anxiety when it's extremely intense, but my experience has proven to me that distraction definitely works.

Choosing to engage in a distracting activity can only be achieved by a determined effort. When an Anxiety Disorder is at its peak, an individual will not only doubt their ability to be distracted but will feel compelled to give all their mental attention to whatever threat the anxiety has latched on to. When a person forces themselves to engage in distracting activities, they will find that doing so offers them some measure of relief, even if only for a brief while.

An instance of this in my own experience happened during that miserable period of anxiety and Religious OCD that I wrote about earlier. I had been suffering for quite some time, but some days were far worse than others. One of those bad days happened to coincide with a meeting that I was to have with some other family members to plan a shower for my niece. I was in "basket case" mode and felt sure that I wouldn't be able to sit through that meeting let alone contribute anything to it. I spent hours debating with myself over whether I should go or not. "What if I couldn't hide my mental state?" (This is the point where guts and grit will serve a person well.) Everything in me was fighting against going. I wanted to stay home, curl up in a ball in my bedroom and hide. Instead, I made the decision to shove back against the grain of my anxiety, suck it up and go. I did my best to look my best. I curled my hair, put on my makeup, picked out a nice outfit, grabbed a clipboard and headed out.

When I first got there, I began to doubt my decision, but every time the anxiety pushed me to flee I stood up to it and stayed my ground. I forced myself to ignore the knot in my stomach. I paid no attention to the trembling I felt in my muscles. I accepted the hot flushing that I knew was evident on my face and neck. But mostly I turned away from the intrusive accusations of my OCD and forced myself to focus on what I could do to contribute toward making my nieces shower special. I listened intently to the other's ideas and eventually begin to offer up some of my own. I took notes on everything we decided on. As the meeting wore on I suddenly noticed that I was feeling much more relaxed and that I hadn't been ruminating about my obsessions during that time. It felt good to behave normally. It felt good to know that I could function in a competent manner even when I was in the midst of a really bad episode of OCD. Even though it was only a brief respite, I'd experienced some measure of relief from the intensity of the anxiety.

Distraction is very helpful when it's used as a method to put off the compulsive activity of OCD. Some things that have been really helpful to me are those which require me to be mentally focused. This might include activities such as playing a game of Tetris or doing a crossword puzzle. But even talking on the phone with a good friend and really tuning in to what's going on in their life, asking them questions and showing concern or support for whatever they may be going through can provide a way to distract yourself from the self-absorbing nature of your disorder.

It's important for each individual to work at discovering what sort of distracting activities are beneficial to them and in doing so they will find that they are employing one more very useful tool in learning to manage their disorder. It's key to realize that when employing this tool against the mental rumination of OCD that you won't feel like engaging in the distracting activity, but that is exactly the reason that you must force yourself to do it. Then, when you've had a few successes, in that the distracting activity has actually provided a measure of relief, you will feel more and more motivated to employ it in the future. If you're not willing to try, then you will be missing out on something that would greatly benefit you.

The most productive way to manage Anxiety Disorders is to take advantage of as many proven strategies as possible. In doing so, you will enhance and speed up your recovery process. Every chronic illness requires disciplined management. Anxiety Disorders are no different. It's also a good idea to explore the plethora of educational materials that are available. You can begin by looking into some of the recommended reading listed at the back of this book. But before you do that, I hope you'll finish *this* book. The next chapter is, in my opinion, the most important one of the whole book. Its main theme involves learning to embrace your Anxiety Disorder as a purposeful and life enriching experience.

So now you may be thinking; "is she serious? All the time I've been reading this book thinking that this woman might have some measure of common sense only to discover that she's a total nutjob! I want to be rid of this stupid disorder and now she's going to try and tell me to "embrace it?!"

At this point I hope your curiosity wins out over your irritation with me and that you'll run the risk of turning the page to find out what I'm driving at. I dare you!

1. "The Anxiety Cure," Dr. Archibald Hart, Word Publishing, Nashville, TN, Page 80, Paragraph 6.
2. "The Anxiety and Phobia Workbook," Dr. Edmund J. Bourne, PH.D., New Harbinger Publications, Page 97, Paragraph 1.
3. "Praise Moves," Laurette Willis, Harvest House Publishers.
4. "The Anxiety and Phobia Workbook," Dr. Edmund J. Bourne, PH.D., New Harbinger Publications, Page 333, Paragraph 2.
5. "The Anxiety Cure," Dr. Archibald Hart, Word Publishing, Nashville, TN, Page 192, Paragraph 2.
6. "The Quotable Lewis," Wayne Martindale and Jerry Root – Editors, Tyndale House Publishers, Inc., Page 557, #1401
7. Romans 12:3 (NIV), (Italics/emphasis mine)

CHAPTER 8

PURPOSEFUL AFFLICTION

C.S. Lewis: "God whispers to us in our pleasures, speaks in our conscience, but shouts in our pain: it is His megaphone to rouse a deaf world." 1.

To COMMENT THAT all is not well regarding the human condition is most assuredly an understatement. Everyone with the ability to think and reason will admit that there's an awful lot that seems to have gone wrong on this planet and that living within a world so marred carries with it the inevitable encounter with personal pain. To take up this topic in an effort to explain *why* there is pain and how it can be reconciled with the concept of a loving and well-intended God would require that I write another book within *this* book.

It is not, however, the purpose of this book to cover such a deep and weighty subject. There are other's far more qualified to do so. What I *will* say regarding this, is that for me, the experience of affliction and pain provides just one of the many pieces of evidence that the world has great need of a Savior – a rescuer. Furthermore, we cannot grasp the meaning of things having gone bad in the first place, unless we understand that "in the beginning," they were good. 2. The work of God in this world is actually a saving and recovery process. That process isn't just a blanketed sort of thing which, in the end, will heal every aspect of creation, but included within that process is the personal saving and recovery of the individual human being.

My own experience with pain and, in particular, the pain of my Anxiety Disorder is that it's been a springboard whereby I've gained a deeper understanding of the character of God and a strengthening of my relationship with Him as He is working to bring about my own recovery. I call this experience a "purposeful affliction" and this concept will be the focus of the remainder of this chapter.

Although willfully choosing to indulge in sinful or destructive behaviors will definitely bring about painful consequences, this is not the type of pain to which this chapter is devoted. Instead, my focus will be on the type of pain that comes into our lives even when we aren't in active and purposeful rebellion against God and His laws. Jesus's own words, as well as the testimony of the scriptures, refer to this kind of pain in the following ways:

"In this world you will have trouble."

"Do not be surprised by the painful trial you are suffering, a righteous man may have many troubles", and "I consider that our present sufferings are not worth comparing to the glory that shall be revealed in us." 3.

So it is obviously clear that these types of trials and afflictions *will* come into our lives, but the reasons for them differ from the pain and suffering which is often the consequence of destructive or sinful choices that we make. Once again the scripture provides an answer as to what some of the reasons are for our experiencing this kind of pain:

"Consider it pure joy, my brothers, whenever you face trials of many kinds, because you know that the testing of your faith develops perseverance. Perseverance must finish its work so that you may be mature and complete, not lacking anything."

"And the God of all grace, who called you to His eternal glory in Christ, after you have suffered a little while will himself restore you and make you strong, firm and steadfast."

"To keep me from being conceited – there was given me a thorn in my flesh." 4.

For the Christian with an anxiety disorder, it can be particularly difficult to see how this type of affliction could produce any of the positive outcomes mentioned above. Yet there really *are* valuable things to be gained from the experience of living with an Anxiety Disorder. John Bunyan suffered many afflictions in his lifetime and while it's true that he was sorely persecuted for his public preaching through imprisonment, the reason for *that* experience of suffering was more easily understood by him as an occasion of "being persecuted for righteousness." 5.

But the main focus of Mr. Bunyan's book, "Grace Abounding", was to relate his experiences and struggles with the painful affliction of OCD. Although he didn't have the luxury of having a diagnosis for his disorder, he did understand it to be an affliction that brought much pain and suffering into his life. At the very end of this transparent account concerning how this affliction impacted his life, he takes the time to list the benefits he'd gained through his suffering:

"These things I continually see and feel and am afflicted and oppressed with; yet the wisdom of God doth order them for my good:

1. They make me abhor myself.
2. They keep me from trusting my heart.
3. They convince me of the insufficiency of all inherit righteousness.
4. They show me the necessity of flying to Jesus.
5. They press me to pray unto God.
6. They show me the need I have to watch and be sober.
7. And provoke me to look to God through Christ to help me and carry me through this world." 6.

When I read those words, I was greatly encouraged by them because I too was learning how God was using my Anxiety Disorder to get me to focus on Him, His grace, His power and His sufficiency. I was learning that God had a purpose in allowing me to live with this disorder – not that getting to that place was easy. There were lots of confusing and faulty notions that I had to get past first. I'm sure that this has been the experience of most Christians who suffer from Anxiety Disorders. The first and foremost reason for this is that the disorder is often wrongfully linked to attitudes of worry, such as a lack of faith in the provisions of God, rather than being attributed to a very real and very painful affliction. Yet it is interesting to note that worry isn't the only thing that people with Anxiety Disorders are accused of. They are also accused of engaging in what is referred to as "the sin of fear." I've found this difficult to understand because fear is most generally understood to be an instinctive response. So there also appears to be some faulty notions concerning the common experience of fear which even falls outside of the realm of an Anxiety Disorder.

I would like to touch on some of those faulty notions before going on so that the person with an Anxiety Disorder would understand that while the emotion of fear isn't something that they are able to prevent, they can, however, make a choice as to what they do in response to it.

Anxiety Disorders And The Spirit Of Fear

I've yet to meet anybody who doesn't have some sort of physical ailment or challenging affliction that crops up during their life. None of us welcome it when it comes. Most of us struggle to understand why it's happening to us, how God expects us to respond to it and how any good can come of it. Every person who lives with an Anxiety Disorder and doesn't understand that it's a valid affliction, uncaused by a sinful choice, will go through a great deal of self-blame and confusion as they attempt to understand how their intense feelings of fear aren't in some way related to the sin of worry.

I went through this too and I'm sure that someone else will also have struggled with trying to comprehend how their experience with "the spirit of fear" even in seemingly non-threatening situations isn't in some way sinful. It' seems like it must surely be their fault. After all, *they* are the one who is feeling the fear as in a panic attack or thinking the disturbing thought as in the case of OCD. But, as covered earlier in this book, it's not the *presence* of the thoughts that are the problem, but the misfiring in the brain that causes the thoughts to *seem* frightening and urgent. It's important to reaffirm that.

I wrote earlier of the intense sting that the following portion of scripture caused to me during those long days of emotional distress when I first became severely afflicted by my Anxiety Disorder; "For God has not given us a spirit of fear but of power and of love and of a sound mind." 7. I felt deeply ashamed at my inability to wrench myself from the grip of "the spirit of fear." And although I came through that long bout of anxiety stronger in my faith, I never really fully grasped the lesson that this portion of scripture held for me until I had the opportunity to revisit it and contemplate it while in a period of remission from my disorder.

A good starting point for understanding what this scripture means is to touch on what is *doesn't* mean. The first thing it doesn't mean is that if you experience fear in any way shape or form that you are, at that very moment, choosing to sin.

Quite some time ago I was taking part in a discussion in an adult Sunday school class which centered on the topic of worry. In that discussion, it was suggested that any or all experiences of fear or anxiety were to be acknowledged as sin and immediately confessed. This really shook me up quite a bit because, for the person undergoing a bad flare of an Anxiety Disorder, this confessing would have to go on 24/7. In response to this suggestion, I began to try and make an illustrative point by sharing with the class that every single time I got up to sing a solo in church, I experienced a huge surge of anxiety. Before I could get any further on in what I was about to say about that, the Pastor who had been sitting in on the class discussion interrupted me and curtly reprimanded me by quoting: "God has not given us the spirit of fear." 7. I could tell by the way he said it that he was faulting me for feeling anxious before I got up to sing. I didn't feel it would be appropriate for me to challenge him in front of the members of his flock so I just sank back into my chair, flushed with the familiar sting of hives that I usually get when I speak up in a public setting. I just let it go, but God was gracious to me at that very moment in that sitting right next to me was a man who had previously spoken with me concerning his own experiences with Panic Disorder. At that moment he leaned in and whispered into my ear; "It's okay Mitzi. If Pastor knew what it was like to have a panic attack, he wouldn't be saying this to you right now." If that Pastor hadn't interrupted me, *this* is what I'd planned on saying; I would have shared that it's not the presence of fear that's the problem but rather what I choose to do in response to it. When I get up to sing the fear and anxiety always accompany me, but they don't rule me. I give myself up to God in obedience to offer up my weak vessel for His use and depend upon His strength and His Spirit to minister through me. I don't allow my weakness, "the spirit of fear," to stop me from trusting in His power. And, He has always been faithful to demonstrate that power in such a way that I've been very aware that it's only in His strength that I am able to sing His praises in front of a congregation.

To insist that every time a person experiences a surge of fear or anxiety that they are actively choosing to sin falls very far off the mark of what that portion of scripture teaches.

Obedience is about choices and an instinctive fear response which is prompted by the fight or flight center of our brains is not a chosen activity.

The experience of fear and anxiety is common to the human condition and is actually necessary for our survival in a world so fraught with danger. While it is true that for some of us, this fight or flight response is firing off in an exaggerated or inappropriate way, as in the case of Anxiety Disorders, for all others it will fire off in response to any dangerous scenario. If this weren't the case, then we wouldn't be able to give a definition for the word, "courage". How is one to say that they have acted courageously if fear wasn't forcing them to *be* courageous? If I see a car on fire and someone inside crying out for help and I'm the only one around who may be able to pull them from that fiery inferno, I guarantee you that I will feel fear if I choose to risk my life in an attempt to rescue them. Every soldier who has fought on the front lines of combat has felt fear and every one of those soldiers who choose to soldier on in that setting is demonstrating courage in the face of fear. So the idea that when we face frightening situations our faith will erase all feelings of fear is pretty outlandish.

I like C.S. Lewis's take on this when he wrote that; "The act of cowardice is all that matters, the emotion of fear, is in itself no sin." 8.

The next even wilder notion that some have suggested is that if you experience fear or the "spirit of fear," in frightening situations that you are being inwardly influenced by demonic activity. Yet the apostle Paul, when he wrote these words to young Timothy never made reference to needing to cast the demon of fear out of Timothy before he would be able to appropriate the gift of teaching for the furtherance of the gospel. It's absurd to suggest that Paul would purposely select or encourage a person who was demonically influenced to "devote *himself* to preaching and teaching" or "to not neglect *his* gift, given to *him* through a prophetic message when the body of elders laid their hands on *him*."9.

It is a disturbing thing that people should give Satan so much credit for every single trouble, affliction or weakness that they might encounter to the point that their fear or trepidation concerning *his* activities are greater than their confidence in the power of God. I can imagine that Satan is pleased by extreme responses at either end of the scale. He might like it very much when people disregard or ignore the truth that he is active and warring against the plans and purposes of God and he might also be quite pleased when people are so consumed by or afraid of what he might do to them that they are continually focused on him rather than on God.

I've heard and read many errant views in Christian communities which attribute the presence of an Anxiety Disorder to one of two things; sinful attitudes or demonic influences. I've heard accusations being flung out in such a way, that those who are afflicted have actually been accused of doing the work of Satan. Both of these faulty and uneducated views are counterproductive as well as harmful to those who are suffering from an Anxiety Disorder.

Having touched on what Paul's reference to "the spirit of fear" 7 is *not* about, next I want to move on to what it *is* about.

Earlier in this book I made reference to my having to get over myself before I could understand what Paul was expounding on in this portion of scripture. As I studied these verses, I felt like I could relate to Timothy in that he also needed to get over himself in order for God to appropriate him for service.

The best way to understand scripture is to study it in its proper context. To do that it's important to look at the verses that are connected to the one being studied. Here's that same portion of Scripture in its proper context.

"I have been reminded of your sincere faith which first lived in your grandmother Lois and in your mother Eunice and, I am persuaded, now lives in you also. For this reason I remind you to fan into flame the gift of God, which is in you through the laying on of hands. For God did not give us a spirit of timidity, but a spirit of power, of love and of self-discipline." 10.

In this scripture, Paul is firstly acknowledging that Timothy's faith in Christ is sincere and alive. Secondly, in light of that acknowledgment Paul is encouraging Timothy to take hold of and appropriate the gift of God which Paul had previously imparted to him as an "apostolic grant of authority" to teach and preach the gospel. 11. Paul is urging Timothy to "get at it!" He wants him to begin his work while at the same time reminding him that it would be God's Spirit and not his which would enable him to carry out this ministry. This is a scripture of *contrast*. The contrast is between Timothy's spirit, which made him feel a sense of inadequacy and fear for this task and the indwelling Spirit of God which would provide the necessary ingredients for him to accomplish the work. Those ingredients which the Spirit would supply were, "power, love, and self-discipline." We know that Timothy was young; "Don't let anyone look down on you because you are young." 12

Timothy may have felt intimidated or shy to teach people much older than himself. He was likely struggling with this and, therefore, hesitant about moving forward in his ministry. He also knew that to do so might include the very real threat of beatings, imprisonment and maybe even death. Paul was, after all, writing to Timothy from the inside of a jail cell; "Don't be ashamed of me His prisoner, and of this gospel. I was appointed a herald and an apostle and a teacher. That is why I am suffering as I am." 13. So Timothy was well aware of what could happen as he moved forward to carry on in the teaching and preaching of that same gospel. Even admitting that he was well acquainted with Paul carried with it the potential for persecution.

This wasn't the first time that Paul had written to Timothy urging him to step up to the plate. In an earlier letter to Timothy, he admonished him by saying, "do not neglect your gift" and "be diligent in these matters, give yourself wholly to them so that everyone can see your progress." 14.

Timothy had to get over himself by switching his focus from his weaknesses, his feelings of inadequacy and the natural tendencies of his old nature to lay hold of and focus on the grace and sufficiency of Christ in him to accomplish the work that God had prepared for him to do. Timothy also suffered from frequent bouts of illness as acknowledged by Paul when he told him; "Stop only drinking water, and use a little wine because of your stomach and your frequent illnesses." 15. *(Wait a second…Paul believed in using medicine?! Shocking!)*

Paul was the perfect person to encourage Timothy in this regard as he too had struggled with his own weaknesses and afflictions. He had battled with the notion that his weaknesses and afflictions were things that had to be removed before he would be able to carry out his ministry on behalf of the Gospel. He spoke openly about this. He explained what it taught him about himself as well as what it taught him about the sufficiency of Christ in him when he penned his letter to the Corinthian believers. It was Paul's personal testimony that encouraged me the most as I began to consider that God's grace was also sufficient for me and that His power could be more perfectly demonstrated in and through my own affliction.

In the past, I had visualized the apostle Paul as a confident, potent and intimidating genius. I couldn't imagine that I would dare to even strike up a conversation with someone as well spoken and imposing as he seemed to be in my mind's eye. Yet the more I read about him in the letters he wrote, I began to see that the reason Paul had such a powerful and brilliant testimony wasn't because of who *he was* but because of who *God was* in and through him. I began to see things that I hadn't noticed before in his writings and those things stood out to me very relatable ways. He suddenly became more *human* to me, and to my surprise even as human as I was. It was in that process of uncovering the human side of Paul that I began to see just how amazing the power of God is.

I'm not suggesting that Paul or even Timothy for that matter were afflicted with an Anxiety Disorder as the scriptures aren't specific as to what their weaknesses and afflictions were. What I *am* saying is that no matter what their weaknesses or afflictions were, that God was not impeded by those things. It's through their testimony that I've come to learn that God is not impeded by my afflictions either, no matter what they may be. Yet, further on in my searching into all of this I was to make the discovery that it wasn't just a matter of God not being impeded by my afflictions, but that my afflictions were also purposeful. It turned out that that they were the very things which God could use to cause me to be more pliant within His hand. So now I am able to say most confidently, that God's grace is sufficient for me not *in spite* of my Anxiety Disorder but actually *because* of it. To get to that place of understanding, I first had to see Paul, a servant of Jesus Christ, through a different lens than I ever had before.

The Apostle Paul: Frightened, Weak, And Afflicted

To tell the truth, in the past if someone had dared to describe the apostle Paul to me in terms such as these, it would have ticked me off. I would have likely confronted them in this way; "How dare you say such a thing as that? Paul was one of God's most courageous, bold and powerful servants." But in saying something like that, I had never taken the time to consider what the things were that made courage a necessity, or what it was that caused him to be such a powerful servant. Was it only his circumstances?

He endured some incredible trials and hardships but when he was in those circumstances did courage come easily to him? Was it in his inborn nature to be courageous? These were the kind of questions that were in my mind as I began to search out the question; who was Paul – the *human* Paul? I wondered; "Was there a sharp contrast between Paul the human and the Spirit of Christ in him?" As I began to ponder all of this, I remembered that I still hadn't fully comprehended what God meant when he told Paul; "My grace is sufficient for you." 16.

One thing that turned my old assumptions upside down regarding Paul was his own description of himself and his inner feelings which he shared concerning his first visit to the Corinthian believers. He said; "When I came to you, brothers, I did not come with eloquence or superior wisdom as I proclaimed to you the testimony about God. For I resolved to know nothing while I was with you except Jesus Christ and Him crucified. I came to you in *weakness* and *fear* and with much trembling. My message and my preaching were not with wise and persuasive words, but with a demonstration of the Spirit's power, so that your faith might not rest on men's wisdom, but on God's power". 17.

I found it quite astonishing to see how willing and transparent Paul was in sharing, that when he first came to speak to them, he felt so weak and fearful that it made him physically tremble. I could relate to that because every time I speak up in a public setting my fear response is so intense that I experience physical trembling. Paul was obviously very aware of his own inadequacy for the work of the gospel. But that sense of inadequacy did not lead to avoidance of the task that lay ahead of him. Instead, he moved forward determined to depend solely on "the Spirit's power" to share the gospel.

I'm not sure whether the purpose for him feeling this way was revealed to him before, during or after his trip. I do know that God definitely had a purpose in allowing Paul to experience this kind of weakness as he shared the gospel. I know that because of two little words tucked within the narrative of these verses. Those two words are; "so that". I've learned that whenever I see those two words in the context of something I'm studying that I need to pay attention because they show forth the intentional purposes of God in whatever setting they appear.

So, as Paul openly revealed his experience of weakness, fear and trembling, he followed it up with the *purpose*, or the "so that" for God allowing him to feel that way. He made it very clear that the only way he could be appropriated for this task was in the "Spirit's power, *so that their* faith might not rest on men's wisdom, but on God's power." 17.

Suddenly as I looked at this scripture it struck me that there was a definite purpose in Paul's experience of fear, weakness and trembling. It was exactly *because* he felt that way that he was keenly aware of his own inadequacy for the task that lay ahead of him and *because* he felt that way he was forced to depend solely on the power of the Holy Spirit rather than on his own strength. This all happened *so that* the Corinthian believers would understand that Paul's message was not his own, nor was it delivered in his own strength, but rather it was the message of God being delivered through a humble, weak - yet willing servant as empowered by God. This wasn't just a one-time eureka moment in the life of Paul. It was something that he would carry with him and be reminded of throughout his ministry.

Later on in another letter to the Corinthian believers he spoke again about his weaknesses and afflictions. This time, he willingly shared with them concerning his struggle with a particularly painful "thorn in the flesh" and how he wrestled to understand how it fit into God's plans and purposes for him. For a time, he focused on getting rid of it. He likely felt that he couldn't go on with that sort of pain and weakness. He may have thought that it had to be removed before he would be able to be an effective servant of God. He may have thought that the removal of it would be a testimony to God's healing power. I really don't know all the things that went through his mind. I only know what my own reactions would have been. One thing I *do* know is that he was desperate to be rid of it.

The appearance of this "thorn" came on the heels of a mysterious and glorious experience he had which he described as "visions and revelations from the Lord." 18 Paul said; "In order to keep me from being conceited because of these surpassingly great revelations, there was given me a thorn in my flesh, a messenger of Satan, to torment me. Three times I pleaded with the Lord to take it away from me. But he said to me, 'my grace is sufficient for you, for my power is made perfect in weakness.' Therefore, I will boast all the more gladly about my weaknesses, *so that* Christ's power may rest on me." 19.

Before moving on to consider how Paul's thorn was purposeful, I would like to touch on his prayers in which he pleaded with the Lord to remove his thorn.

It would be wholly dishonest for me to say that I never have in my past or present circumstances asked the Lord to remove my Anxiety Disorder. Nor would I suggest that others should refrain from making that same petition. I say this because God is the only one who is truly able to determine whether our thorns should stay or go. In thinking about this; I'm reminded of how Job, after undergoing the first onslaughts of his horrific trial made this comment; "The Lord gave and the Lord has taken away; may the name of the Lord be praised." 20. While I don't pretend to know the mind of Job, I can't help but think that he was acknowledging the sovereignty of God concerning the things that are given and taken from us. I think Job was able to bless the name of the Lord because although he couldn't understand the "why's" concerning these events, he did understand that God is good and, therefore, He must have had a purpose for allowing him to experience those losses.

When I consider my own experiences with regard to the things God gives to me or takes away from me, I must acknowledge that it isn't the loss of or the receiving of the thing that matters as much as it is the effect it has on my entire being. How does it change me? I've come to believe that the Lord's giving and taking away always has a purpose. This purpose can often be that the taking away is done to make room in me for the giving of something better. When God enters our lives, He is not content with mediocrity or underachievement. As a loving Father, He wishes for His children to grow, to mount up new heights, to be lifted up. But just as little children often resist or rebel at the loving intentions of a parent we also resist and rebel when God is in the process of growing us. There may be things in us which fight against that process which He needs to alter or remove. Or it could be that we've shoved down the good things which He has intended to use and He must lift those things back up. I see the following verse in the book of Isaiah, not just as an example of the promise of God to reclaim and restore His creation to all that He intended for it to be, but also as a way for me to understand the transforming work He is doing in my person. "Make straight in the wilderness a highway for our God. Every valley shall be raised up, every mountain and hill made low; and the rough ground shall become level, the rugged places a plain. And the glory of the Lord will be revealed." 21.

There are certainly things that I've shoved into the valley of my life, mountains that I've given prominence, paths that I've twisted by my actions and rough places which have come about due to my own rebellious nature. All of this has created a landscape which isn't fitting for the life of Christ in me. All of this must be transformed and rearranged in order that the glory of the Lord can be revealed in me.

Therefore, when I approach God with my petitions, I need to be aware that ultimately He must decide what needs to stay and what needs to go so that I can become the person He created me to be.

As I pondered these things, I penned the following poem as a reminder that I need to trust God as He directs the events of my life, I must trust that He is working to bring about changes in me which will benefit me and draw me further and further into the realm of His kingdom purposes.

THOUGHTS ON PRAYER
Do my prayers to God cause any change?
Or can they, His purpose, rearrange?
What's caused this distance I perceive?

Which one of us has taken leave?
Who's left the road? Whose feet have slipped?
Who's placed these rocks on which I've tripped?
Who's thrown up hedges filled with thorns,
His godly feet to scar and scorn?
Who's made it hard for Him to grace,
My life with His all caring face?
Oh yes, there *is* great need for change –
It's *my* landscape He must rearrange,
To make it fitting for His feet,
And *this* is why in prayer we meet.
And in those prayers He's teaching me,
This rightful and foremost of pleas;
"God, let it be for Jesus sake,
That I to you my prayers do make,
And not for selfishness alone,
Let me approach your loving throne.
Instead, align my will with Thine,
So that you may reign in me divine.

Returning to the topic of Paul's thorn, I must say that this passage of scripture has comforted and encouraged me more than any other regarding my own "thorn" of living with a chronic disorder.

First off I notice that Paul's affliction was purposeful. The purpose lay in the fact that God was aware that Paul would be tempted toward an attitude of conceitedness. This was because God chose to communicate great truths to Paul through glorious and miraculous revelations. This wasn't just a rare event; it was also an indescribably high privilege and honor. It would be very hard indeed for Paul not to have an inner attitude that went something like this; "God must be very pleased with me that He would entrust me with this vision of glories that He has kept hidden from others." Suddenly he may have been tempted toward an attitude of self-importance. It would be very hard for most of us to resist this inherent tendency toward pride if this had been our experience. In light of this, Paul needed something to remind him of who he really was; a frail human vessel- "a jar of clay". 22. He also needed something which would, in effect, force him to rely on the sufficiency of God's grace rather than his own strength.

The next thing I noticed was the role of Satan in this event. Paul referred to his "thorn" as a "Messenger of Satan." 18 When I read this, I recalled how God permitted Satan to afflict and torment His servant Job. At the end of that account, I saw Job standing firm in his resolution to continue trusting in his God; "Though He slay me yet will I trust Him." 23.

Time and time again the scriptures reveal the activity of Satan as he attempts to thwart God's plans by attacking his servants. And time and time again we see how God takes those attacks and makes good use of them in turning them around into something whereby He accomplishes His plans and purposes. Nothing can impede or interfere with His larger kingdom purposes or with His purposes in the individual lives of those who belong to Him. Satan's intentions and motives in oppressing Paul were definitely meant for evil, but you'll notice that Paul, while he *does* acknowledge Satan's activity, moved very quickly past that fact directly to what was most important which was the activity of God in his life. His focus was fixed on what God was accomplishing in him due to the thorn rather than the fact that Satan was attacking him. I find this to be a great example of where my focus should be when Satan attacks. Rather than being intensely focused and horrified that Satan is attacking, I need to be shifting my focus directly to God with an expectant and trusting heart.

The next thing that I noticed was that Paul's thorn wasn't some mildly annoying event. Paul used the word, "torment" to describe the effect it had on him. This thing was somehow so intensely painful and distressing for Paul that he "pleaded with God to remove it", not just once, but on three separate occasions. He really wanted this thing gone. I could totally relate to that. The time and effort I had spent in pleading with God to remove my Anxiety Disorder was not only lengthy; it was also a period of great distress and torment. I could hear God telling me; "My grace is sufficient for you", but I just couldn't grasp what He meant by that. How was it sufficient? What could His grace do for me? Couldn't it just wipe out the feelings of terror? How in the world could I move forward or be of any further use to God with something so distressing plaguing me? I figured that once I'd learned what it was that He was trying to teach me that He'd surely completely remove my thorn, but just like Paul I really needed to grasp the purpose of the thorn before I could learn to embrace it.

Just about now you may be shocked or irritated with me for suggesting that anyone should or could ever "embrace" an affliction like, Panic Disorder or OCD and I need to tell you quite plainly that I completely understand why you'd feel that way. There are still days when I struggle with my decision to embrace my disorder. I grow weary of the chronic waxing and waning of my disorder. I grow weary of myself, of my weakness and my feelings of inadequacy. I want to *feel* strong and confident. Instead, God asks me to give up on those ideas and invites me to depend solely upon Him for those qualities which I am lacking. In doing so, I begin to realize that the affliction is actually something beneficial to me. It's part and parcel of God's dealings in my life and I'm grateful that He's using it to shape and mold me into someone who can fit into His plans. If my confidence, my strength and my adequacy for His work belonged to me, then I'm quite certain I would be getting in His way on a regular basis. The work would cease to be His work and it would become mine. I know that's what I'd be like and have come to realize that this is the reason for His giving me this thorn. It is suitable for me. Its design is custom made in a specific way to address those things in me which need to be altered.

It's taken quite some time for this to happen, but now I am finally able to chime in with Paul when he said; "Therefore I will boast all the more gladly about my weaknesses, so that Christ's power may rest on me. That is why, for Christ's sake, I delight *in* weaknesses, *in* insults, *in* hardships, *in* persecutions, *in* difficulties. For when I am weak, then I am strong." 24.

I would have to say that the uppermost thing I've learned about myself in all of this is that I'm a proud person. As a matter of fact, pride seems to be inherent in my human nature. I don't think a single day goes by where I don't somehow focus on who I am, how I'm doing and what other people may think of me. I'm a very self-conscious person in the worst of ways. In light of this tendency to which I am all too easily inclined I am able to understand how my Anxiety Disorder is actually helpful to me. It continually prompts me to not only look to God for strength and power but to acknowledge that it's only *in* His strength that I'm able to accomplish anything for His kingdom purposes. My Anxiety Disorder has revealed the real me to myself in ways I could have never imagined and in seeing the real me I am able to look to God to rearrange those things in me which inhibit the life of Christ from flowing freely through me. And that makes my disorder purposeful.

Even in writing this book I've been continually aware of the inner leanings of my nature toward pride; *If it fails, you'll look like an idiot for even thinking that you could do something like this. If it succeeds there will likely be some folk who mock or berate you for writing it. Then you might feel the need to defend your character. Others might praise you for writing it and when or if they do you will like it and you might begin to pat yourself on the back.* All these inner leanings go completely against the real purpose in my writing this book and if I pet them or allow them to grow unchecked, then I'll lose sight of who I really am and the proper role of Christ in me. I won't be acknowledging His strength, grace, and power, but instead I'd be attributing any good that comes of it to me.

I figure the only way to keep my pride in check is to be continually *aware* of its presence. If I begin to think that I've conquered it, then sadly I can quickly become proud about that; "I'm a very humble individual and I take pride in that fact."

This verse comes to my mind a lot when I contemplate my tendency toward pride; "So, if you think you are standing firm, be careful that you don't fall." 25. It's a good reminder of how easily the attitude of pride can trip us up. I finally ended up penning a poem to tuck away in my mind as a reminder to be on my guard for this tendency.

PRIDE
There is a road within called Pride,
On which my feet with ease do glide.
A well-worn path so often trod,
That turns my heart away from God.
Sometimes when light comes flooding in,
I recognize this trail of sin,
And turn to take the better way,
And on His road I try to stay.
Then for a while with Him I go,
And feel His presence in me grow.
But then my thoughts will often say;
"How *good* of me to walk this way."
Then I look down to find my feet,
Upon that old familiar street,
That well-worn path of mine called Pride,
On which my feet so easily glide.

The thing that greatly heartens me about such struggles as these is that God is right now in the very process of undoing all the snarled knots of my old nature. I can't imagine what it will be like to finally be rid of them when He calls me home. I wonder how light and free I'll feel to have all of them undone and to finally be able to stop being so self-absorbed, self-conscious and self-promoting? It's hard to picture while I'm in my present state. For now, though, this affliction is definitely something that pushes me away from my pride and self-sufficiency and turns me toward the real source of strength and power which is Christ in me.

As I continued to examine this portion of scripture, one little word stuck out amongst all the rest which has made it even clearer to me that my thorn is something to be embraced. The *little* words in scripture are so important and the more I study the Bible, I am able to see how if you pluck out or change even one of them it can distort the whole meaning of a particular verse. For instance, if you take the word "the" out of the following scripture; "I am *the* way, *the* truth and *the* life" 26. and substitute it with the word "a", suddenly Christ just becomes one of many paths to God instead of the one and only true path to God. Many have done this regarding both the identity of Christ and the reason that He stepped into our world and the consequence of this has been that our society is more pluralistic and varied than ever regarding their concept of who God really is.

In light of the ramifications of this, I always try to pay very close attention to the little words when I'm studying scripture. The little word that became so significant to me in Paul's letter concerning his thorn was the word; "IN". It is used in Paul's relating what God's response was to his plea to have it removed. This is what God said to Paul; "My strength is made perfect *in* weakness." 27. That little word, "IN", just jumped off the page when I read that portion of scripture. I immediately began to think; "Wait a minute, God told Paul that His strength would be made perfect *in* the weakness – the thorn – the affliction, not *out* of it!"

As I was dwelling on this, another scripture came quickly to my mind. This scripture, penned by Paul and found in his letter to the Romans was one that I'd read many times before but suddenly there was a new lesson in it that I'd never considered before.

Paul wrote; "Who shall separate us from the love of Christ? Shall trouble, or hardship, or persecution or famine or nakedness or danger or sword? As it is written; 'For your sake we face death all day long; we are considered sheep to be slaughtered.' No, *in* all these things we are more than conquerors through Him who loved us." 28.

There it was again – "IN all these things". So it would appear that it's actually when we are *in* the throes of any persecution or affliction that God is making us into conquerors rather than when we are *out* of them. Of course this makes perfect sense; why should we need to be a conqueror when there isn't anything to challenge us – anything that actually needs conquering? And of course, God is completely clear that we don't become conquerors by relying on our own strength but once again we can only conquer through the power of Christ in us. I knew this to be true, for when we are at ease and aren't facing a challenging or afflicting circumstance we don't tend to seek out His help. It is all too easy to become self-reliant, self-assured and apathetic toward God. We forget that "it is He who has made us and not we ourselves." 29. *And*, it's just at this point that He must often do something to get our attention in order to put us back into our rightful relationship to Him. In my own life, I've found that when things are going well I forget to look up but as soon as I'm in the pit, I've no choice but to look up. How much better it would be to always look up and depend solely on Him rather than to try and make a go of it on my own.

Living with an Anxiety Disorder has been good for me. It's been the very thing that has kept me looking up and depending on Christ to lay hold of my life so that He could fill and empower me as a vessel made ready for His service. Yet even with the knowledge of this, there still remains some difficult questions such as; "What if when I'm looking up, I feel no comfort because He just seems too far off. What if I can't feel His presence in me or the comfort of His hand upon me? What do I do then?" These were the questions that helped me toward understanding that I cannot depend on my emotions as evidence for or against God's dealings with me. What follows is the invaluable lesson that God taught to me from my experience of living with a disorder that oft times completely robbed me of my emotional reassurance when it came to my standing with Him.

The Volitional Faith Of The Christian With Religious OCD

C.S. Lewis: "Obedience is the key to all doors; feelings come, (or don't come), and go as God pleases. We can't produce them at will and mustn't try." 30.

I really hate referring to this particular manifestation of my OCD as "religious", as I think it falls short of describing the root fear of everyone who is afflicted with it. The root fear is that our *relationship* with our loving God might or could be eternally cut off. It's still the better choice, however, to refer to it in this way when you are seeking professional help for it. Otherwise, a doctor might not really be able to grasp what theme or category of OCD you are struggling with.

There is a Psalm of David which has really encouraged and aided me in being able to press on through those distressing times when my disorder had robbed me of the ability to feel any emotional reassurance concerning my relationship with God: "How long O Lord? Will you forget me forever? How long will you hide your face from me? How long must I wrestle with my thoughts and every day and have sorrow in my heart? How long will my enemy triumph over me? Look on me and answer, O Lord my God. Give light to my eyes, or I will sleep in death; my enemy will say, "I have overcome him," and my foes will rejoice when I fall." 31.

When I read this Psalm, it was as if I, through my own experiences, had written it. It made me weep as I considered each sentence. I too felt that God must surely have turned His back on me. I cried out to Him, but it seemed as if He didn't' hear me. Why wouldn't He answer? I couldn't *feel* my faith in Him as my thoughts attacked and assaulted me relentlessly. I wrestled with them day and night. I felt overwhelmed and desperate for an answer, a sign, a moment of peace or assurance that He had not abandoned me or left me for Satan to do as he pleased with me. My focus was on my disturbing thoughts, my fear, my mental pain, my anguish and all of those things that stood as continual accusers. They made me feel ashamed and conquered. I could picture Satan, (that old liar), gloating over me; "You're done in now! The God you trusted in has abandoned you."

It all made me want to die, except that to die was too dreadful because I feared that to die in that state might mean the ultimate/eternal separation from the only One who could give me life.

But the Psalmist didn't end his message there. I noticed a pause or break in the Psalm and then an entirely different shift in the tone and the message. He goes on: "But I trust in your unfailing love; my heart rejoices in your salvation. I will sing to the Lord, for He has been good to me." 31.

I was confounded by this. Why the shift? What changed? Where were the answers and the explanations for what he'd been going through and what God was up to? There wasn't anything between the first section of the Psalm and the last section that indicated that there had been some sort of change in his circumstances. So what *had* changed? I went back and read it again. It was then that I noticed that the Psalmist had done a complete turnabout in his *focus*.

In the first part of the Psalm his entire focus had been on his circumstances, his fear filled emotions, his suffering, anguish, and confusion. Not only was he intensely focused on all these things, but he was also giving credence to them as evidence that his Lord had turned away and abandoned him to his enemies. It was then that it hit me; *When has it ever been a good idea to define who God is or what He's up to according to my circumstances let alone my fluctuating emotional state?* So I began to think about who God was, who He'd always been and what His Word had to say about His intentions toward me. As I did this, I realized that this was the same thing the Psalmist had done. And in his consideration of who he knew God to be, he made a choice to affirm those things. This was not because his circumstances had changed or his pain had been alleviated but because God is exactly who He says He is and nothing can ever change that. No circumstance, no act of any human, no act of Satan and in my particular case, no strange and confusing emotional state. I too had a choice. I could side with my feelings or I could choose to move forward and press right on through those feelings in order to get to what was really true. While my emotions might not line up to validate that choice, I could still make it. I could still chime in with the Psalmist and say: "I (too) *will* sing to the Lord for He had dealt kindly with me." 31. Not only would I sing to Him and praise Him because of His worthiness, but I would also go to church, read my Bible, pray and do my level best to obey Him. I could do all of these things even *while* I was experiencing those inappropriate surges of fear.

It was then that I began to think again about Job and how he too had no explanation for his suffering. He wasn't privy to the meeting between God and Satan where Satan had been so hoping that if God allowed suffering in Job's life that he would turn away from Him. When all those horrific things began to happen to him, he had many unanswered questions. He also had a lot of accusers who tried to make him feel that he was to blame for his suffering. None of them were right because they were viewing the entire scene through their limited and errant human understanding. They were assuming way too much about the plans and purposes of God in the life of His Servant Job. Job had nothing tangible, no word of reassurance, and no earthly comfort by which he could say: "see this is why I know God loves me." Then just when his pain and suffering couldn't seem to get any worse his closest remaining family member, his wife, offers up this encouraging word; "Curse God and die." 32. The accusations, false assertions and misguided counsel that Job encountered were relentless. When I considered all this I couldn't help but compare it to the relentless false assertions and accusations that my OCD was continually throwing into my face. How in the world did Job hold up under such an onslaught? Two words came to my mind as I contemplated that question; allegiance and obedience.

The scriptures tell us that: "In all this, Job did not sin in what he said." 33. Job never turned away from God or from his affirmation that God could be trusted. He even went so far as to make this proclamation, "Though He slay me, yet will I hope in Him." 34. Later on, he affirms the rock solid assurance of his eternal salvation, not because of his own worthiness but because he knew that it was the redemptive work of God on his behalf that would save him; "I know that my Redeemer lives, and that in the end He will stand upon the earth. And after my skin has been destroyed, yet in my flesh I will see God; I myself will see him with my own eyes – I, and not another." 35. Even further on he shares his anguish at the silence and seeming absence of His God, yet even in that dry and numb condition he still affirms that God is at work and he reveals his steadfast decision to follow Him. He says; "If I go to the east, He is not there; if I go to the west, I do not find Him. But He knows the way that I take; when He has tested me, I will come forth as gold. My feet have closely followed His steps; I have kept to His way without turning aside." 36.

There have been days when the relentless thoughts and haunting emptiness paired with the hollow abandoned feelings that this disorder creates have been so intense that I can't seem to find even the smallest trace of emotional reassurance to bolster my faith. It is just then that I must acknowledge that I still have a choice. I have the choice to walk in obedience and allegiance. I have the choice to chime in with the Psalmist in saying; "I will bless the Lord at *all* times. His praise shall continually be in my mouth." 37.

I realized that I could make the exact same choice as Mr. Bunyan.

Bunyan: "I am for going on and venturing my eternal state with Christ, whether I have comfort here or no; If God doth not come in thought I, I will leap off the ladder even blindfolded into eternity, sink or swim, come heaven, come hell; Lord Jesus, if thou wilt catch me, do; if not I will venture for thy name." 38.

I've learned that no matter how many intrusive thoughts come or how intense the anxiety gets; my will remains intact. When the accusations shout out something like; *you'll be lost forever to hell!* I choose to assert this; "Even in hell I would still praise the name of Christ my Lord."

This kind of faith is volitional. Its foundation does not rest upon circumstances or emotional validation but rather on the solid and unfailing character of God. This is the faith that allows me to "get over myself" with all my weaknesses and feelings of fear and inadequacy. And this is the faith that encourages me to get up and walk! It's the kind of faith that every individual who is afflicted with OCD or any other type of Anxiety Disorder can exercise even in their darkest days.

You may say; "but it hurts so much to walk like this." Yes, it does. But it's in the walking that the pain is eventually healed. Imagine that you had a badly broken leg which, if it were ever to be healed, would require that you go through intensive physical therapy. Imagine that when you went to therapy that those first few steps were so painful that you just wanted to quit. Then imagine the therapist informing you that the only way for that leg to get stronger was for you to put weight on it and move forward. Would you quit? Or would you walk in the knowledge that it would be in the process of that pain filled walking that your leg would eventually be healed?

This is how it is concerning the volitional faith of the Christian with OCD. It may hurt for us to walk, but walking is the only choice which will heal us. So we pick up our Bibles, even though to do so might stir up our fear. We approach God in prayer, even though when we do the OCD shouts out accusations in our heads. We go to God's house to learn and to worship even though when we do the OCD might flare up and take things in the sermon and twist them round to accuse us. We sing His praises even though we feel unworthy to even speak His name.

This is how we exercise the legs of our volitional faith and the more we exercise them, the stronger they'll get and the stronger they become, the less pain we will feel. We don't avoid the things that stir up the OCD we walk right into them. And eventually the walking will turn into running and the terrified feelings will fade away and the joy of our salvation will return to us. But we cannot get there unless we are willing to endure that painful and sometimes very prolonged period of walking while the OCD is attacking.

The greatest example of volitional faith was manifested in the willing suffering of Christ on our behalf. It's far greater than anything we could ever boast in because we don't *choose* our afflictions. They happen to us. We never see the cruel road up ahead in the way that He did.

In the book of Isaiah, He says: "Therefore I have set my face like a flint." 39.

He said this regarding His attitude concerning the suffering that lay ahead of Him as He willingly walked toward the cross on our behalf. He was obedient, "to death – even the death on a cross."40. And those of us who know *why* He did it are astounded at such love and grace. The wonder and depth of what He did for us can never be fully comprehended. "This is love; not that we loved God, but that He loved us and sent His Son as an atoning sacrifice for our sins." 41.

So while we choose to obey because quite clearly He is worthy of our obedience, he chose to obey because of who He is; a God of perfect love, grace, and mercy. This knowledge of who He is, assures us that we can trust Him and because we trust Him we can obey Him. Please get this: To trust Him *is* to obey Him and to *obey* Him is to demonstrate that we do indeed trust Him. They go hand in hand in the manifestation of the life of faith.

One day as I was thinking about all of this, I was reminded of a beautiful illustration that God had used to teach me more about the harmoniousness of faith, trust, allegiance and obedience. The illustration came to me through the simple trust, loyalty, and obedience of our family dog, Patch.

A Dog Story

Every *good* dog owner who actually loves their dog will be patient all throughout the training process. They will understand the *nature* of their dog. They will correct the dog, not to be mean, but with the intention of making the dog into the sort of animal that can be a trusted and obedient companion for the span of his whole life. In doing so, the dog will reap the benefits of sharing his life with a caring master who not only provides him with food and shelter but also holds a deep love and affection for him. It's really a win, win scenario for the dog *and* his master. The other thing that every good dog owner is aware of is that dealing with a puppy requires a determined effort. You have to really stick with the training process for as long as it takes for the lessons to finally sink in and become natural to the pup. It's really a matter of taking an animal, which if left to his own devices, would never be able to enjoy the benefits of a loving home and helping him to become a beloved and well-fitted member of the family.

When we first brought our adorable English Setter puppy home and gave him the name "Patch", he was pretty much untrained and clueless as to how a dog should behave in the home of his master. He peed on the floor and romped about wildly and recklessly knocking over whatever happened to be in his path. He chewed on whatever he liked, (including our hands), barked and whined whenever he felt like it and the thing he rebelled against the most was the leash.

When we first put his collar on and snapped a leash onto it in an attempt to lead him, he completely balked. He pulled in the opposite direction, flopped down on the floor rolling on his back and took the leash into his mouth to try and gain control of it. It wasn't as if we could sit him down and give him an explanation as to why he needed to learn how to walk on a leash. We could only keep repeating the process of standing him up, removing the leash from his mouth, and giving a few sharp tugs along with vocal commands so that he eventually got the idea that he wasn't in charge and that the leash was to be obeyed.

When he'd cooperate by walking alongside of us for a short distance without straining to get away we'd give him much praise and encouragement – sometimes he'd even get a treat. It wasn't long before he began to understand that the leash meant good things like; going on long walks in the neighborhood or taking a ride in the car, or a visit to Grandma and Grandpa's or best of all getting to go out into the country where the elusive game birds lived. Nothing could equal the joy of stalking and hunting those birds. Patch was made for that very purpose and everything in him yearned for it.

There were so many lessons to be learned both on and off the leash and the person who Patch looked to the most to learn these lessons was his master, my husband, Dennis.

In the process of training, Patch had to learn to obey Dennis even off the leash so that he could eventually take part in the sport of hunting birds. When he finally learned to sit, stay, heel and come within the confines of our fenced back yard, we took him out to the country for his very first lesson in how to behave off leash - in the open field. He needed this lesson because to disobey out in the field could spell disaster for him.

Things were going along fine at first. Dennis had been using a loud police whistle along with vocal commands so that if Patch ran too far ahead of him he could call him back in. We were having a lovely time together as he crisscrossed back and forth through the tall weeds trying to pick up the scent of a bird. But as we went along Patch began to become overconfident and careless. As we approached a corn field, he bull-headedly dove headlong into it ignoring Dennis's blasts on the whistle and his vocal commands to "come!" We ran after him as fast as we could but within just a few moments he was swallowed up by the tall stalks of corn and we had no way of seeing which way he'd went. We kept calling to him, but the both of us were terrified that he might not ever find his way back to us again. As we called, we could hear him yelping somewhere in the midst of the field in anxious fear.

It didn't take long for him to realize that he was lost and suddenly his cocky attitude dissolved and he was reduced to a scared and frantic pup that was desperate to get back to his master. Dennis continued to use both his voice and the whistle and as he did so, it soon became obvious that Patch could hear him and was following his voice. But Dennis wasn't just calling out the word "come," he also used Patch's name in the command as had been his practice all during training. It was always; "Patch sit, Patch stay, Patch come, Patch heel, etc.

As Patch listened and responded to Dennis calling out his name, he was eventually able to navigate his way back to us. I'll never forget that scene when he finally burst out into the open. He raced to Dennis as fast as he could and literally leaped into his arms. Dennis was hugging him and comforting him while Patch, wriggling with joy, covered his face with wet puppy kisses. Dennis wasn't quite ready to let go of him so he chose to carry him back to the car and as we walked back together, Patch fell fast asleep in Dennis' arms. So great was his own feeling of relief and comfort that he just melted into the warm embrace of his master. It was a well-learned lesson for him – one that he never forgot. That was the one and only time he ever went astray when out in the field with Dennis.

Over the years, Patch developed such a deep sense of trust and devotion to Dennis that the occasions where he needed to correct him became rarer and rarer. His level of obedience far exceeded those very few times where he chose to ignore his master. His favored position was to be in a place where he could both see and hear Dennis. He followed him everywhere. He kept his eyes on him and listened intently to every word that Dennis spoke to him. When they played together, he was ecstatic because nothing made him happier than to have the privilege of Dennis's undivided attention. He would even choose a romp with Dennis over a bowl of his favorite food. He had learned that the best and fullest way to be a dog was to be a dog that obeyed and followed a loving master.

The fact that Patch had learned this lesson carried him through some very difficult times as he began to age. The first thing that happened to him was that he began to lose his hearing. This affliction, we thought, would surely rob him of his ability to hunt. But we were so wrong about that. We began to notice that when we took him out in the field he stayed in even closer than before and he constantly did visual checks to keep Dennis within his sights. If he got a bit too far ahead, Dennis had only to lift his hand up and motion for him to come back. We began to notice that he understood Dennis's body language just as well as he understood his spoken commands. That was how careful his observance had been of his master. He knew and understood what his master expected of him. Dennis could get him to sit, stay, come, heel, leave it, and be quiet as well as numerous other commands just by using hand signals.

As his hearing decreased his focus on his master became even more intense. As his eyesight began to dim somewhat with the development of cataracts, he chose to stay in even closer and used his nose in order to assure himself that he was in close proximity to Dennis.

Patch and Dennis were still able to go on long hikes or runs in the country which was something that gave Dennis just as much joy as it did Patch.

Eventually, he developed a serious condition that would rob him of his ability to go out in the field. If he became too overheated or too excited, he would actually begin to suffocate from this condition. On several occasions, Dennis was right at hand to calm him down by petting him and talking soothingly to him and during those times he seemed able to get over the attacks fairly quickly. But there were several other times when Dennis wasn't around that he nearly died before we could get him to our veterinarian. This horrible condition finally robbed him completely of his ability to hunt or to go for long runs and he seemed to suffer greatly from the loss of those things. He wanted so badly to go out with his master but to do so was just too risky.

This really broke all our hearts, but it especially broke Dennis's heart to see his buddy suffer in this way and, therefore, he finally made the painful decision to give Patch back to his creator. Patch was fifteen and a half years old, which for a Setter was a good and ripe old age.

Patch's very last activity on the day of his death was to take a calm and familiar walk with Dennis in the neighborhood. They walked for a mile with Patch's tail beating wildly against his master's leg. He was so full of joy on that walk, but Dennis's heart was heavy with grief knowing that this was the very last time they would walk together at least in this life.

We drove to our vet's office with stricken hearts but also with the knowledge that this was the right choice to make for the sake of our beloved dog. Patch was so calm, so at peace because he was with his master. He obediently climbed up onto the examining table as we discussed what would soon take place with our vet. At first the vet said he should probably give Patch a shot to relax him so that he wouldn't feel any anxiety when he was given that final injection. But as he stood there observing how calm Patch was he commented that for Patch, he didn't think that the first shot would be necessary. Patch was quiet, calm and confident because his eyes were completely locked on Dennis as had been his practice. His confidence wasn't dependent on his circumstances but on his relationship with his master. His tail was lightly thumping the examining table and I swear to you that as he looked up into Dennis's eyes he was smiling.

As the shot went in Dennis's hand was resting on Patch's lovely silken head. He blinked a couple times then just lowered his head, closed his eyes and sighed out his final breath. The tears flowed freely as Dennis gathered his beloved companion into his arms and carried him back out to the car. We took his body out to Dennis's folk's house and buried him just inside the edge of the woods within eyeshot of the house. We did this because he was a dog who loved the outdoors as equally as he loved being a part of a household. Our son Denny helped us dig his grave and we all stood there sobbing but also thanking God for the blessing that Patch had been to all of us.

We've not had another dog since. We tried one time to adopt another English Setter rescue dog and although he looked nearly identical to Patch, he was nothing like him. He didn't know or trust his master in the way Patch did. Therefore, he seemed unable to obey. Perhaps had Dennis raised him up from a puppy he would have learned to trust and obey but he was too far gone in his long-held practices of disobedience for Dennis to be able to get him to change his ways. We regretted having to take him back to the rescue organization, but it had to be done. He was not Dennis's dog. He didn't know his ways. He didn't trust his commands and, therefore, he couldn't enjoy his companionship. Dennis chose instead to enjoy the memories of his beloved Patch.

In thinking about the blessing that Patch had been to all of us, I never realized just how much God would use him to teach me about my relationship with Him. It's those lessons that have stayed with me. It amazes me how God can take the seemingly ordinary experiences in my life and use them to cause me to see Him more clearly. The lessons that I've learned through my observation of Patch and Dennis's relationship were that of Master and servant and trust and obedience.

"Then in fellowship sweet, we will sit at His feet – or we'll walk by His side in the way. What He says we will do. Where He leads, we will go. Never fear only trust and obey. Trust and obey – for there's no other way to be happy in Jesus, but to trust and obey." 42.

Trust And Obey

Many of you who are reading this may be quite familiar with that often sung and well-loved old hymn. Even though I've sung it innumerable times it never really sunk in or spoke to me as profoundly as it did after walking through the difficult and confounding seasons when my Anxiety Disorder was at its most severe. Yet later on it spoke to me with even deeper meaning as I pondered the lessons God had taught me through observing the simple and yet moving example of Patch's trust and obedience toward his master. It was during that time that the deep truth and significance of this hymn really began to hit home.

If you are at all familiar with this hymn, you will note that verses two through four walks us through some very difficult terrains. The hymn writer speaks of "shadows, clouds, doubts, fears, sighs, tears, weighty burdens, sorrows, grief, toil, labor, and sacrifice." Those paths are all too familiar to many of us and when God, our Master, is taking us down them the strain of the leash will often send us into a fit of fear, confusion and doubt.

I am certain that Patch was pretty much clueless as to why he had to wear a collar, why Dennis put a leash on him and most of all why he couldn't just run off in any old direction his canine heart desired. When Dennis first began to teach him how to walk on the lead, his confusion and fear about the whole matter was quite obvious. That's because he was unable to see the big picture. There was absolutely no way for him to grasp why Dennis was restraining him or why he needed to be led. Dennis certainly knew why he was doing it, but for Patch the only choices he had before him were to either submit to the lead or continue to strain against the leash. So what was it that made him choose to obey? The only conclusion that I could come up with was that he was gradually learning that the person at the end of the leash was a "good guy." He was the one who fed him, gave him shelter, stroked him, played with him and even gave him treats. He was learning that he could trust his master.

When I thought about this, especially regarding the confusing and painful circumstances of my Anxiety Disorder, I realized that my encouragement to move forward in obedience wasn't motivated by my focusing on my circumstances or my feelings but rather by my focusing on the person at the end of the leash. That person was my Master, Jesus. He had, after all, not only provided for my needs in so many gracious and loving ways, but He had also demonstrated His love for me by giving His life for me on the cross. "But God demonstrated His own love for us in this: While we were still sinners, Christ died for us."43. If anyone was to be completely and wholly trusted in all circumstances, it had to be Him and Him alone.

I mentioned earlier that a dog left to his own devices would never be able to reap the benefits of a loving home and family. This is quite obvious because a dog left alone without the influence of a master will act like a wild beast without any regard for rules or discipline.

The only way for a dog to enter into a companion relationship with his master is for him to learn the rules of obedience. In the same way – God, because he loves us and wants for us to enter into a love relationship with Him will not leave *us* to ourselves. He must and will often have to use a "collar or leash" to teach us that to trust and obey Him, will in the end benefit us greatly. For we are more fully and completely ourselves when we are rightly related to Him. We are derived from His very being – created by His very hand and, therefore, the place where we are most fully human is in our being rightly related to Him in accordance with His loving intentions for us. If we choose to bull-headedly run in the opposite direction of His plans and purposes for us or if we attempt to "chew through the leash" we will be cutting ourselves off from the very source of our being.

While it may be true that we don't or won't necessarily like the strain of the leash because obedience training can be hard, we can know that the one who holds the leash has our best interests at heart. "And we know that in all things God works for the good of those who love him, who have been called according to His purpose."44. "Trust in the Lord with all your heart and lean not on your own understanding. In all your ways acknowledge Him and he will make your paths straight." 45.

It was only when Patch learned to just trust and follow Dennis's leading, although incapable of seeing the big picture, that he was able to enjoy a walk without Dennis continually having to tug on the leash. In this same way, it is only when I learn to acknowledge *who* it is that is directing my paths that I'm able to move forward with a measure of calm and confidence.

What I've also discovered is that my learning to trust is born out of my willingness to obey just as my willingness to obey is born out of knowing that I can trust the One, who is asking me to obey. In this way, the two are always linked together.

Each and every path, even the dark and scary ones that we come through together only serve to deepen and solidify my relationship with God and the consequence of this is that my allegiance to Him as my loving Master becomes as natural as breathing. "Who among you fears the Lord and obeys the word of His servant? Let him who walks in the dark, who has no light, trust in the name of the Lord and rely on His God." 46

This scripture prompts me to ask myself these questions; "Am I following my Master so closely and are my eyes so fixed on Him that I can follow Him in any and all circumstances? Can I walk with Him when the questions of *why* or *what* He is doing are still a mystery to me?" The answer has to be a resounding; yes! This is not because of who I am but because of who He is. He is my God *and* my Lord and He is wholly trustworthy. I must remember that His is the only name to which the words faithful and true are continually and perfectly applicable. 47.

The other thing that reminded me of the ways in which God deals with me was reflected by how Dennis had not just named his dog "Patch" but, that he used that name to call him and to identify him as *his* dog so that others would know that there was a person who cared for him. It was a name that Patch learned to respond to. He had that name on the dog tag attached to his collar and right alongside it was the name of his master.

If Patch had wandered off and been picked up by a stranger, they would know who he belonged to by the name of his master which was engraved on his collar. Whenever Dennis needed to get Patch's attention he always called him by his name.

Christ also calls each one of His children by their name and he also puts his name on them. He knows them intimately and they know Him and recognize His call.

"He calls His own sheep by name and leads them out. I am the good shepherd, I know my sheep and my sheep know me." 48. "They will see his face and his name will be written on their foreheads." 49.

I can tell you for certain that Dennis knew and understood his dog. He knew what was good for Patch far more than Patch could understand himself. He knew what things were safe for Patch to eat. He knew that he was allergic to bug bites and that he needed repellent and medication whenever he was bitten. He knew that there were some very unstable dogs in the neighborhood that Patch needed to avoid. He knew that some paths out in the field were far too thorny or treacherous for Patch to navigate. He knew where the streams were shallow enough for Patch to cross safely. He knew that the shots that our veterinarian gave to Patch were for his benefit. He knew that burrs were best removed by using a brush rather than a dog's tongue. He knew that a smelly dog wasn't likely to get very much affection.

As Patch's master, Dennis knew more about what was good for him than he could ever know on his own.

Yet my Master knows me on and even deeper and much more intimate level. He is far more aware of what's best for me than I am able to discern on my own. He knows this not just because He's my Master but because He is also my creator. He formed me and, therefore, He knows every detail concerning my life including my inmost thoughts.

"O Lord, you have searched me and you know me. You know when I sit and when I rise; you perceive my thoughts from afar. You discern my going out and my lying down; you are familiar with all my ways. Before a word is on my tongue, you know it completely, O Lord." 50.

Last but not least of these lessons concerns the fact that Dennis understood what Patch was created to do. He knew the gifts and abilities that God had placed in him. He knew and understood that it would be training and discipline which would eventually allow for Patch to make the most of those gifts and abilities.

Patch was able to lead a fulfilling life doing what he was made to do. He may not have liked or understood the training processes, but those were the very things which enabled him to engage in the thing he loved the most – which was to hunt.

Patch was made for hunting, he yearned for it. When he was a puppy, he hunted bees and butterflies but when he was a grown and mature dog, he hunted game birds.

When Dennis brought Patch home, he did so with a plan in mind. It wasn't a plan that ran contrary to Patch's God-given abilities but rather it was a plan that would increase those abilities in such a way that he would eventually be the very best hunting dog that it was possible for him to be. So the training and disciplines toward that goal began straight off.

I suppose you could say that it was Patch's calling to hunt birds but it was also his master's delight to train him to be a hunter so that he could experience an abundant and purposeful life.

My Master, Jesus, has made His intentions in this regard quite clear;

"I am come that they may have life, and have it to the full." 51.

We humans are inclined to think, just like bullheaded and ignorant pups, that God's plans for us will be something we abhor. We are born rebellious and prone toward running in the exact opposite direction that God knows we need to go.

"We all, like sheep, have gone astray, each of us has turned to his own way." 52.

It is only when we enter into a loving relationship with our Master and focus on really knowing who He is and what His intentions are for us, that we are able to willingly choose to trust His leading in our lives. Thankfully, He has not left us to our own devices. He has given us His Word to teach and guide us and, His Spirit to encourage, lead and convict us. He invites us to intimacy with Him – to really get to know Him more and more with each passing day. And when that intimacy is firmly established we are able to follow Him confidently through even the darkest valleys and the most treacherous terrains. We can do this because we have learned to trust in His loving intentions toward us. We have learned that our Master loves us and that it's His greatest joy to see our life's purposes fulfilled. He has and always will be bringing us to "our desired haven." 53.

We may ignorantly think that running around in loose traffic is the way to go but He knows that there are lovely fields full of promise and adventure that await us if only we will trust in His leading.

"For I know the plans I have for you, declares the Lord, plans to prosper you and not to harm you, plans to give you hope and a future." 54.

It's all a matter of where we are placing our focus. Is our gaze firmly fixed on our Master? Are our feet aligned with His? Will we both trust *and* obey Him? When we set our hearts in earnest devotion to Him, we can be confident that He will never leave our side. It's then that we will know that we have the assurance of His companionship in this life as well as in the life to come - where the field's bloom eternally, where the sun never sets and the adventures will no longer be fraught with danger or peril.

"Then in fellowship sweet, we will sit at His feet, or we'll walk by His side in the way. What He says we will do, where He leads we will go. Never fear, only trust and obey. Trust and obey for there's no other way to be happy in Jesus but to trust and obey." 42.

On Being A Comforter

This book wouldn't be complete without touching on how the experience of suffering and trials enables us to support and encourage others. This is, in fact, the greatest motive for my decision to go ahead and write this book. As I stated before, there has been nothing as comforting to me as finding even just one other person who understands what I've experienced in living with my Anxiety Disorders. There is a kinship in suffering that is like no other, but more importantly there's support, understanding, and encouragement that comes from hearing from another just how God has helped them throughout their trials.

John Bunyan's book did this for me in the same way that the words of comfort and encouragement that I've received from others who share my affliction have helped me. There's tenderness in the tears of others who really understand, from personal experience, what this kind of affliction feels like. There are fervent and sincere prayers offered up on our behalf because the other person really understands exactly how it feels to live with this affliction. We are heartened by their words, encouraged by their stories, enlightened by the knowledge that they've gained. So this must always be a part of why we go through our trials.

Someone, somewhere, someday will need to hear our story and in turn, need to tell us theirs. They will need for us to pray for them, need for us to encourage them and show them compassion and love.

I pray that this book has encouraged *you*. I pray that you will keep on walking not only *with* God but *for* Him. In doing so, you will be walking in step with "the God of all comfort." 55 You can experience the great privilege of being His hands and His feet as He reaches *through* you to comfort another individual who is hurting.

Now: "Praise be to the God and Father of our Lord Jesus Christ, the Father of compassion and the God of all comfort, who comforts us in all our troubles, so that *we* can comfort those in any trouble with the comfort we ourselves have received from God." 55.

Now; Go forth and be a comforter!

1. "The Problem of Pain," C.S. Lewis, Harper Collins, Chapter 6, Page 91, Paragraph 1
2. Genesis 1:1 KJV
3. John 16:33, 1 Peter 4:12, Psalm 34:19, Romans 8:18, NIV
4. James 1: 2-4, 1 Peter 5:10, 2 Corinthians 12:7 NIV
5. Matthew 5:10 NIV
6. "Grace Abounding to the Chief of Sinners," John Bunyan, Penguin Books, Pages 83-84, #7
7. 2 Timothy 1:7 KJV
8. "The Screwtape Letters," C.S. Lewis, Broadman and Holman Publishers, Chapter 24, Page 139, Paragraph 8
9. 1 Timothy 4: 13-14, NIV, (Italics/ emphasis mine)
10. 2 Timothy 1:5-9 NIV
11. 1 Timothy 4: 13-14 NIV
12. 1 Timothy 4: 12 NIV
13. 2 Timothy 1:8b & 14-12 NIV
14. 1 Timothy 4:14 – 15 NIV
15. 1 Timothy 5:23 NIV
16. 2. Corinthians 12:9 KJV
17. 1 Corinthians 2: 1-5 (Italics/emphasis mine)
18. 2 Corinthians 12:1 NIV
19. 2 Corinthians 12: 7-9 NIV

20. Job 1: 21b NIV
21. Isaiah 40:3-5 NIV
22. 2 Corinthians 4:7 NIV
23. Job 13:15 KJV
24. 2 Corinthians 12: 9b – 10 NIV (Italics/emphasis mine)
25. I Corinthians 10:2 NIV
26. John 14:6 KJV
27. 2 Corinthians 12:9 KJV
28. Romans 8: 35-37 KJV
29. Psalm 100:3 KJV
30. "The Quotable Lewis," Wayne Martindale and Jerry Root – Editors, Tyndale House Publishers Inc., Page 462, #1146
31. Psalm 13 NIV
32. Job 13:15 NIV
33. Job 2:10b NIV
34. Job 13:15 NIV
35. Job 19: 25-27 NIV
36. Job 23: 8-11 NIV
37. Psalm 34:1 KJV (Italics/emphasis mine)
38. "Grace Abounding to the Chief of Sinners," John Bunyan, Penguin Books, Page 82, #337
39. Isaiah 50:7 NIV
40. Philippians 2:8 NIV
41. 1 John 4:10 NIV
42. "Trust and Obey," J.H. Sammis, Verse 4
43. Romans 5:8 NIV
44. Romans 8:28 NIV
45. Proverbs 3: 5-6 NIV
46. Isaiah 50: 10 NIV
47. Revelation 19: 11 KJV
48. John 10: 3b & 14 NIV
49. Revelation 22:4 NIV
50. Psalm 139: 1-4 NIV

51. John 10:10 NIV
52. Isaiah 53:6 NIV
53. Psalm 107: 30 NIV
54. Jeremiah 29:11 NIV
55. 2 Corinthians 1: 3-4 NIV (Emphasis mine)

Appendix

Some OCD Questions and Answers

What follows are a few examples of OCD questions which I've responded to from people who suffer from OCD. Many of them fall into the category of Religious OCD or Scrupulosity.

It was suggested to me that it might be a helpful addition to the book for me to share some of my responses to these types of questions. My answers reflect of how I would try to handle my own OCD in these various scenarios. The approach that I take in handling my own OCD is based upon what I've learned about the use of Exposure and Response Prevention Therapy or (ERP) in the treatment of OCD. These responses are not meant to replace or overrule the recommendations of a professional therapist who specializes in the treatment of OCD.

Q. I have bad OCD thoughts on the theme of harming myself or others. Today I have been reassuring myself by saying; "I am not capable of harming myself or others...I don't want to do that!" Is this counterproductive to the therapy?

A. I'm speaking here from my own experience with these same types of obsessions. It is my experience that, yes, when you provide mental reassurances in response to the thoughts that it *is* counterproductive. Here's the reason; by saying those kinds of things you are giving the OCD thought weight and validity. You are treating it as if it's worthy of your responding to it. You're actually answering it or fighting against it with those kinds of statements. This kind of attending to OCD themes will always cause them to get larger and more persistent. It's better to just let the thoughts be there without attending to them at all.

Q. I write out my OCD thoughts and then read them back to myself. Sometimes I am able to do this without feeling any fear at all. But then later on when the thoughts come back I can feel very anxious about them. Why is this?

A. It was my experience that to just write out the exact thoughts and read them back to myself wasn't all that helpful. Just like you, I could do this in sort of a detached way without really entering into the fear. I needed to really stir up the fear. Therefore, the thing that *was* helpful, (and this is hard), was to write out the horrific *outcome* if the thoughts turned out to be true. For instance, with the harming thoughts that I had about my children, I would have to try and visualize, in as much detail as I could, what it would actually be like if those thoughts were to come true. After I had that picture in my head, then I would proceed to write all of that down and then read it back to myself. Then I would just have to sit with that ugly scenario and allow the anxiety to do its worst to me while refusing to respond to it by mentally fighting back. I like to refer to this as "lighting my own back burn". Instead of trying to douse water on the flames of the obsession with mental reassurances I do the exact opposite - I turn up the heat. The obsession cannot claim any more territory in my mind if I've already used up all its fuel by lighting my own obsessional fire. Only I voluntarily choose to make *my* fire a whole lot bigger. I exaggerate it, so that when the obsession tries to advance, it can't, because I've already visited every single worst case scenario of my own accord by lighting my own back burn against it.

Q. I have experienced OCD/scrupulosity symptoms for a number of years and the main issue has been in my prayer life and this intense urge to keep repeating prayers until they are "perfect." I have really been arming myself with the Word of God and I am slowly but surely conquering these horrific symptoms. I still have some days though when the idea of praying is too overwhelming. During these times, I would call my mother or sister and as they pray I would repeat after them (this has helped me a great deal) or I would write a prayer out and ask my husband to say it for me.

I know that sometimes family members can unknowingly enable their loved one who has OCD symptoms by participating in their rituals and I was wondering if having my family pray for or with me is a form of enabling? What do you think?

A. That's a really good and insightful question. This shows that you understand how your disorder operates and that's key to understanding how to manage it.

I suppose you'd have to ask yourself *why* you ask your family to help you with these prayers. Is it to make sure you've done it correctly? Is it to pass off the feeling of responsibility for you praying "correctly" onto them? If the answers to those questions are, "yes" then I think it's safe to say that you are asking them to help you with the compulsion because you are depending on what they do to make you feel comfortable or reassured.

This could be compared to a person with OCD locking the door and then asking a family member to 'check' it for them. That's definitely asking for help with the compulsion. I suppose it might be helpful for you to write a prayer down in order to focus your thoughts when you pray, but my concerns would be; how long would that take you? Could you write it out in a matter of minutes without a ton of revising and scrutinizing it? Then, could you just read it as a prayer to the Lord, just once, and leave it at that? That's what you'd need to do or else the writing and checking what you wrote over and over would then become the new compulsion.

Q. I have a question. I have made so many compulsive and perhaps genuine vows to God on so many things. I feel that the right thing to do is probably to keep the vows as best as I can. Do you think God requires that I keep all these vows to the best of my ability? If yes, can you tell me why and if no, why not? I think of Psalm 15 where David says those who will dwell on God's holy hill keep their vows even when it hurts.

A. OCD vows are unwanted and intrusive. God is well aware of that so I'm going to recommend that you don't bother about them at all. I don't have any idea of how you categorize a "genuine" vow. But for me a *genuine* vow would be something that I really desire to do to show allegiance to God and His statutes. This would be a joyful act of allegiance not a terrifying; "Oh no, I think I made a promise to God and if I don't keep it he's going to strike me dead!!" A genuine vow would be something like a marriage vow. We really do intend to be faithful to our spouse because we really do love them and wish to be devoted to them as a part of our obedience to God in that matter. If you have an OCD theme that centers on vows and the possible consequences of making them and not keeping them, then your brain will be making automatic vows even when you don't want it to. These type of vows would definitely be categorized as unwanted/intrusive thoughts. None of them would be valid and every one of them should be ignored even if it feels terribly wrong and scary to do so. Otherwise, your entire life will be spent in attending to a bunch of meaningless vows that you didn't really want to make and that would rob you of your ability to really live freely in Christ *and* to live in freedom from the bully of your OCD.

Q. I know that I have severe OCD. I just pray that I have not committed the unpardonable sin. I think the thoughts are OCD, but I just want to make sure. I know that the miracles of Jesus are divine through God. I guess the best way I can try to express my problem is like that of a tic. I keep saying "the works of Jesus were through God" out loud and have become afraid of a slip of the tongue that I had. I then contributed them to _____. (OCD sufferers know what I am afraid to type). I know the thoughts are of little substance. I just want to make sure I haven't committed the unpardonable sin if I accidently had a slip of the tongue and accidently SAID that the miracles of Christ were of (the enemy in Hell). So, if I did that have I committed the unpardonable sin?

A. When you said; "I just want to make sure" that is classic OCD statement. You were demonstrating just how easily OCD gets us to do its bidding. It's that need for 100% proof or certainty that drives the disorder. But OCD questions/doubts aren't something for which we can obtain 100% certainty. The more we try, the bigger the fear becomes. Learning to live with the feelings of uncertainty that these thoughts create is the key to learning to manage the disorder - no matter what theme it's latched on to. There will *never* be a reassurance regarding an OCD theme that lays it all to rest. You can't out- logic OCD.

Ask yourself this; what if this tic was a true tic as in Tourette's syndrome that was happening automatically? Would you think that every tic caused by Tourette's was meaningful or reflective of how the person with Tourette's really felt or believed? So whether there is a slip of the tongue or not has no bearing on what the intent of your heart is.

In your case, though, I'm not sure that you repeating that phrase is an automatic thing like a tic. I suspect that you are likely saying it as a compulsion to undo or cancel out the obsession? It's alright if it actually is automatic as in a tic rather than a chosen statement, but if you're using it to try and calm yourself down about the obsession, then you need to stop doing that. Furthermore, if you have some idea of what blaspheming the Holy Spirit is and you are very afraid that you'll end up doing that, the OCD is going to cause you to automatically think blasphemous thoughts. These thoughts are referred to as unwanted/intrusive. Some psychologists also refer to them as automatic negative thoughts or ANTS. They sicken us and freak us out. But if we make "much" of them by attending to them or by trying to somehow reverse or undo them we will be feeding the OCD. So, my best counsel to you is that you just let the thoughts as well as the doubts and fears they stir up, just lie there without attending to them. Do your best to ignore them and find something to distract yourself from attending to them. Try to imagine that they are like angry bees. If you keep swatting at them by giving them so much attention, they'll sting you all the more. If you just let them be, "put that fly swatter down" they'll eventually leave you alone and die a natural death.

Q. I need advice in discerning a situation. I was asked to come to an interview for a job tomorrow. This morning I wanted to call first thing, but felt convicted to take my supplement for my anxiety first (as my OCD rages when not taking my supplement and I need it most first thing in the morning). Well, I really wanted to call first, and felt angry and had the thought; "damn you" and then right after that I visualized the Holy Spirit. Now I am wondering if I should even go to the interview because of this. Please help????

A. These unwanted and intrusive thoughts and images have to be ignored. They are meaningless and shouldn't dictate your decision. If I were you, I'd go to the interview. If you don't go, you will be giving these thoughts power over you in that you will be validating the fear/doubt they've stirred up. I realize it will feel scary to do so, but if we let the fear cause avoidance that only serves to ramp up the OCD machine.

Q. How do you tell the difference? I am having thoughts about something I've chosen to do for the future, that it's wrong. But then I say to myself "It's just OCD or it's the devil", and I pray to God asking Him to help me be sure I really know it's not Him giving me these thoughts and I also ask Him to make me be SURE if it is Him .... but then I still think "What if it's Holy Spirit's conviction?" and then I tell myself, "it's not, it's just the devil", but then I wonder whether that's my sin nature trying to do away with convictions. Does anybody have any advice for me how to know which is which?

A. I think most of us with OCD second guess a lot of our decisions. We are so hyper-scrupulous about "doing the right thing" that we tend to overthink something to the point that our OCD starts to put some pretty strange notions in our head about it. The root of our fear really lies in our doing something to displease God and if that were to be true, we become afraid of the consequences.

Anyhow, my counsel to you is that unless you can find a certain scripture that states very specifically... you should not do such and such or so and so, that you should continue on in your plan. You need only acknowledge God and ask Him to direct and guide you as you proceed in implementing your plan. Just ask Him to open and close doors according to His good purposes. Then move on. All those unsettling "thoughts" are just your OCD pushing you to ruminate or check about something because OCD is always looking for something to chew on. Ignore the thoughts or you'll be giving them validity.

Q. *Forgive me, if this sounds a bit crazy, but for some reason, I may have made a vow to God that if anything should fall down and touch the floor on a certain side of my bed, I can no longer use it. If I do, I'll lose my salvation. Just today, I can't use a white dress shirt because of that. And just now, my blanket fell on that section of the floor and now I'm afraid to use it. Can anyone out there help me to reason this thing out? I'm at a loss.*

A. No... I won't help you reason it out because that would make your OCD worse. What I mean is that you shouldn't try to figure out whether or not you need to keep this unwanted vow because that makes the question valid. Now here's what I would do, if I wanted to get over this obsession super-fast. (You won't like it.) I'd take a bunch of things that I really like and throw them all on that section of the floor. I'd expect to feel really anxious as I did this and I'd just force myself to sit there and accept that feeling. Then after sitting there for a few minutes, I'd pick them all back up and put them away but I'd see to it that I used each and every one of them at some point over the next few days. For starters go ahead and wear that dress shirt. This serves to teach your brain that the intrusive thought isn't valid. If you treat it as valid, it will really *seem* valid and you'll be feeding the OCD. It may seem like I'm being pretty tough on you, but I'm actually being tough toward the OCD, not you.

Q. *(Continuation) So for instance, regarding an intrusive thought I had today about me vowing not to write anything (besides in email and forums) or else God might send my soul to hell--you're saying that I should go ahead and write and write some more, because not only is that "vow" not real, but this would "desensitize" my brain against it?*

A. Bingo!! You got it. I know that seems to be the exact opposite of what you feel you *should* do and that it will, in the beginning, make you feel anxious but if you keep doing it, your brain will accept that it's no big deal.

Q. *What do you do when you are in fear that you are 'becoming' what your thoughts are telling you? I have this fear even though I really don't agree with the thoughts. The thoughts are absolutely disgusting to me and I hate them and don't want to be or do what they are telling me.*

A. The answer to this question, within the context of treating OCD, is that you do absolutely nothing. You must refuse to *attend* to those thoughts as well as the fear that you might become what the thoughts are telling you. OCD always makes us feel as though having the thoughts is tantamount to acting on them. If you take any type of action to attend to this, you'll be giving the whole matter such a great measure of weight and validity that your brain will latch onto it all the more. By attending to these matters, you place them at the very top of the list in your brain as being the most important or urgent things that you must sort out. You don't want to do that or you'll perpetuate the cycle of the disorder.

Q. *a).What is ruminating? b).What is a spike? c).Can these lead to other thoughts?*

A. a.)Ruminating is the compulsive activity of a form of OCD referred to as; "Purely Obsessional". Ruminating is when you spend hours and hours in mental debate about your OCD theme. This involves trying to mentally reassure ourselves that the fearful and disgusting thoughts just aren't true. It's a kind of mental warfare. Ruminating about the "theme" will get the obsession more embedded in the mind and that will trick the mind into thinking that it really *is* a valid or threatening issue and, therefore, must be attended to more than any other thought.

b.) A Spike, (a term coined by Dr. Stephen Phillipson), is a sudden unwanted thought or idea that pops into your mind which intensifies the anxiety. It will usually be related to your root OCD fear.

c.) Yes – spikes, unless you choose to ignore them, can certainly lead to more thoughts. This is because when you are trying to mentally argue or fight against a spike your OCD will usually come up with yet another, "what if" or "what about this" type of thought in order to make you feel even more compelled to try and figure it all out. It will then become a vicious cycle of; a. spike, b. anxiety response, c. compulsion/rumination and then once again a. more spikes, b. more anxiety and c. even more rumination. The Rumination and reassurance seeking is what must be resisted even though the anxiety will try and push you to do those things.

Q. I want my fear back. Is this wrong? Lately, I haven't been feeling any fear when I have the bad thoughts about God. Yet - I just know they're wrong. In the beginning, I was terrified of them. Then when I learned that this was OCD, I stopped being afraid of them. But now that I'm not scared I feel like I should be. I don't want these thoughts to be acceptable to me so how do I get my fear back?

A. Sorry to have to tell you this, but the fear is NOT gone. It's just changed up tactics. This is a common thing with this kind of OCD. Here's how the fear is still with you; "I'm *afraid* because I don't *feel* afraid of the thoughts. This must mean that I'm OK with them. I should be upset about them. If I'm not upset about them, this might mean that I don't really care about God or whether or not I'm sinning against Him. That might mean I'm not a Christian after all. And that really SCARES me." The OCD is trying to get you back into ruminating about them. If you chase after this and make a big deal of it won't be long until you're right back on that miserable hamster wheel. This seemingly *new* thought is still an OCD thought. Ignore it! Don't give in to the bully. Refuse to attend to it even though it feels so wrong to do so.

Q. *I would NEVER commit suicide, but I constantly have the thoughts that I will overdose or something like that. I find these thoughts stronger some days than others. Does anyone else have this problem?*

A. Do you mean like; "what if I just walk into the bathroom open up the medicine cabinet and swallow a bunch of pills even though I really don't want to? UGH!!"

I've struggled with this obsession before *and* for a while I was afraid for my husband to leave me alone because - "it might not be safe." Like you, I had no desire to do such a thing but the OCD made me feel like I might do it anyway. I don't know for sure if that's what it's like for you, but thought I'd share just in case it might comfort you to know that someone else has experienced that.

Q.(Continuation) *That's exactly what it's like! I love my life and am happy, (when I am not obsessing), but I would never overdose on pills. That's so opposite of how I really feel! OCD can be tricky and deceptive. Thanks for your response. It made me feel that I'm not so alone in this mental struggle!*

A.(Continuation) You are welcome! I know just what you mean. There's nothing quite as comforting as finding someone else with OCD, who has struggled with the exact same obsessional content as I've had. Suddenly I know that I'm not the freakish anomaly that I thought I was.

Now... the first thing you should do is to just go ahead and let that obsession ring out in your head but don't fight against it. I mean don't try to do any mental debating with it. Just totally ignore it and go about your business. If you engage with it or attend to it, you'll find out that it will bother you a lot more.

The second thing you can do which will help you get over this a whole lot faster is something that I had to do. I decided to expose myself even more aggressively to this fear by going to the medicine cabinet and taking out one of my prescription drugs. Then I dumped the whole bottle of pills out into my hand and just stood there staring at it while my brain told me that I was probably going to swallow all of them and die. This stirred up quite a bit of anxiety so I just stayed put and held on to the pills until the anxiety started to go down. Then I dumped them back into the bottle and went about my business. I had to do this a few times a day for about a week but after that I didn't struggle with this obsession anymore.

Q. *I know this is Obsessive-Compulsive Disorder, but what are the obsessions and what are the compulsions?*

One common symptom of mine is that I organize my computer to ridiculous perfection. I spend days and days organizing the file names of documents and placing them in a hierarchy of appropriate folders. What forces me to do this is the uncontrollable thought that my files need to be organized perfectly. I wish I did not care about these stupid photos and music and document files, just like I didn't care about them before I got OCD, but now it's different, now the thought of my files not being organized causes me a lot of anxiety, so much anxiety that I cannot do or think about anything else other than organizing them.

Can someone explain to me what the obsessive and compulsive parts are in my example?

Is the part where I feel the urge to organize the compulsive part of my OCD?

A. Yes, I can but first I want you to know that it's okay that you *feel* that urge. However, if you actually organize the files in response to that compelling feeling to assuage the anxiety *that* is the compulsion.

Having said that, I still think it's a very good thing that you are trying to categorize the components of your OCD cycle. It shows that you are taking a clinical approach to it and trying to understand how it gets a foothold with you. This is how I'd categorize the components in your example:

1. The obsession: "I feel compelled to organize my computer and my files to perfection or else _____." You fill in the blank. What is it that you fear might happen if you don't keep your computer organized? This is the obsession.
2. The Anxiety response. This is what will happen if you refuse to keep your computer and files organized to perfection. So then because you are feeling anxious you will begin to have that urge to engage in…..
3. The Compulsion: Organizing your computer and files over and over to try and shove down or quell the anxiety response.

To treat this OCD cycle properly, you must apply the brakes just before you begin to engage in step 3, which is the compulsion. If you continue to perform the compulsion, you validate the obsession that something bad will happen if you don't keep everything organized to perfection. This perpetuates the cycle and if you continue on this path, you will have to organize it more and more in order to alleviate the anxiety response. The more we engage in the compulsions, the more valid and frightening the obsession seems to us.

If you force yourself to let it be and ride out the anxiety then over time, the anxiety will die out. You have to do this in small steps. Set goals for yourself to leave off organizing it for longer and longer periods of time, even though it makes you feel very anxious. Then just allow the anxiety to be there without giving in to the compulsion.

Q. About a month ago this numbing feeling toward God came upon me and it has become a fight to hold on to the idea that I still have faith. The thing is that I used my anxious feelings to combat my OCD. Having those feelings at least made me feel that I still cared. Now with this numb feeling I find it so hard to go on and this depression and anger are harder to fight against than the feelings of anxiety that I used to have. Has anyone felt like this before? I just want my love and feelings of zeal to come back, but I know deep down that we are supposed to live by faith, not by sight.

A. Yes, I think I might understand what you're trying to convey. As I was training myself to ignore the content of my OCD obsessions, eventually I seemed to calm down about the thoughts. But then, what I was left with, was this numb or dead feeling toward God. I felt that maybe, just maybe I would never experience the joy of my salvation again. That's a desperate and depressing way to feel. But please keep in mind that it takes quite some time to climb out of the pit of this kind of OCD. It can be a very long process. I found that if I started to make too much of the fact that I felt numb toward God that I would often begin to obsess again about whether or not this might be some kind of sign or evidence that maybe I really wasn't saved after all. You have to avoid going down that path. I know it's a distressing feeling, but you are right, it *is* just a feeling. It doesn't mean a thing other than the fact that you've been going through a very difficult season with your OCD.

Try to tell yourself... this too shall pass and do just like you said; try to live by faith, not by sight. Doing that means choosing to walk in faith and obedience toward God even while we cannot seem to feel the comfort of His presence. But as we continue to walk our feelings will eventually catch up with our actions. I always say that to trust *is* to obey and that if I really trust God then I will choose to obey Him. You can't separate one from the other.

Q. *Do you know that just thinking about purposely exposing myself to the idea that my obsession might be true makes me feel like I'd collapse from the inside out?!*

A. Yes, believe it or not, I *do* know that because exposing ourselves to our obsessions in this way will always create a tremendous surge of anxiety. But, here's the thing - what you said, just here, is exactly *why* you must do it and it's also why doing it would work for you. Even though it's awful, exposure *should* create this kind of feeling. You have to remember that to refuse to do exposure to this fear is the very thing that's keeping you afraid of it. Running from a bully always gives him power and it's the same with OCD obsessions. Standing up to them and being willing to consider every ugly scenario that they dish out without flinching, (which would be to engage in any sort of checking or reassurance seeking), will retrain your brain to quit reacting to the obsession as if it's valid.

Having struggled with a long held obsessional theme will mean that you absolutely have to do active exposure in order to get over it. And even taking baby steps in exposure is better than taking no steps at all. Just take it one day at a time. Forget the past regarding how long you've dealt with it and don't worry about how long it might take to feel better. Expect ups and downs so long as you keep coming back and trying again. Then if you can, try to visualize or imagine how many people you can help after you beat this obsession. Be inspired by that. Ask God to give you that future privilege. Be inspired as to how you might be able to help your children or grandchildren should they suffer from OCD in the future. Be inspired about all that God is going to teach you about His grace and sufficiency in and through this. Then take all that inspiration and use it to motivate you to learn to manage your OCD. I know you can do it. I'll be praying for you.

Q.I want to get your take on a situation that happened tonight that I am hoping was OCD and not me, but please be honest in your assessment of the situation?

I was invited over somewhere, I went there. There were these gummy bears on the table. I was told I could have some. I did, but while doing so I mentally said something to the effect that I shouldn't eat much more because of my food sensitivities, and it having a negative effect on me. The person hosting also made popcorn, and I had some. After some bites of the popcorn, I thought; "I guess I'll have a gummy bear to push some of the popcorn residue in my throat down." As I was about to eat the gummy bear I had this thought that I shouldn't because I would be going back on what I said earlier in my mind about not eating too many. Anyway, as I started to eat the gummy bear, I felt convicted that I shouldn't be eating it.

Then I felt frustrated that I felt convicted. I am not sure if I was frustrated at the Holy Spirit or not; I may have been. I started to hear the phrase "Get behind me Satan." come out in my mind and I began to resist that. But then I gave into that thought and it came into my mind anyway. Now, I do not think the Holy Spirit is Satan at all. But I do think I felt frustrated at that moment, and maybe that frustration was aimed at the Holy Spirit because I felt convicted to not eat that gummy bear and convicted when I was doing something I shouldn't have been doing. As I was chewing it up, I thought; "I need to go spit it out to show my repentance and love toward the Holy Spirit", but instead I kept chewing it and swallowed it. I felt awful that I did this. Wow! I told myself that I needed to immediately go pray and ask God to remember my transgressions toward His Holy Spirit no more. I discovered I had one small piece of the gummy bear left in my mouth so I spit it out. Does this sound like I genuinely sinned against God's Spirit tonight? Or does this sound like it was OCD? Please explain why? Please be totally honest in your assessment.

A. This episode has OCD/Scrupulosity written all over it. Scrupulosity is this intense scrutinizing of everything we do or think or say, in order to gain some kind of reassurance that we haven't offended God or, in this case, His Holy Spirit. Eating one more gummy bear after thinking you probably shouldn't have too many is, of course, no big deal. But when you went ahead and did it and that hyper-scrupulous or convicted feeling came on, you naturally felt very frustrated because it's just so darn tiring to constantly be that scrupulous about every little thing in your life. Then, of course, because you thought the Holy Spirit was convicting you, the very last thing you wanted to do was to offend Him. So then your OCD does you this lovely favor of sending you an intrusive thought that seems to be aimed at the Holy Spirit even though you don't agree with the thought. Remember that all these kinds of thoughts are unwanted and intrusive and that you don't choose to have them pop into your mind. What happened to you was a classic example of just how over the top OCD can get when it's running the show.

Now, this isn't going to seem right to you and it certainly wouldn't have felt right at the time but the best thing you could have done in response to this whole OCD episode would have been to go and get even more gummy bears and eat them. Then to force yourself to sit there and ride out the torrent of accusations and the firestorm of anxiety that ensued without trying to undo any of it through confession or reassurance-seeking behaviors. This whole episode was normally/abnormal in the realm of OCD experiences and responses.

The proof that it's OCD is that it's still so upsetting to you that you now feel compelled to come to this forum to try and obtain some kind of reassurance about what happened. Not much fun is it? Best to just let it all go and maybe even go buy a bag of gummy bears and eat the whole bag just to show the OCD that it can't shove you around.

Q. *I've been avoiding a lot of TV shows lately because I don't wish for a TV show to trigger any obsessive thoughts. I have to read the summaries before I watch a movie, TV show or read a book. Entertainment is upsetting to me yet I find myself drawn to it. This sometimes causes me to wonder if avoidance is actually a good thing. That is why I don't watch most TV shows and I hate award shows for fear that something bad will happen on those shows. I was wondering if avoidance is a good coping mechanism or does it make the thoughts worse? I have this fear that I will have another series of thoughts that are triggered just by watching TV or a movie or reading a work of fiction. What is wrong with me? What do I need to do?*

A. This is a really insightful question. In general, I would have to say that avoiding the things which trigger our OCD obsessions isn't a good thing. I do, however; want to qualify my answer by saying that if a TV show is inappropriate in that we know deep down that watching it is displeasing to God that we shouldn't watch it. But the reason for doing that wouldn't be inspired by a fear of it prompting obsessions; it would be inspired by a desire to obey God. Do you see the difference? For me, I avoid R-rated movies just because I know there's a good possibility that they might have some very inappropriate scenes in them which God wouldn't want me to see. But the reason I avoid them isn't to keep me from having fearful OCD thoughts. I avoid them because I really *do* feel that watching them would be displeasing to God.

Anyhow - as to avoidance – when we avoid the things which trigger our OCD fears we are basically running from them. When we run from them, we are training our brain to believe that the threats they pose are actually valid or real. This would be akin to running from a big bully rather than facing up to him. Run from the bully and he knows he scares you. Stand up to him and face him and he loses his ability to bully you around.

So as long as any form of entertainment is something, which when viewed outside of the context of OCD fears, would still be deemed appropriate for a Christian to watch, then you should go ahead and watch it. You should watch it expecting and accepting that it might trigger some kind of obsessional thought and anxiety, but if you stick it out, you will have scored a major point against your OCD. This is called, "exposure." It's the same thing we'd do regarding any phobia. For example; what would be the only way to get over being afraid of riding in elevators? The answer to that question is; go ahead and ride in elevators until your brain just gets over being afraid of them.

About The Author

Mitzi VanCleve is a self-published author who began writing out of a deep desire to provide awareness, support and advocacy for those who share her experience of living with anxiety disorders. She was particularly inspired to share her experiences within the body of Christ in order to help eliminate the stigma, lack of understanding and lack of support for Christians who suffer from mental illness.

Mitzi experienced distressing bouts of anxiety in the form of obsessional themes and social anxiety from childhood to early adulthood. Sadly, she remained unaware of her disorders up until her mid-twenties which resulted in her feeling isolated, alone, and, as she puts it; "like some sort of freakish anomaly." At that point in time, she began to experience debilitating panic attacks which led to the discovery that she had Panic Disorder.

Mitzi was immensely relieved to find out that she had an actual disorder which could be managed, but still remained unaware that some of her longest and most excruciating seasons of distress were due to a type of OCD called Purely Obsessional OCD. *That* answer didn't come until, at the age of fifty, she went through yet another crushing season of anxiety due to severe obsessions about her faith in Christ.

As Mitzi became educated about OCD and was able to obtain professional help, this resulted in a greater level of relief as she became more skilled at learning how to manage the OCD.

Eventually, she began to communicate through online forums with other Christians who were afflicted with anxiety disorders and found that she was able to provide a great deal of comfort, encouragement and hope to those who were suffering in isolated silence. This is what led to her publishing her first book: "Strivings Within – The OCD Christian." After publishing that book, she felt a desire to reach out to teens because that's when anxiety disorders will typically become much more distressing. Mitzi thought that the best way to do that would be in the form of an easy read/ fictional novel which portrayed what it's like for a teen who is struggling with some of the things she went through at that age. This is how "In Your Dreams" was born.

Mitzi resides in Michigan with her closest friend and supporter; her husband Dennis. They have been married for thirty-eight years and have three children and seven grandchildren.

Helpful Resources

1. "Grace Abounding to the Chief of Sinners," By John Bunyan, Penguin Books
2. http://www.ocdonline.com   Articles and video by Dr. Stephen Phillipson
3. "The Obsessive Compulsive Trap" By Dr. Mark Crawford, Regal Publishing
4. "The Anxiety Cure," By Dr. Archibald D. Hart, Word Publishing
5. "S.T.O.P Obsessing!" By: Edna B. Foa, Ph.D. And Reid Wilson, Ph.D., Bantam Books
6. "Brain Lock" By Jeffrey M. Schwartz, M.D., Regan Books
7. "The Anxiety and Phobia Workbook – Third Edition" By: Edmund J. Bourne, Ph.D., New Harbinger Publications, Inc.